RAW LIFE, NEW HOPE

Mem getting ready for a Friday night outing in The Park

RAW LIFE, NEW HOPE

DECENCY, HOUSING AND EVERYDAY LIFE IN A POST-APARTHEID COMMUNITY

FIONA C. ROSS

UCT
PRESS

Raw Life, New Hope:
Decency, housing and everyday life in a post-apartheid community

First published 2010
UCT Press
First floor
Sunclare Building
21 Dreyer Street
Claremont
7708

ISBN 978-1-91989-527-7

PROJECT MANAGER: Debbie Henry
EDITOR: Helen Hacksley
PROOFREADER: Ethné Clarke
TYPESETTER: Guineafolio
COVER DESIGNER: Guineafolio
INDEXER: Sanet le Roux
PRINT MANAGEMENT BY Print Communications

Printed on Triple Green, an environment-friendly paper which comes from sustainable resources

The authors and the publisher have made every effort to obtain permission for and to
acknowledge the use of copyright material. Should any infringement of copyright have
occurred, please contact the publisher, and every effort will be made to rectify omissions
or errors in the event of a reprint or new edition.

Photo credits: All photos Fiona C. Ross except top two images p. 17, Luzanne Jacobs

Contents

For Luzanne (left) and Meitjie (right)
and in memory of those who have died.

Preface

This is a heart-work. It has taken many years to write; a slow layering of knowledge and experience that would not have been possible without the patience, trust and courage of many people. I thank, firstly, my friends and neighbours in The Park, without whom there would be no book at all. I want particularly to thank Dina, Sandra, Ponkies, Bernie, Baby, Raymond, Gerald, Aubrey, Ou Rose, Big Anne, Lien, Price, Attie, Queenie, Luzanne, Hybrie, Mem, Meitjie, Mitha, Tassa, Erica, Tol and Aunty Maggie. Some of the people I have thanked are dead.

Janine Pheiffer has been a marvellous research assistant, astute observer and good companion in this work. I thank her for her judgement, her compassion and ongoing commitment to this project. Robyn Rorke worked with great verve and care. Thanks to Patti Henderson who has been an intellectual companion without compare. A circle of friends has sustained me. Thanks especially to ACR, for unfailing encouragement. I am grateful to my colleagues in the Department of Social Anthropology at the University of Cape Town, particularly to Mugsy Spiegel, who was there at the beginning. Jess Auerbach, Megan Greenwood, Thomas Cousins, Simon Eppel and Marlon Burgess read and commented in detail on an early draft, and students and tutors in an introductory anthropology course in 2008 offered careful engagements with the work. I have enjoyed working with – and puzzling over – their feedback. My thanks to the anonymous readers who read this manuscript and the articles that preceded it. It has been a pleasure to work with Sandy Shepherd of UCT Press, my editor Helen Hacksley, and Debbie Henry and the talented design team. Some of the materials presented here appeared in different forms in the *Journal of Southern African Studies*, *Social Dynamics* and *Africa Today*. I am grateful for permission to reproduce portions of these articles.

Aspects of this research were funded by the National Research Foundation (NRF), grant numbers 2050283 and 63222 (Effects of Home Ownership, 2002 and Ethnographies of/and the Marginal, 2007–2010), and the University of Cape Town Research Committee (URC). The views expressed herein do not necessarily represent those of the NRF or the URC.

Finally, my thanks to Andy and Sarah, who put up with my wandering mind and sudden 2 am writing fixations, and who centre my universe.

While selecting photographs for the book, I realised once again how many people whom I came to know have died or disappeared. I dedicate this book to all of them, and in particular to Meitjie and Luzanne.

'Teen die pad, Die Bos'
(Alongside the road, The Bush)

Nongwase's post box was blue. It stood proudly on the fence pole of a yard edged with straggling flower beds in The Bush, a shack settlement on the outer perimeter of the city of Cape Town, South Africa. The home Nongwase had built for herself and her children was typical of others in the settlement; a single room assembled from wood off-cuts collected from a nearby timber merchant, cardboard boxes, estate agents' 'For Sale' boards, and roofed with corrugated iron. The post box marked her home from the scurry of surrounding shacks. It seemed simultaneously incongruous and bold: a statement, an affirmation of presence. I once asked Nongwase whether she ever received mail. She replied that she did not – too few of her relatives were literate. If they could or did write, I pressed, what address would they use? 'Teen die pad, Die Bos', she replied.

In 1991, when I encountered Nongwase and her family, The Bush was an illegal settlement that had already been razed several times by the apartheid state and which was again under threat by local landlords. The post box has stuck in my mind all that time as a symbol of Nongwase's aspirations to an ordinary urban life in Cape Town, an expectation that an African woman and her family would remain in one site long enough to receive mail and would do so legally. That aspiration was shared by many of the residents of this and other shanty settlements across the city and in cities elsewhere in South Africa, and slowly came to fruition in the post-apartheid period.

In apartheid South Africa, such aspirations were almost revolutionary for a black woman. From the 1950s, the apartheid state had legislated against permanent African presence in towns under any but the most stringent circumstances. African women were considered perpetual minors, under the guardianship of their fathers, husbands or brothers. The City of Cape Town and surrounds were declared a Coloured Labour Preference area in 1954: under this legislation no African person could be offered a job if there was a Coloured person to do it. The Group Areas Act of 1950 was stringently implemented from the mid-1950s and the city that prior to the Second World War had been the most integrated in the country quickly became the most segregated (Western 1981; Pinnock 1989; Besteman 2008). The pre-apartheid city's apparent racial integration overlay a cruel class structure that apartheid re-rendered in crude racial terms. Despite massive post-apartheid change, Cape Town remains South Africa's most segregated city.

The city stopped building housing for Africans in the mid-1960s and its housing provision for Coloureds was limited. Informal shack settlements sprang up as migrants and urbanites tried to establish themselves in a context of dire housing shortage. Living in 'squatter camps' was dangerous: settlements were razed throughout the 1970s and 1980s and African people without 'rights' to reside in urban areas were 'endorsed out' – sent back to overcrowded ethnic 'homelands'. By the mid-1980s, there were tensions between different leadership factions of informal settlements. Manufactured and manipulated by the apartheid state, they gave rise to sporadic violence characterised by the state as 'black on black'. Meanwhile, housing provision for Coloureds had been drastically limited. Existing housing was massively crowded and there was a rapid growth in 'backyard shacks'. By the mid-1980s, the city was ringed with informal settlements. The Bush, later renamed The Park,[1] was one of these, populated mostly by Coloured and some African people who sought to establish their homes and secure their families.

Less than a kilometre long and at its widest point not more than 500 metres, the settlement was wedged between a road and a railway line. It was nestled between the forested windbreak of a wine farm and the nearby mountains where Rastafari meditate and collect herbs. The setting was stunning, the squalor scandalous. Residents had long complained about their appalling living conditions. Outsiders looking in saw only chaos and disorder; one resident of The Bush described the settlement as 'too wild' to be considered anything but temporary living, but for many people, this had been home for extended periods. After many years of 'squatting' (illegal residence in shacks), the residents eventually won rights to muurhuise (Afrikaans:[2] lit. wall houses, the vernacular term for formal houses in planned residential suburbs), and moved from The Park to The Village at the turn of the millennium. The move afforded residents an opportunity to reflect on their ideals and everyday lives.

Raw Life, New Hope takes the move as the centrifugal point around which to consider social relations and their changes over time. In the period between

1995 and 2000, residents' hopes crystallised around the notion of *ordentlikheid* (respectability, decency); they hoped that new housing and job opportunities would enable them finally to live decent lives and to be recognised as respectable people. Their aspirations and the contexts in which they tried to accomplish them bring to life the enormous social costs of apartheid and colonial capitalism, and the tragic limitations of the current state's efforts at remedy.

The period of my research (1991–2004) has been characterised by radical social change in South Africa and internationally, among them apartheid's official demise, changing global geopolitics as a result of the end of the Cold War and the beginning of the 'war against terror', the 'liberalisation' of global economies and massive population movements. Global shifts in geopolitics and economic relations have shaped a neo-liberal economic agenda in South Africa that stresses property ownership and a partially deregulated market alongside an attempt to broaden access to state social support and services. Political changes since the end of minority rule in 1994 have been considerable but old legacies endure and are replicated in some of the effects of neo-liberal economic policies despite changes in state policy toward the poor. Focusing on a small site allows us to see these tensions play out in people's lives. For South Africans, the greatest post-apartheid changes have been the removal of racially defined rights, universal adult franchise, the repeal of much apartheid-era legislation, the amalgamation and streamlining of formerly racially defined bureaucracies, and a commitment to Constitutionally defined human rights. Closer to home for those with whom I worked, change has been manifest in access to state housing grants through a public–private partnership that enabled them to move from shacks to new houses in The Village in 2001.

When I first began working in The Bush, residents did not have rights to the land on which they lived or over the shacks that they built and there were many attempts to evict them. Living conditions were abysmal. Residents were un- or underemployed; making ends meet was a daily corrosive struggle. There was no water provision, no sanitation and no refuse collection in the settlement. Against this backdrop of negligible material support and state abandonment, many thousands of people in this and other cities attempted to craft everyday lives that accorded with their ideals and personal sensibilities while grappling with the alienation inherited from apartheid's cruel intrusions on social life. So, brought together by historical contingencies, themselves partly shaped by colonialism and apartheid's systematic assault on social life, residents of the settlement have, together, unevenly, wrought a sense of community. It is fragile and beset but also has endured much, including the very conditions of its making.

In The Bush's early years, people were subject to the scrutiny of the apartheid state through the restrictions imposed by the Population Registration Act (1950), the Group Areas Act (1954), the Prevention of Illegal Squatting Act (1951), the Trespass Act (1959), the Slums Act (1970), the Coloured Labour Preference Policy (1954) and a host of other legislation, most of which served to segregate people and had the effect of limiting life opportunities for many. While many of these laws have been repealed, in the present, people grapple with their legacies.[3] The city remains largely segregated on class and racial lines; conflicts arise between those who were formerly advantaged by the Coloured Labour Preference Policy and those who seek to establish lives for themselves in areas to which their access was formerly constrained; contradictions abound. Residents struggle against the ongoing humiliations of being poor in a context in which job security seems to be increasingly undermined by neo-liberal economic policies. Ordinary social relationships are undercut by poverty's cruelty and by forms of violence – both structural and interpersonal – that shape and taint everyday interactions. The effects of apartheid and poverty play out in residents' lives, relationships and social structures: forces against which people pitted themselves and in relation to which they sought to forge meaningful and fulfilling everyday lives in conditions of humiliating impoverishment and contexts that can only be described as ugly. Theirs is a story of constant effort in the face of ongoing erosions of family, work, stability and residence, created by what I call the 'raw life'.

My formulation of raw life differs somewhat from that of Achille Mbembe (2001: 197), who uses the same term to describe the form of life of the postcolony: a time and space in which, he claims, life and death are so entangled that living has the form of an ongoing partial death to which human meaning cannot be ascribed. My thinking about the rawness of life's conditions in The Park has been shaped primarily by observation and conversation with people enduring its harshness and seeking to make meaning and relationships in its midst. It has also been shaped by philosopher Giorgio Agamben's (1998) reflections on the ancient Greek distinction between two forms of life, zoé and bios. [4] Zoé is bare life, the life common to animals and humans, life itself. In contrast, bios is political life; a life shaped by and recognised politically; a life with meaning, which is, he says, a life particular to humans. In contexts such as The Park, where ideal forms of sociality were eroded but not absent, the contingent quality of both zoé and bios becomes clear. What forms and modalities of living are part of the repertoires of those who must live, knife-edged, in contingency's wake?

A further source of my thoughts about raw life derives from a description of poverty offered by the feminist theorist Susan Griffin. After seeing an etching called Poverty, created in 1897 by artist Käthe Kollwitz which depicts an impoverished mother and her dying child, Griffin writes, 'Never have I seen so clearly that what we call poverty is simply a raw exposure to the terror and fragility of life' (1992:

127). And nowhere have I seen this exposure more visibly manifest than among those with whom I worked, where attempts to create predictability and routine in everyday lives are punctured by violence and lack, where stability is limited and even the most strenuous efforts often secure only temporary well-being, and where interpersonal and structural violence sometimes intercept to render life in its crudest terms. While people are busy trying to make and live ordinary lives, they do so in contexts that lay bare social and institutional failures to support, transform and care. Reduced material circumstances and opportunities mean that people must make extraordinary efforts to achieve stability and routine in daily lives marked by ugliness and the slow erasure of hope that is poverty's grinding legacy.

It is enormously difficult to write about ugliness in social life, and there are great risks in doing so – of pathologising, of generating fixed positions, of blaming victims. Where life is punctuated by loss, disruption, violence, abjection (Kristeva 1982) and what Achille Mbembe describes as 'the distress of experience deprived of power, peace, and rest' (2001: 12), people must put much effort into developing and maintaining relationships and ordinary rhythms of everyday life. This does not mean that there is no regularity to everyday life, but rather that it is achieved against great odds, and, as we shall see, often holds only temporarily. As Baby, one of the *eerste mense* (first people: original inhabitants) of The Park put it, 'Every day we're *deurmekaar*' (confused, disoriented. The word implies irrationality and emotionalism, and, for some, the threat of violence).

Novelist Milan Kundera has an entry for 'ugly' in his personal dictionary, 'Sixty-three words'. He writes,

UGLY. ... the word 'ugly' is irreplaceable: the omnipresent ugliness of the modern world is mercifully veiled by routine, but it breaks through harshly the moment we run into the slightest trouble. (1988: 150–1)

Kundera traces here a connection between the moral and the aesthetic, a connection that, as we shall see in Chapter Two, has significant bearing on people's ideals. For Kundera, ugliness is the result of fracture in routines and rhythms. His ideas are useful for thinking about the rawness of life in The Park, where it is difficult for people to make their lives coherent over time, if by coherent we mean regular and predictable, and where violence – both interpersonal and structural – and forms of what might be characterised as 'uncare' puncture everyday life.

Social forms may always contain traces of ugliness; certain forms of relationship are saturated with and structured by inequalities, exploitation or depravity. Occupying such zones is painful, difficult and humiliating. It can be risky and, for some, may carry a frisson of excitement. Everyday routines that are taken for granted elsewhere can be easily destroyed – the loss of a job, an illness, threats of eviction, violence, lack of income all threaten hard-won senses of security. For some, daily life's unpredictability is related to the difficulties and discomforts of extremely impoverished lives, in which holding oneself together takes ingenuity and resourcefulness. Others describe the ways in which the daily contexts of being poor erode one's sense of coping, making one feel senuweeagtig ('on my nerves', as the phrase is locally translated), or, as isiXhosa speakers say, 'uyacinga kakhulu' – she thinks too much. When problems (iingxaki) have no apparent solutions, thought can spill over into suffering (-sokola) and illness. Where relationships are stretched to their utmost and tempers are fraught, small incidents may precipitate disproportionate responses: violence lurks in social encounters. Substance abuse, particularly of alcohol, plays a role in creating unpredictable behaviour and cruelty. As in all human life, tragedy traduces people's everyday lives, but here, as we will see, it compounds other vulnerabilities so that kinship and other intimate relations become still more fragile. For some, this gives rise to a sense (too often justified by experience) that their everyday lives are unstable, their relationships unreliable, and that networks of care and support beyond the family or neighbours are limited or absent. And yet, people have created solidarities, the 'community' exists, both in people's imaginations and in practice; durable relationships, even if fraught, are possible.

The people you will encounter in the course of this book are not necessarily related, although there were widespread kin networks in The Bush. They do not all hail from the same areas, although there are agglomerations of people who activated 'home person' networks to secure permission from community leaders to reside there. They have diverse life experiences but their lives have been shaped by the same historical processes. All were classified Coloured or African – that is, 'non-white' – under the apartheid regime. This fact is significant, for when The Bush first came into being in the late 1980s, one's racial classification determined in large measure the kinds of resources and life opportunities to which one might have access, or rather, from which one was excluded. All the residents were extremely poor, and in some instances had fallen through the (limited) security nets that kin, friends and networks provided.

Some of the residents have been rejected by mainstream society – the destitute, very ill or disabled, those whose kin have disowned or displaced them, addicts, ex-convicts. There are also those who reject the values of mainstream society (such as the Rastafari), those who have lost jobs or stumbled on hard times and found social support networks elsewhere insufficient to their needs. In this respect, early residents of The Bush were unlike those of most other shantytowns in the Cape, which are more usually home to people who were historically excluded from the city on the grounds of race, and who, owing to the city's poor building record and the backlog in housing, have been unable to access formal houses. Then there are those who came to The Bush/Park in search of privacy, a chance to begin lives afresh, those who have decided to move away from parents and kinsfolk in order to start their own families. In this respect, the settlement is like other shantytowns. In short, the study site comprises people with different life experiences and a wide range of hopes and expectations for the future. What residents do have in common, for the most part, is that they are poor and utterly exposed to the rawness of life. Their poverty renders them extremely vulnerable to even small negative changes in their social and financial circumstances.

Mine is not a study of poverty along the lines of Oscar Lewis's (1959) *Children of Sanchez*, a now classic (and highly contested) study of 'the culture of poverty' in Mexico; instead, it is a study of how, in contexts of extreme impoverishment and marginalisation, people make meaning, make do and get by, and sometimes succeed in goals set by a mainstream society that, for the most part, does little to support them and has little sense of either the constraints they face or the ingenious ways in which they attempt to overcome them. This is not to validate everything that happened in the sites. There are many aspects of social life there that I – like its residents – find deplorable, tragic, unethical, upsetting. There seems to be a reciprocal relationship between forms of social abandonment and living with abandon. For example, one of the ways in which some people deal with the humiliations and eroded life chances they experience is through drug use and alcohol dependence. These are temporary fixes and their effect is to reinforce lack of opportunity. Predatory courtship styles work against the well-being of girls and women. High rates of domestic and other forms of violence have shattering effects on attempts to build sociality and caring relationships. Cruel (*wreed*: also means barbaric) environments and histories are materialised in people's cruelty to one another. The effects on children in particular can be devastating. Alongside trying to secure stable jobs in adverse employment conditions, making ends meet can involve theft, drug sales and prostitution. Sometimes there is a very fine line between intimate relations and terrible abuse. In order to understand these, events must be contextualised in colonialism and apartheid's savage histories that have undermined or complicated the possibilities of coherent social lives for many.

One might see in The Bush/Park similarities with the forms of life revealed in João Biehl's study in Vita, an asylum on the outskirts of Rio de Janiero, Brazil. Like the earliest residents of The Bush (see Chapter Two), the people living in Vita are often ill or deranged, or, as Biehl shows, left without or evicted from the limited shelter of the family. Medical services there are virtually non-existent and bureaucratic forms of care make a mockery of individual efforts to find assistance and social sustenance. People are considered by themselves and others to be 'leftovers', 'castaways', or, as Biehl hesitantly describes them, 'ex-humans'; located in a place where 'the living subjects of marginal institutions are constituted as something other, between life and death' (2005: 317). The Bush was established by those who society considered derelict, and the forms of sociality possible there were severely constrained. And yet, unlike Vita, where people are so reduced by their circumstances that sociality seems almost impossible and where relationship counts as an accomplishment; where love, affection, anger, joy are undercut by alienation so that one is left only with a sense of dismay in the face of the other so isolated and abandoned, residents of The Bush/Park created solidarities and a sense of community. Desperately afraid of being considered *weggooi mense* (throw-away people; it has connotations of being discardable, reject, surplus), they worked hard against the prevailing stereotype, to reframe themselves as valuable. Indeed, *weggegooi* (thrown-away, discarded) remains one of the most violent and ugly epithets that can be levelled at someone; far worse than the traditional *jou ma se* *** (your mother's ***), itself a term so derogatory that to utter it is an invitation to violence. Unlike the residents of Vita, residents of The Bush/Park were able to get things done in their name: refuse collection, water supply, rights to remain on site; state welfare grants; state housing subsidies; houses. The new state and its social policies figure large in these gains. There are thus dimensions of life in The Park that I admire enormously: people's determined efforts to sustain kinship relations and friendships, their insistence that they are not *weggooi mense*, their lively efforts to remain on site in the face of multiple attempts at eviction, the fact that they have secured rights to housing and have been able to do so as a community, their critical assessments of lives – their own and others – in the settlements, and their acerbic commentary on the contexts of reduced life chances and abject poverty. These efforts transform everyday life from what might otherwise have become what Biehl describes as 'a zone of social abandonment' into something that one might characterise as 'a community'.

On method

Why read a monograph about poor people and their changing lives in what residents called 'the ghetto', particularly when it is not necessarily representative of the poor in the city? What is the value of a small-scale, intensive study, with limited generalisability? Why study at the micro-level? Why read ethnographies at all? In *The Interpretation of Cultures*, Clifford Geertz addresses the issue in his famous, somewhat elliptical remark, 'Small facts speak to large issues' (1973: 23). Statistical data can reveal much about the general features of social life, but they cannot tell us about how people experience the world or attempt to make sense of the events and processes that shape a life. People may live in a world in which connections are global and events in far-off places can substantially change everyday lives, and thanks to the media they may be quite well informed about global events, but the fact is that people live locally, however inflected by global processes that local may be. Anthropology's cultural relativist approach recognises that humans are meaning-making creatures and anticipates that human behaviour makes sense, even if the sense that a given set of people make, the forms of their behaviours and the explanations they offer for these, are not universally the same or accepted.

Being part of a research project can be uncomfortable. It involves subjecting oneself, one's beliefs and practices to the assessing eye of an outsider unfamiliar with the nuances of daily life and the histories – personal and political – that shape one's actions and relations in the world. The people with whom I have worked over an extended period (intermittently since 1991) have been extremely generous with their time and their contributions to the project. I hope that the book both conveys the extent of my gratitude and does justice to the complexity of their everyday lives. People do not accept their way of life unquestioningly, especially when that way of life is blatantly unjust and clearly the result of discrimination. I have been fortunate in that people have shared with me their assessments of their own lives and those of people around them. This is not to say that my account is uncritical. Rather, I have tried to offer a critique that, like their own, is sensible of the specific circumstances that give rise to the general forms of social life and relationship, and that locates these in a broader historical and social context.

I consider anthropology to be a form of disciplined curiosity. In its attentiveness to social life, ethnography offers the tools for a careful, sensitive and sensible assessment of people's lives and contexts such as these. Ethnography differs from other social scientific accounts in that it attempts to make sense of people's experiences using people's own everyday categories and models. Sometimes this involves comparisons that highlight differences between ways of doing, seeing and saying. Sometimes the ethnographic process reveals similarities between social systems and relations that on the face of it seem markedly different. The value of ethnographic approaches is double. Part lies in seeing people's lives from the inside, as it were; showing how they organise social life and make sense (or not) of what happens to them. This emic perspective is complemented by an etic approach which entails systematising that knowledge, extending it through abstraction, generalisation and comparison so that we can say something more broadly about the human condition. One might accurately describe the anthropological approach as 'inside-out'.

'Participant-observation' is one among many ways of being attentive. As a research technique, it involves coming to know others through experiencing what they experience. The anthropologist becomes the tool through which knowledge is gained; the approach is both subjective (drawing from one's own experiences) and objective (in so far as one develops methodological tools to verify subjective experience, personal observations and interpretations). This kind of knowledge demands a kind of intimacy; a coming to know others not through the categories assigned to them by mainstream society or theoretical ideas imposed from outside, but in their relationships and routines, through sharing the rhythms of daily life. In other words, fieldwork is an effort, consciously directed, a means through which to come to know other people and their ways of life. According to the founding myth of ethnographic fieldwork (Malinowski 1922), this means living with people in their own social contexts and coming to learn the rules, often unspoken and unacknowledged, by which they live and make meaning, and also how the rules are broken and with what consequences. I lived in The Bush in 1991–2 and have returned to the site regularly since then, sometimes to do research (1993, 1995, 1999–2002) and sometimes just to catch up and chat.

Attentiveness requires setting aside one's ideas about how things 'should' be in order to find out how they actually are (or are not). It may mean stepping outside of conventional ways of seeing; conventions are often established and enforced by the powerful. This was brought home very strongly to me one day when I was talking with a woman about her desires to live a life that other people would recognise as 'decent'. Waving her hands at the 'zinc' (corrugated iron) walls of her shack, she commented,

> People look at our houses, these squatter houses, and they think 'Ag, these people' (i.e. dismiss us). But they shouldn't just look – let them rather come and see what's in our hearts …. We are not our houses.

Her comment was heart-felt. People who happen to live in shacks are frequently described by mainstream society as deviant. There is among the comfortable classes too often an assumption that those without permanent dwellings are little more than animals. They are homogenised and called by a generic name – 'squatters' – and all kinds of assumptions, usually negative, are made about them. The word 'squatting' alone is indicative, associated as it is with defecation. Discrimination against people with no fixed abodes endures in our modern world – for example, city planners refer to the shack settlements that ring the city as 'the septic fringe' and one need think only of the epithets applied to gypsies, slash-and-burn agriculturalists, nomads and herders around the world to see the weight of prejudice (notwithstanding recent theorising that seeks to recuperate nomadism). The roots of this discrimination go far back. In the Cape in 1655 Jan van Riebeeck noted disparagingly that the Khoisan peoples of the Cape had no homes. In Europe, by the eighteenth century, people without homes were considered a threat to society and stringent laws were enacted to force them to remain rooted in one place. These were implemented still more stringently in colonial states, where indigenes were excluded from the state's civil and political life, where racial laws enacted spatial separations and where gendered ideologies intersected with these to limit women's legal participation in urban life and their citizenship even more than men's.

There are echoes of these ideas in many of the laws that governed (and continue to govern) our cities – Acts that prevent vagrancy (such as Ordinance 50 of 1850 that enabled the colonial authorities to put 'vagrants' to work), thus turning certain kinds of mobility into crimes; Acts that determined who could live where and for how long (such as the now-abolished Group Areas Act) and who could work where (such as the apartheid-era Coloured Labour Preference Policy that governed employment relations in what is now the Western Cape). Ordinary people, activists and scholars continue to try to convince those in power that homelessness and mobility have little to do with an individual's intrinsic worth and everything to do with political will, economic relations and social classifications.

My methodological approach might perhaps be described as a disciplined eclecticism. My main interest is in everyday life; in what people take for granted as they go about their daily activities, the social rules – both implicit and explicit – that they follow, the tacit knowledge that they bring to bear on everyday activities and the consequences of these for their lives. I am interested in concepts and practices as they arise in a social field and in how people recognise and solve social problems. I pay particular attention to conversation and observations in order to try to trace key concerns as they were generated, articulated and acted on publicly. Being able to do so rests on a long-term commitment to a fieldsite or project, an aspect that is at the core of anthropological research. The book draws on nearly a decade and a half of working in The Park and thinking about everyday activities and unusual events. I trace concepts – such as *ordentlikheid* (decency), or *weggooi mense* – that were fashioned in public talk, and follow the ways in which they were discussed and debated and acted on – that is, as they acquired a social life and became naturalised in practice.

Over time, I have drawn on a range of tools, including surveys, questionnaires, structured and semi-structured interviews, informal conversations, structured observations, attendance at community events and ritual occasions, academic conferences and workshops. I made maps of the settlement as respondents saw it, and, for comparative purposes, encouraged fieldworkers to do the same. I gave cameras and diaries to children and asked them to record their daily lives, and developed food logs with adults as one way to track changing food and monetary incomes. Discussing observations with residents, colleagues and friends enabled me to refine the research questions and develop methods to address them.

There is a powerful founding myth in anthropology that fieldwork is conducted alone (see Clifford and Marcus 1986; Schumaker 2001). But all knowledge is produced in relation to others – those with whom we work, those with whom we share our ideas, those against whose ideas we set our own findings, and so on. My work has been enriched by the local expertise of residents of The Park and by astute assistants who worked on specific subsections of the project. Janine Pheiffer, who conducted interviews in Afrikaans on 'home', 'work' and 'illness' and transcribed and translated most of them, has been a delight to work with. She brought with her sunny disposition an acute ability to code-switch between the different forms of Afrikaans that signal different social statuses, and with that a marvellous capacity to engage people in linguistic forms in which they felt comfortable, respected, valued and understood. Our conversations, including her comparisons of The Park with the gang-ridden area in which she grew up, were endlessly illuminating. People with whom she worked remember her fondly and regularly ask after her well-being. Robyn Rorke assisted with the project on 'work'. Those with whom she worked say of her, sy't hart – 'she has a heart' – a great compliment. Years after her research in The Village was over, some residents still keep in touch with her by SMS. Siphiwo Bayi-Bayi was present for a short period during which he conducted interviews in isiXhosa on 'home'. His assessments of what he found in The Park with his experience of both shanties and hostels in Cape Town and with rural lifeways were illustrative, and his ability to work with young isiXhosa-speaking migrants, with whom I had had little contact, was a wonderful addition to the project. In addition to these three, over the years I have been fortunate to be able to work with undergraduate and graduate students in the Department of Social Anthropology at the University of Cape Town, conducting surveys, and so on. I am particularly grateful to Sean Cozette, Rhoda Louw and Kate Spann for their assistance in survey work, and to Sean for introducing me to Janine. Zanine Wolf and Cecelia Bermudez-Holsten both conducted short research projects on illness in The Park in 2001 with assistance from Janine. Their findings provided an important means through which I could track changes in people's ideas about illness causation.

A note on language

Most residents of The Park/Village speak Cape Flats Afrikaans (taal) as their mother tongue. Expressive and tonal, taal is specific to region and class. It is inventive and lively. Words are crafted to occasions, new expressions catch on flash-quick, spread fast. Throughout the book I have stuck close to local ways of speaking, even where these are technically 'incorrect'. I have also tried to retain the local flavour of words by rendering them as they are spoken. Thus *shebeen*, the common word for an informal bar, apparently derived from the Gaelic, is rendered here as *subeen* to retain the distinctiveness of local speech.

IsiXhosa-speakers account for approximately ten percent of the population of The Park/Village. AmaXhosa are usually proficient in several languages and most of our interactions were conducted in English or Afrikaans, or, more often, an *ad hoc* mixture of both with smatterings of isiXhosa thrown in. Where I have investigated concepts and practices that have particular cultural inflections (such as the various understandings of 'home', funeral practices, the relationship between sickness and suffering), I use the appropriate isiXhosa terminologies. I benefited greatly from conversations about my findings on these topics with Ntombizodumo Ngxabi, who at the time was working in a different part of the city, completing her research on amaXhosa migrants' conceptions of home and urban space, and with Siphiwo Bayi-Bayi.

On race and racialisation

South Africa's horrifying experiment with racial classification has had lasting effects on people's access to material means of survival and also in their explanatory models of the world. All of the residents of the Park/Village would have been classified as 'non-white' (Coloured, African/Black) in terms of apartheid legislation. Their life chances and those of their ancestors were constrained by the pernicious and cruel ways that racial categorisation – both colonial and apartheid – shaped ordinary worlds. I take this as the terrible givenness of the world into which people are thrown and through which they must navigate. I explore the contours of apartheid's structural legacies. I have tried to remain faithful to the ways that race materialises in everyday discussions. As a result, racial terminology appears when residents themselves made use of such terms to question or explain events and processes in their lives and encounters.

On idiosyncrasy

Raw Life, New Hope is both idiosyncratic – it derives some of its focus from the intersections of events or speech with my own experiences and expectations – and concerned with idiosyncrasy. Idiosyncrasy does not mean the absence of social rules. Rather, it marks the intersections of relationships and convention – of the social and cultural – at a particular time and in relation to particular persons. Idiosyncrasy is a relational term: something can only be judged idiosyncratic if it does not mesh neatly with one's own categories of thought, knowledge or experience, themselves socially and culturally derived. One's expectations are shaped by one's position in a set of social relations – class, gender and, in South Africa, racialised privilege play an important part in shaping these, as do value systems, cultural practices, ideology, training and so on. In other words, one's ideas and actions are always given shape in relation to multiple sites and systems of power. Reflexivity – an awareness of the ways in which present and past forms of power and history shape our expectations, positions and actions – is an important part of the anthropological research approach.

Idiosyncrasy implies that one's expectations are, in some way, exceeded. In many respects, anthropology encourages such a stance. I take delight in the discipline's readiness to be surprised. 'It may be said that the task of anthropology is to create astonishment, to show that the world is both richer and more complex than it is usually assumed to be', notes Thomas Hylland Eriksen (2004: 7). Brian Massumi writes that 'Reality is not fundamentally objective. Before and after it becomes an object, it is an inexhaustible reserve of surprise' (2002: 214). Surprise unsettles existing knowledge, making anthropology a powerful tool for thinking about and in the world. Social life always overflows the categories that we create for thinking about it, and sometimes a willingness to be surprised can generate novel – and useful – insights into social arrangements and relationships which themselves are always in a state of flux.

Everyday life in The Park

ABOVE (left to right) **Aunty Maggie on washday;
Nongwase's postbox; Tomega, Sakhiwe and Trica
catching fish in the sloot**

BELOW **The Park seen from the railway line, 1995.**

CLOCKWISE FROM TOP **The water tanks, erected in 1995; Andries and Gwen at work in Koos's spaza shop; Seven Leaves, The Park's Rastafari soccer team; Korporal and Callie and friends playing dominoes; Hendrik collecting firewood.**

ABOVE **Luzanne's photo of Donna Jean, Hybrie and Shirley posing in Charmaine's garden.**

ABOVE LEFT **Shirley near her home.**

I gave the children disposable cameras to take pictures of their everyday activities. Luzanne chose to take photos of her friends in Charmaine's garden. When I asked why they had posed there, she replied 'because it's *ordentlik* (proper) and pretty'. Being *ordentlik* was a core concern in people's aspirations and it shaped the organisation of everyday life.

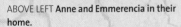

ABOVE LEFT **Anne and Emmerencia in their home.**

ABOVE **Themsy and Aunty Jane. Washdays were sociable in The Park.**

RIGHT **Nikitha visiting Bernie's house on washday.**

2

'I long to live in a house'

The Bush was really strange (snaaks) … Each of us could write a book about our life there … because there was always something. Every day something different happened. Big things, not small things.

Clive, interview 2004

We're going to build a model community. That's the only way forward for people.

Developer, interview 2000

'We are not *bergies* or *weggooi mense*', stormed Margaret angrily.

Someone had described her child as a *''n bergie se kind'* (a bergie's child), her home as a *weggooi huis* (throw-away house). The terms were disparaging. They cut her to the quick, undermined her efforts to secure her family and home. They resonated with older histories of displacement and racism. They made her *senuweeagtig*, caused her to *skel* (scold, shout), made her feel cold and shaky. People in The Park differentiate *bosslapers* (lit. bush sleepers; homeless people)[1] from *bergies* (lit. mountain people; tramps) and both from *plakkers* (squatters). *Bergies* is used only to describe people who live on the streets, and not to describe homeless people in general, as is the case in much public discourse in Cape Town. For residents of The Park, *bergie* is pejorative, implying a lack of morality and an inability to care for oneself and others, or to have sufficiently close relationships with others to be properly cared for. While many residents of the metropole referred to squatters as *bergies*, residents of The Park identified themselves initially as *bosslapers* or *eerste mense* (first people) and later as *plakkers*. They were careful to differentiate themselves from *bergies*. They were concerned not to be seen as '*weggooi mense*' (lit. 'throw-away people'), although for many years this is how other people, better-off than they, viewed them: a perspective shared by the apartheid state. Yet, among those who did not live in formal houses, there was a clear sense of place and commitment to site; so much so that despite several eviction attempts, they remained on site for more than a decade and some even longer.

Initial settlers, the bosslapers, at night, built small shelters beneath the pine trees. Several were migrants from the Aberdeen area of the Karoo, some 600 km away, who came to work in the metropole. They seem to have become relatively settled in the area of The Bush sometime in the late 1980s. The early bosslapers had a hard time of it. Unless threatened by police or landowners, they tended to remain in the area over quite long periods, although not necessarily in exactly the same site. During the day, they worked in town, working in domestic employ, seeking odd jobs or begging. If they did not find work, the bridge near the 'Pick and Pay' shopping centre offered a quiet space. They were frequently persecuted for vagrancy. In order to find work or food, and to avoid being arrested for loitering or vagrancy, the bosslapers usually moved away from the site during the day and returned near dark to share food, wine, fire and stories of the day. Their temporary shelters, locally known as hokkies (chicken coops), were originally little more than long low structures, often made from branches and plastic. One, a clear plastic structure into which its owner wriggled at night, is recalled with laughter as 'the greenhouse'. The shelters offered minimal cover from the elements and from the surveillance of police and town residents. Most people had formerly been farm workers and alcohol consumption was a central part of daily activities for several, particularly but not only men. In this, the routines of daily life matched and echoed those implemented in the Western Cape with the arrival of the first settlers and the establishment of farming systems based on slave and coerced labour, subdued through the dop system.[2]

The settlement grew and its inhabitants became bolder in the last years of apartheid. Shacks replaced the low-slung shelters and people acquired furniture and consumer goods. The increased size and visibility of the settlement did not go uncontested: old residents date the 'real' establishment of the settlement to when state agents razed the structures in about 1989. Shortly afterwards, Dina, who lived nearby and had 'rescued' people's belongings, moved into the settlement and, in her words, 'began organising'. By October 1990, when the Human Sciences Research Council (HSRC) conducted survey-based research in the area, the settlement had consolidated and there were fifty shacks on site (Emmett 1992). A survey I conducted at the end of my first fieldwork in The Park in July 1992 identified 132 structures (Ross 1995). At that time the area officially fell outside of the municipal boundaries, prompting the mayor of the nearby town to tell me in an interview in 1992 that 'There are no squatters here'. Partly consisting of road reserve, partly of rail reserve and partly of private property, a section of which was owned outright by a local landlord and another section of which was leased out, the administrative responsibilities for the area were complex. People's presence was constantly under threat. When I began my first research there in 1991, residents had already resisted seven eviction attempts by a variety of agents – local landowners, their tenants, and representatives of the state – to remove the settlement, either by forced removal, eviction notices, bulldozing the shacks, or, later, by attempting to negotiate with the leaders to have the settlement move to a large 'transit camp' built nearby, to which a number of other informal settlements in the area had already been moved. The latest of these ostensibly voluntary removals had just occurred when I began my research in the settlement. The removals occurred despite recommendations arising from research conducted by the HSRC (Emmett 1992) that proposed that one way to limit the violent conflicts over leadership and resources that plagued other large squatter and informal[3] settlements was to retain small, autonomous settlements with individual leadership. The Park's leaders, assisted by churches, journalists, the local Black Sash Advice Office and human rights lawyers, successfully resisted relocation efforts.

In the early 1990s, living in The Bush did not appear to hold any prospects of improvement. While other settlements in the Western Cape had at least some likelihood of future development, there was no hint that this would be the case for The Bush when I began work there. At that time, no services – water, electricity, refuse collection, sanitation – were provided. Residents had to collect water from a dam on a neighbouring farm. Women were afraid to venture far into the forested regions; violent attacks were common and they feared rape. Men had therefore to be sent – and paid – to collect water. By 1995, two storage tanks held potable water provided by the municipality. People used wood, paraffin and gas to cook on, and lit their homes with candles. They performed ablutions in the nearby forests. Refuse was occasionally collected by the municipality but more often gathered at the edges of the railway line until residents burnt it, smudging the settlement with thick, dark, smelly smoke. A strong smell of human waste permeated the air.

Despite its squalid conditions and lack of basic amenities, The Bush's population increased from 300 people in 1990 (Emmett 1992) to approximately 600 people in 2001 and from 50 to 180 structures (Developers 2001, personal communication). There are a number of reasons for the growth in the settlement between 1990 and 2000. There was a considerable influx into the settlement in 1992 as (im)migrants from the former homelands of Transkei and Ciskei (now the Eastern Cape) sought work in the city. In the post-1995 period the settlement expanded again; incomers were mostly labourers evicted from nearby farms, many of which were 'shedding labour' as they diversified, mechanised or were sold for urban development.[4] Other newcomers were the product of what local planners call 'urban overflow', largely of boarders, seeking their own residential spaces. In later years, the growth factors of urban overflow and farm eviction were joined by the loss of 'sleep-in' domestic work as domestic employment patterns changed. Young couples seeking independence from kin established new households in The Bush/Park, reasoning that it was better to live independently in a shack than to share personal space with others. These people usually phrased their move to the shack settlement in terms of 'privacy' and the opportunity to set up nuclear family households, although longer-established residents complained about the lack of privacy in the jostling settlement.

'Hok, dok, paleis, so the saying goes'

Children on The Cape Flats play a counting game, a fantasy about their future homes. You, they point, 'hok' (chicken coop). You, 'dok' (pondok – hovel). You, 'paleis' (palace). The categorisation marks a hierarchy: coop at the bottom, palace at the top. Well aware of the negative stereotypes that are attached to shack settlements, many people were ashamed of living in The Bush. They felt the sting of others' damaging evaluations. As an elderly resident, Attie, put it,

> Look, these people aren't riff-raff just because they live here. Some of them come from good communities. Do you understand? So, like me, they also lost their way once they started living here. But it's not too late for them to change. They just have to believe in themselves.

Attie's comment reveals the ambivalence people felt about life in the settlement. His pronoun – 'they' – and the term 'these people' (which, in South Africa is usually racially inflected and patronising), seems to refer to people unlike himself, but as he makes clear, he is one of the people who've 'lost their way'. Nevertheless, here and throughout the interview from which this extract is drawn, he insists that people are not to be equated with their circumstances. Others concurred. Asked by Janine to describe her feelings about a squatter camp, Wilma commented,

> You know, the first time my mother visited me, she was shocked. For the first few minutes, she felt a bit strange, but you know I made her feel comfortable. I mean, I was also shocked the first time I came to the squatter camp. I couldn't believe those were really homes.[5] I wondered how people managed to get by. [But] It's really not that bad and people are there because of circumstances beyond their control.

A little later, she added,

Wilma: To us, it's a home. But [to] others it's strange. I have a nephew in Port Elizabeth who wants to visit me but I don't know how to keep him away, you see?

Janine: Do you want to keep him away?

Wilma: Yes, but I don't know how to do that.

Janine: But why do you want to keep him away?

Wilma: Ooh, no! He doesn't know that I live like this, you see? So he'll be shocked, but if he comes then he'll just have to be shocked. If he doesn't want to sleep here then that's up to him. I don't know, he's such 'high society'. That's why I don't really want my real family to [visit]. You know, they do visit me and no one's ever had a problem but whenever I go home my sister would say, 'Oh no, you're obsessed with that shack of yours'. But it's a house, it's my home. It might be a shack but it's my home and I'm proud of it. When I asked her where her house is, she couldn't answer me. But it's true, I love my shack but they can't seem to understand that. Look, when I left home, I also didn't understand, because I grew up in a brick house.

Wilma's comments foreground several themes in this chapter, among them, the judgemental evaluations of non-residents, class and status differences and the consequences of these for (intimate) social relationships, shame and its remedies, pride and decency. Freddie, reflecting on stereotypes, said,

Many times I hear people saying, 'Oh, you live in a pipe' .... I don't know if miss ever heard of a pipe-sleeper (pypslaaper)? .... It's when people working on the roads dig trenches then they lay the pipes down for the storm water and at night you'll find people forcing themselves into those pipes if they have nowhere to sleep.

When asked how he felt about the appellation, he replied,

[It makes me feel] very sad. To think, to humiliate and to make that person feel so small ... It's bad enough that he doesn't have a house and then to be called a pipe-sleeper on top of that. It's not pleasant for me. My heart just breaks .... I long to live in a house.

Ponkies, one of the first people to befriend me when I lived in The Park in the early 1990s, commented, 'People think because we are squatters we are bergies.

But we are not, we are ordentlike mense' (decent people). On another occasion she commented that she was glad when the committee changed the shack settlement's name from 'Die Bos'[6] to The Park because she felt that 'Die Bos' made it sound like people 'slept under trees, without houses', which in turn made them seem 'unrespectable'.

Frustration and hurt at being judged by appearances was widespread. Strangers were not the only people to offer negative assessments of shack residents: as the quotations from the interview with Wilma cited above demonstrate, stigma rendered even close relationships fraught. One elderly man described it thus: 'Jy hoef nie skaam te wees om iemand daar van Stellenbosch te nooi daar na jou plek nie' [you needn't be ashamed to invite someone from Stellenbosch to your place]. ('People from Stellenbosch' operate in the local imaginary much as the proverbial Joneses.) Indeed, one woman explained that her partner's family had severed contact with them when they moved to The Park because they were so ashamed of the ugliness of the shanties, the poor appearance of the couple's shack and the kinds of people with whom they now associated. She hoped that the move to new houses would enable them to 'invite the family over for tea' and thereby restore proper relationships. Doubtless other factors figure in why kin relations had been severed. Nevertheless, her identification of the problem as lying in appearance and its complex relationship to respectability remains pertinent. In 2001, Lien told me that she was excited about living in a brick house because now perhaps her kin would not be embarrassed to come to visit her. Her comments were reiterated by others who claimed that relatives were so ashamed of their kin or afraid of the rough living of squatter camps that they refused to visit.

That one might believe oneself abandoned by kin because of where one lives may seem strange, but, as Wilma's discussion with Janine suggests, the fear is widespread and, it would seem, not unjustified. Under apartheid, racial classification for Coloured people rested partly on with whom one associated, and family relations were stretched and torn by the requisites of 'passing' in class and race terms. Apartheid's legacies remain powerful. Fine gradations – such as association, comportment, place of residence, manners – continue to mark people's social standing. It is horrifying but not surprising that residents' relatives feared that they would be negatively judged because their family members seemed less than decent. Disgust at the conditions in which squatters live often sours familial relations. Sometimes kinship relations cannot sustain the demands that people may make of them. Despite an ideology that holds kin as core, the family is a social institution that may crumble under the weight of poverty.

These dimensions are graphically revealed in the following extracts from an interview conducted by Janine with Anthony:

Janine: Okay. Tell me ... what do you think when I say the word squatter camp?

Anthony: It's very tragic. I actually grew up on a farm, and if my father and sisters have to find out that I'm living in a squatter camp ... I don't know if I'll be able to invite them for a visit .... The rest of my family will be too scared to visit me because I live in a squatter camp. They don't know anything about a squatter camp. They don't know anyone ... I mean, they don't know about building a house with zinc sheets. They wouldn't consider my place to be a home.

Janine: Is that so? So, you haven't told them yet?

Anthony: I never told them ....

Janine: You said that your family would be too scared to visit you, why is that so?

Anthony: Because they're not used to squatting. They don't know any squatters. Besides, things are rough around here and they are not rough people. It's alright for me though because I also used to be a rough guy.

As a young man, Anthony had spent a total of almost ten years in jail for murder and attempted murder. While in prison, he had been recruited into the notorious Numbers prison gang structure (see Steinberg 2004), in which he was a member of the 27s, the gang associated with assault. Striking in his model is that living in a shack of one's own was inferior to life in the impoverished and extremely dependent contexts of the commercial farms of the Western Cape. And living in a squatter camp was considered more ignominious than to have been a gangster and to have spent time in jail for attempted murder. So ignominious, in fact, that his family did not know where he lived because he was ashamed to tell them.

Attie responded to Janine's question about what came to mind when he heard the words 'squatter camp':

Attie: Uh ... It makes me think of an informal place where people squat because they have nowhere else to live. I think about the authorities, and how they don't care about those people. Before I knew anything about a squatter camp, I thought no one cared about those people living there. But then I moved to one myself, and I've discovered that there are still people who care. People still drop by to see how you're doing, or to do something for you. But at the beginning, it seemed as if these people were simply thrown away (weggegooi), and that nobody would ever think of them again.

Janine: So, the ones who still care are they outsiders, or do they live here?

Attie: It's the people who live here, for example the committee members and the people who come to our aid in times of need. The people from the Welfare Office and Red Cross are the ones who still care. The residents here also care about each other. We help each other wherever we can, you see?

This model of a caring community was one that was frequently offered to outsiders, although the reality was more complex and dynamic. Early in 2001, Janine asked Wilma about her sense of community. Wilma laughed:

Wilma: Oooh, the way things are going right now, I'd say it's chaotic. When I first got here, I looked up to people in the community. But later I got to know them better ....

Janine: Chaotic? Why do you say so?

Wilma: Man ... it's the alcohol that's tearing us apart. But when it comes to standing together, then everyone's there, especially when the police (boere) come in here. Otherwise, everyone does his or her own thing and life goes on. But there are a few good people around here. If you have a problem you can go to them and they'd help you. Really.

Vicky endorsed her point of view, saying, 'Look sometimes people here are good and sometimes they're disorderly (I almost said moer-in). I think sometimes people just lose control and when that happens, there's nothing you can do or say'. Both women longed for the privacy afforded by a formal house: 'then we won't have to listen to our neighbours fighting' as Vicky said.

The desire for privacy was frequently expressed, usually in terms of the desire for 'peace and quiet'. Yet, as Helena Broadbridge points out in her study of a new residential suburb in Cape Town, '[F]ulfilling the desire for privacy requires a collective understanding of what leading a private life means, and how it can be achieved, as well as a collective effort to achieve it' (2001: 243). It also requires conditions that are amenable to privacy, and there were few such spaces in The Park. Although many of the residents who settled there in the 1990s came seeking privacy, shack living made a mockery of public–private distinctions. Residents complained that neighbours' sounds impinged on their own attempts to create privacy and that the crowding and thin walls of shacks rendered privacy vulnerable. Anger, enjoyment, arguments, conversation and love-making were easily audible, making precarious people's attempts to establish 'private lives'. Noisiness was a core issue in conflicts in The Park. Sound was thought to affect one's comportment and emotion: women frequently told me that the noise from subeens 'worked on their nerves', causing them to be tense, shrill and irritable. Noise produced nervous tension which, they said, disposed them to quick anger which required careful self-control to overcome.

One of the community leaders, Sandra, who had lived in a shanty for some twelve years, described her frustration with the lack of privacy and her desire to live in a muurhuis (wall house – i.e. brick structure) thus:

Sandra: For instance, nè, my neighbours got a fight and I hear everything and in a wall house it doesn't happen like that .... I think that's much better, yes, because I think it's not useful for people to know each other in the, hoe kan ek sê [how can I put it], the finer details. I think it's not right.

Fiona: It's a nice way of saying it, not to know the finer details. It's a very nice way.

Sandra: Ja. And my feeling is that it's better that we can [should] move there fast ... We know a lot about each other and I think it's not right. ... Because I think myself that the moment we move we will stay away from each other, like the finer details, we will go to each other but not like we know each other so well like we do in the squatter camp, you see. ... And everybody knows. It's not right.

Fiona: So what you're saying is that you still want to have the sense that people know each other but not in so much detail. A little bit more distance maybe.

Sandra: A little bit more, ja. Some of the people said, 'when I move I will put a wall around my house so no one can see', you see.[7] Like we are at this stage, we've had enough from each other's knowings, knowings, knowings.

People anticipated that formal housing would offer respite from the forced intimacies of close living.[8] As Vicky put it,

When I have a decent roof over my head, I want to put my head out the door without knowing everyone's business. As long as I can open my door, not to throw out my water, but to admire the view, I'll be happy .... When I get my house, my business will be nobody else's but my own.

The complaint that 'everyone knows my business' was justified. In the over-crowded spaces, public and private life cannot easily be distinguished, and social tensions arise easily. Maintaining one's relationships in these circumstances is difficult; there are few resources available to assist people to manage interpersonal difficulties, especially when these take the form of domestic violence. The reality of unequal and often violent gender relations impinges on people's ideals and expectations of the new community. What appears from the outside to be a cohesive and homogenous 'community' is actually cross-cut with different schisms, gender being one of the foremost among them.

Options and constraints

Given that shack dwelling is generally considered by outsiders to be shameful and disgraceful, why do people live in such conditions? There are many answers. The first, and most obvious, is that peoples' options are constrained by a lack of opportunities. The legacies of apartheid planning, a severe shortage of housing in the city, overcrowding elsewhere and the lack of work (and thence access to a regular income that might allow one to pay rent in a more respectable area) are some of the main factors that precipitate the move to a shack settlement. In some instances, people have even less choice. Those who have served time in prison, for example, often find life difficult on the outside; work is scarce for ex-cons and the more so if one has a history of gang-activity – a history that is literally tattooed on the body. Sometimes social institutions such as the family fail people and they are forced to seek refuge elsewhere after their support networks have drifted apart or kinship structures are no longer able to sustain the strain of caring. In some cases, extreme destitution or illness combined with addiction problems propels individuals into squalor. And sometimes the move is the result of changes in the political economy of a region, as when ex-farm workers were evicted when farms were sold or farming mechanised.

People were not always pushed into living in a shack settlement. In some instances, people sought privacy or the chance to begin life anew. This was often the case later in the settlement's history for young people who sought to establish themselves in new relationships away from their parental homes, and who, given the lack of housing, found squatting to be a solution to their housing needs. Men who had been released from prison and who had been unable or unwilling to activate old (gang) networks often ended up squatting in The Park. Some saw the squatter camp as offering a place to 'get on your feet', as Anthony put it, but soon found themselves lodged there by the lack of opportunities to leave.

Sometimes people chose to live together in order to retain community ties. Such was the case for the many Rastafari in the settlement, who had forged a sense of community and wanted to live in proximity to one another so that they could carry out their desired form of life with others who shared their faith. It was also the case for family members who sought to retain strong kinship links despite material hardships.

A few people were attracted by the spontaneity of life in the settlement, the marginality and apparent lack of inhibition it seemed to offer. Strange offerings these, but some people celebrated a sense of the anarchic – the wildness – that they found there, where life was unpredictable and where, if they chose, it could be lived on the flipside of the law. For them, the settlement offered a kind of living on the cusp – risky, violent, extreme, exciting and attractive for precisely these reasons.

Drink and what was considered 'reckless living' were two ways in which increasing numbers of people tried to offset the instabilities of daily life. Reckless living offers men and a few women an escape into the excitement that comes with violating norms and conventions: it transforms lack of stability into an adventure. People whose lifestyles are extremely reckless, hinged into violence, are considered rou – raw, rough, anti-social, unformed. They represent the obverse to the aspirations for *ordentlikheid* (decency, respectability) to which many residents aspired. Yet there are attractions to living in the moment and doing away with inhibition, chief among them being setting aside worries about the future by behaving as if only the present matters.

This is also true of alcohol consumption, a defining feature of everyday life for some people. Wine (either the ubiquitous *papsak*—a five-litre sachet of cheap wine shared with friends, or bought by the glass at *subeens*) and beer were the usual drinks. Brandy was usually drunk only on weekends, mainly by men. While residents held that they were responsible for their own behaviour – 'If you drink, it's your fault', as Vicki put it – they also commented on the trying circumstances of everyday life, on the presence of *subeens* which made it easy to obtain alcohol and on the nature of addiction which made for repeated drinking (and drug-taking, though this was seldom mentioned as openly as references to alcohol).[9] Some people were clearly addicted, finding it difficult to give up alcohol even for a day. Alcohol was widely associated with the devil, and people here and elsewhere in the Western Cape hold that one of the only effective ways to relieve oneself of the devil's tight grip is to become *bekeer*, a convert (i.e. a 'reborn' Christian. See De Kock 2002). At the time of my research, several denominations including some charismatic churches were operational in The Park, but there were no drug or alcohol prevention programmes.

Drinking offers a routine to the day – a routine that had, for generations, cadenced the working day on the farms from which many people came. Noting that many people in The Park had 'drinking problems', Vicki described herself as longing for a drink, 'to get rid of stress and stuff'. She recognised the short-term and self-defeating nature of her alcohol use: 'It's not alright ... You think you're drowning your problems when you're only gaining more problems.' But, on the other hand,

> I get to forget my troubles for a little while, this way I also get to sleep throughout the night because most nights I just lie awake and think about lots of things ... When I wake up in the morning, I tell myself I won't touch another drink. But when I get up I feel way too terrible and the next thing I know, I'm taking yet another drink.

Alcohol (and drugs) blurs the edges of ugliness that holds lives in thrall, and allows the emergence of particular forms of sociality – the institution of drinking friendships among them. At the same time, however, it generates other kinds of ugliness, particularly interpersonal violence, including rape.[10] It renders people unpredictable; it is thought to undo inhibitions and strip aside culture. It is held that alcohol makes men 'horny',[11] lustful[12] and *woes* (fierce, furious). Drunk people are thought to be at the mercy of their emotions, particularly 'green eye' – jealousy. And jealousy is considered the root cause for domestic violence which was rife in the settlement (see Ross 1996). My observations suggest that alcohol-use deadens the experience of structural violence but enlivens the possibilities of interpersonal violence.[13]

Many people remained in The Park because they could see no alternatives. When the ugliness, repetitiveness and drudgery of everyday life set in, the expectation of new housing and improved prospects kept some people in a situation which might otherwise have been untenable. Nevertheless, over time they came to know one another, to have a sense of community. They had struggled to remain on site and to secure limited rights, and despite the problems that beset the community, they desired to remain with those they knew, anticipating that the move to new houses would permit a reformulation of everyday lives and routines, and might create the space to stabilise relationships and behaviours that they viewed as rendered precarious by the context in which they lived.

The consequences of these forms of life are many and diverse. As we will see, for some, insecurities give rise to short-term strategising. Fluctuating incomes, shattered personal lives, illness and long histories of being undermined and humiliated meant that some people did not always easily recognise long-term possibilities or know how to actualise them. Ongoing humiliations produced a lack of confidence in knowing that they could negotiate, or made them uncomfortable with formal structures, so that even relatively simple tasks, like asking for credit extensions, negotiating loans or registering children for schooling were haunted by the fear of appearing stupid or incompetent. Unable to secure the material means through which to activate their ideals, some people sank slowly into the squalor of their surroundings. Others struggled hard against prevailing conditions to raise their children with a sense of hope for the future.

'Where the community can find each other'

One way of dealing analytically with the diminished nature of everyday life's possibilities is to try to understand people's fears, their aspirations and desires for the future. I was fortunate to have conducted fieldwork at a time when new opportunities for housing meant that people were engaging with their ideals in a very practical way as they anticipated moving into a formal residential area. While excited, many people were anxious that leaving the shanty settlement and moving to the formal township would bring about an end to neighbourly relations and their sense of belonging to 'a community'. Here is Dina, one of two long-time leaders of The Park, talking to me in November 2000 about the impending move:

Dina: The one thing I will really miss of this community, I will miss the water tap.[14]

Fiona: You will miss the water tap? Why?!

Dina: Because everybody comes there. Even I'm there by the water tap. Even Sunday mornings, Saturday mornings, you will see everything. You can see jokes, you can see people standing and talking to each other and that music by the *subeen* is very hard [loud], people dance. Oh, it's nice, really I will miss the water tap .... No, when we are in our houses, when are we going to see each other? Do you understand what I mean? This water tank here means a lot to us, I must tell you.

Fiona: Interesting. Because I suppose it's a place where the community comes together.

Dina: That is it.

Fiona: So what's going to replace it?

Dina: [Interrupting] ... So it's like where the community can find each other you see? ... Hey, Fiona, I must tell you, you hear all the stories by *die water kraan* [tap]. If you don't know, you want to hear something, just go there to the water tap.

Fiona: So you'll see me every day now with my notebook!
Dina: If you want to find something just go there to the water tap.

In the period immediately prior to the move, the water tanks and the social interactions that occurred there as women and children waited in queues to collect their water allocations came to function as a metaphor for 'community', in all its complexity. Here, people problematised their living conditions and considered alternatives. New housing and the hope that it would enable more dignified living were frequent topics of conversation.

Making a model community[15]

By the mid-1990s, the Provincial Administration had finally recognised the settlement and begun to pay rent to a local landowner for part of the site. When the land on which the residents lived was sold in 1995, an agreement was gradually reached between The Park, the new land-owning consortium (The Consortium), the municipality and local government. The Consortium planned a security estate situated on a former wine estate. Its first phases have already been completed. The area is electric fenced, the single access road is barred with two boomed entrances that are manned twenty-four hours a day, and each of the townhouse developments is also secured with walls, electric fences and booms. The roadside is dotted with signs advertising an elite lifestyle and large signs at the town's entrances warn that trespassers on private property will be prosecuted.

One of the trustees of The Consortium described the development as 'a private township (with) private roads, private houses, private parks. (It's a) totally secured town ...'. The project manager for The Consortium commented:

The idea is to allow a community to develop in this area that feels free to walk to friends that live on the other side of the development, to create an area where people feel safe enough to do that and in the society and country security is a problem, so we're trying to provide some form of control without trying to create a little bastion of one's own, you know .... Whether that's practical or will happen remains to be seen. ... I think it's really trying to build an area that people can live, work and play all within walking distance and create a community that operates as communities of old used to operate, you know.

In such an environment, a shantytown is more than merely an eyesore: it is a deterrent to prospective clients. The Park was located on prime property alongside the development and partly occupying land that The Consortium had purchased. After protracted and frequently tense negotiations, The Consortium donated a section of land to the residents of The Park on condition that they secure funding for forms of housing that matched The Consortium's aesthetic vision of 'a model community'. (It is both a historical irony and a sign of continuities with the past that the sites to which Coloured people in the Cape were forcibly removed under apartheid legislation were described as 'model villages'.) A housing estate of low-density, low-cost housing was designed: five rows of houses built around tarred cul-de-sacs, with a central public open space and a single road access.

Anxious to create a new township that would be a 'model community' of fully urbanised residents with strong urban commitments and not a 'dormitory town', planners, developers, The Consortium, local leaders and community members alike envisaged urban planning as a means to curb 'disorderly' and unconventional social relations epitomised by the organic forms of the shanties and their spatial layout. Describing their intervention in housing provision as 'humanitarian' (letter to CEO, local authority, 18 June 1997), the Consortium's vision of 'the model community' was expressed in terms of education, aesthetics and responsibility – ideals that were closely linked with the developer's notions.

Home ownership is a central tenet in the post-apartheid state's provision of housing for the poor. Developers and community leaders alike described it to me in terms of having to educate people: responsibility and property are linked in a discourse that locates the residents of shanties in terms of their lack. The core trope used to describe the deficiency was flush toilets.[16] Differences between The Park residents and people who previously lived on a neighbouring farm were frequently described in terms of the latter's access to proper toilet facilities, and the former's lack. Developers, committee members and Trustees alike commented on the need for residents of the shanties to learn to use flush toilets as part of the process of becoming 'ordentlik' (respectable; decent). One developer said, '... I think that is for them the [main] part of ordentlikheid. To be clean and not to go into a bliktoilet (bucket toilet) or something like that.' Another commented that a model community consisted of:

> a decent built house with their own toilets and their own houses. And that for people that have never had access to things like that, there should be training. Although it sounds stupid. But the one thing is the health issue: that they have to clean the toilet twice a day and so on and what kind of chemicals to use and all that.

These ideas were not specific to the middle-class developers. One of The Park's community leaders told me,

> we are going to give them some workshops you see. So we are going to learn (teach) them, what is a house, now, you see. ... Because some of us don't know how to use even a flush toilet. So you have to do workshops with them.

This, despite the fact that most of the adult women – even those who have never had toilets in their own homes – have been or are domestic workers and are only too well acquainted with these activities. The anticipated workshops for women never actually took place, but the idea points to the ways that 'gender sensitivity' in development discourse – educating women – can actually disguise outright sexism and racism.

All development projects have a myth of origin. That accompanying the move to the new site goes something like this:

> Residents are poor. Housing is substandard. There are limited or no services. People are ill. Relationships are often short-lived. These features of urban living are not the result of state failure, planning, capitalism's unequal distributions of wealth, or even of apartheid planning's horrifying success, but are failings of the residents, who can only be saved by education.

The roots of this model are old: as with the eighteenth-century missionaries described by Jean and John Comaroff (1991), education was seen as primary in the development of a new kind of person, someone fit to live in a formal house. It was a model that many, including some residents, believed. It was linked with ideas about the need to take responsibility, ideas that were sometimes expressed in ways that verged on racism. For example, a Consortium trustee commented:

> I mean, it's a free enterprise society that we're in. They must take responsibility for themselves .... They are not like children: they must take responsibility for their own community ... [and] their own selves. And this is what I keep saying to them as well. It's no good all this time with the attitude give and take; we give, you take. They must learn they've got responsibilities. They are being given something, they must run that thing and they must run it properly. ... They have to learn to be responsible. There's too much of this bending over backwards for these people. They must learn now. They've got the vote, they've got the rights, now they've also got the responsibility of conducting themselves as organised citizens. They must organise themselves.

Others, more cognisant of the historical production of homelessness, shack settlements and unemployment, still identified education and responsibility as solutions to producing 'proper' people capable of living in formal houses. Here is how the Consortium's project manager described the task of educating people to be responsible homeowners:

> This thing has to be managed in a particular way to maintain standards .... What is home-ownership about? One of the concerns that I have – and I think you see it in other projects – is that people who are given homes without any 'sweat equity', without having to put anything into it, go into those homes and never lift a finger to maintain them. They don't see it as their responsibility, they don't realise that if you don't maintain, if you don't look after the property that over a period of time it will degenerate and depreciate .... We are looking at creating a Code of Conduct: the way we expect people to live and how we would expect them to interact with other people.

For him and the Consortium he represented, a model community consists in rules and adherence to them. Other 'key players' – committee members and members of The Park's Board of Trustees – held a similar view. For all, a model community does not arise as a natural product of upgraded housing, but is produced through carefully instilling new forms of social life, mainly through educational processes, and especially workshops. Developers and residents alike saw a link between urban planning, the spatial layout of homes and morality (Broadbridge 2001; Robins 2002). What Helen Meintjes (2000, 2001) calls 'propriety' is seen by key players as central to the emergence of an established working or even lower-middle class.

The creation of a model community was an ideal held by residents, too, but their terms of reference were wider. There was much emotional and social investment into prospects of new houses, which were seen by the residents as offering a way into respectability. Prior to the move, residents were excited. The new site was far larger than the area in which they were living, and as Vicky said,

> We'll have a beautiful view of the oceans and mountains. Around here, though, we only see cars driving by. I visited the site two weeks ago and the views are incredible and I imagine it will be great to sit in your front door on a Sunday afternoon.

Many agreed with Anthony that 'living at the new place will be better than ... living in this rubbish'. Others were anxious. Here are Baby's concerns:

Oh, the friends are happy to move but they're also very sad. Sometimes when they are all together they talk about how nice it could be if all of us could still live here together. Here we all know each other but we don't know what it will be like over there. Do you understand? The thing is, once we get there, we'll have to worry about our children. Here they can walk around late at night. They can go dancing in the *subeens* and nothing will happen to them. They can come home late and no one will be raped or lying dead somewhere. That's how it is around here.

Some people were concerned that they would not be able to afford living in new houses, with rates, water and electricity bills and with all the demands for material investment – decoration and maintenance – that go along with property. As Aunty Maggie, one of the *eerste mense* who hailed from Aberdeen and Baby's neighbour, put it, 'Houses are so expensive and I don't understand [how] we have to pay for those houses. I don't know about the paying story but whoever has to pay has to pay'. And Baby again: 'There's no money. Who's going to pay for it? I don't have a husband.' [17]

Her comment about lacking a husband signals the power of gender relations in The Park, where 'Die man is die dak en die vrou die vloer' (The man is the roof and the woman the floor). These ideas were universal among respondents, although women frequently pointed out that in practice the notion justified male domination (after all, a floor is walked on …) and was not an accurate representation of household roles. As Ponkies said, 'Hulle sê die man's die hof, maar dis ons wat die werk doen' (they say the man is the head, but we [women] do the work). Here, for example, are Regina and Vicky talking to Janine about their hopes for the new houses. They had just explained that, in a proper house, a woman is subservient to a man when Regina suddenly commented,

Regina: But why does it all of a sudden seem like women have a harder time? These days, men have it so easy … but we have to go on with these men.
Janine: Do you think there's something you can do about this or do you just have to accept it?
Vicky: Man, we call in the help of the law but they only ever tell us that domestic disputes are none of their concern. They're probably waiting for our bodies to lie somewhere before they step in. Women are beaten around here. I'm afraid that things won't get any better once we move to the new houses. …

Some people were extremely anxious that they would not be able to live up to their own ideals of propriety and were concerned that if they did not measure up, they would be ostracised. People fear ostracisation. As a researcher on the project, Siphiwo Bayi-Bayi pointed out:

> Sometimes … in the informal settlement, you can't say this is your border, like you don't even have a yard. … You might plan not to buy anything while you are living in an informal settlement and then when you are moving you might decide to buy luxuries. … At times you might say, 'No, I am not going to buy anything while I am living here. The shack can burn any time, you know'.[18] So you are hiding yourself as to what kind of person you are when you are living in that informal settlement.

In other words, the circumstances of shack living were such that people lived similarly (although, as we will see, there were exceptions to that rule), but the move into new housing had the potential to lay bare latent hierarchies and social divisions based on the accumulation and display of material goods, and indeed, this was the case.

While residents shared with developers a concern about the appearance of houses, they were also concerned about *ordentlikheid* and social relations. They actively dreamt of an 'elsewhere' that would not only be a material improvement on their current living conditions but that would also lead away from what they perceived as the moral decay of The Park. Indeed, early in the research, one of the community leaders described the goal of moving to formal houses as being to create 'a moral community'.

Ordentlikheid and the making of a moral community

The making of a moral community rests on both available material resources and on local conceptions of decency. In contemplating the new residential opportunities that faced them, many people spoke of 'ordentlikheid'. 'A lovely old-fashioned word', is how Etienne van Heerden, Professor of Afrikaans literature at the University of Cape Town described *ordentlikheid*. It has connotations of gentility and restraint, aspects of life both markedly absent from the rough, impoverished and improvisational conditions of daily life in The Park. It was a word in common use there and one that cropped up frequently as people spoke of their hopes for the future. It was widely held that the slum conditions of The Park gave rise to indecent behaviours and thence to people who are disrespectful of themselves and others. Attie explained: 'Ek sien hoe lewe jy, nou sien ek, nou kry ek skaam jy's my buurman. Ek kry skaam' (I see how you live, now I see, and I'm embarrassed that you're my neighbour. I get embarrassed).

Some people describe ordentlikheid in terms of respectability marked by external appearances. For example, all respondents described an ordentlike person as being 'skoon en netjies' (clean and neat), and ordentlike places as being visibly cared for and well maintained. Ordentlikheid is clearly a relational concept, one usually (but not only) deployed by women. It was widely held that women were responsible for ensuring that houses and family life appeared respectable. Here is Wilma: 'If that house isn't tidy, then you're not a woman', while Vicky noted of an ordentlike house that,

It has to be tidy on the outside as well as on the inside. In fact, it has to be even tidier on the outside, especially in the morning. You might not be able to clean your house in the morning because you have to go to work, but at least your house will be clean and tidy on the outside. First you have to clean your kitchen or your yard. Your yard has to be clean, especially if you have a garden with flowers or plants, then you have to greet them in the morning and you have to talk to them as well. If you don't talk to a plant then it will ultimately die. My mother got me to talk to plants because they understand what we say. For instance, if the atmosphere in a house is tense, then the plant will also look ill, even though you've watered it.

Both women anticipate the scrutiny of outsiders: residents know that they are assessed on the basis of appearances. The assessment can be harsh, even violent: men consider it justified to beat women who do not adhere to social norms.

Respondents described ordentlikheid by describing people and places using words like maniere (manners), leefwyse (lifestyle), netjies en skaam (neat and modest), groet (greet, or say goodbye), gedrag (behaviour), bedagsaam (considerate). In a delightfully Victorian turn of phrase, one elderly man described an ordentlike appearance as spoggerig (natty). A few other people described ordentlikheid in terms of a disposition that suggested to me a Christian framing, particularly as it relates to personal comportment and gender roles. My interpretation was confirmed in other quarters (see Salo 2004 and Ogden 1996), but most women respondents in The Park rejected the idea of Christian influences, although Ponkies commented in response to a question about the link between ordentlikheid and the church, 'Oh yes, Fiona, because cleanliness is next to Godliness'.

Others described ordentlikheid in terms of (self-) respect (see also Bourgois 1996). Respect has class and status components. One shows respect to those deemed different and of higher status: parents, strangers, church people, officials, senior people in the settlement. Subtle signs offered in people's bodily orientation and their linguistic bearings offer clues to the degree of formality that is appropriate in social interactions. For instance, during a discussion while we were standing outdoors one day, surveying the destruction wrought by a terrible fire that had razed one third of the shacks on the site, Tol suddenly straightened, quickly tucked in his shirt, turned the peak of his cap so that it shadowed his face, and greeted an elderly couple walking past. Neither of us recognised or knew them. His tone and the formal gestures that accompanied the greeting were unlike his usual informal mode of interacting with residents and visitors to the settlement. When I commented on the change in his comportment, he explained that the couple were clearly ordentlike mense. He had been able to tell from their clothes and style of walking that they were 'church people', and had adjusted his comportment accordingly, affording to them the respect that demonstrated his awareness of their status as ordentlik. His own 'proper' behaviour was modelled on his interpretation of their comportment and on his understanding of the kinds of behaviour this required of him. He illustrated his point with a description of behaviour in a subeen: 'If a man walks in and the peak of his cap is facing straight forward, then I know he's ordentlik and I hide my beer bottle. If his cap is skew or backwards, then I know he's a tjommie (chum, mate), one of us, and I offer him a swig.'

Drinkers, particularly women, often hide bottles behind their legs when strangers enter subeens. Outward signs of respectability in the other – read from bodily disposition and comportment – trigger 'respectable behaviour'. The slightest manipulation of objects is sufficient to code respect or its lack: the movement of a bottle behind a leg, the twitch of a cap from side- to front-facing. Here, where the appearance of respectability is desired, responsiveness to slight cues in the social context is important and conformity is valued. To gesture inappropriately or to fail to make the gesture when it is called for is a sign of poor socialisation and of lack of respect. To be self-respecting implies policing one's behaviour to ensure that one is not judged and found wanting. Small gestures and shifts in intonation are freighted with meaning and mark differential social status. These are so 'practised' – that is habituated, so deeply embedded in the taken-for-granted aspects of comportment in everyday life – that people do not notice them except in their absence or their misuse.

Informants hold that people are diversely socialised into ordentlikheid, and while 'ordentlike mense' are considered easily recognisable, ordentlikheid is not uniform. In one discussion, I asked people I know well to give examples of ordentlike mense. Only one of the three people whose names I was given corresponded with the model of decency I had internalised. Bernie runs a spaza/subeen. Her home was always sparkling, neat, with a kitchen area full of appliances and a fully furnished sitting room decorated with knick-knacks, a TV, video and hi-fi imposingly lodged on a new wall unit, wedding photographs proudly displayed. The other two names surprised me. One was of a man who lived and maintained his household alone. Unlike other single men, he did not hire a woman to do his washing, clean his house or cook for him, but managed, 'like a woman', on his own. He was well-liked for his 'friendly face' and charming manners – he never passed someone in the settlement without greeting them. Given that single status is eschewed in the community, and that it was widely known that he abused drugs, I was surprised that he was identified. The other is Evalyn, an elderly woman who was well known in the community. I was surprised that her name was listed because she was alcohol dependent and had a tendency to dance and sing and cry loudly in public when drunk. The group responded that this is precisely what made her *ordentlik*: 'She will always greet you, she brags, laughs, and when she's drunk she likes to sing, even if it is twelve o'clock at night. She reads her Bible in the window so she can be seen.' All three people were described as being '*altyd dieselfde*', always the same, unchanging; [19] '*hulle het altyd dieselfde gesiggies*' (they always have the same faces; that is, their demeanour does not change according to circumstances). This is considered an important trait in communities where poverty, violence, substance abuse and stress shred one's nerves and activate sharpness, jealousy and violence.

In short, *ordentlikheid* manifests as reliability in the conduct of social relations. It has to do with approved forms of sociality as the latter is manifest in appearances and interaction, both in recognition by others and in self-projection. A further dimension to sociability is characterised by 'conviviality' (Illich 1973; Overing 2000; Nyamnjoh 2002), manners of living and sharing in the everyday that elicit a sense of belonging through pride or sociability. Properness entails a careful weaving between possibilities. Taken to extremes, *ordentlikheid* may be interpreted as airs and graces, posturings of the 'hoity toity' that militate against dependable, 'real' relationships. Such people are described as having lost their *nederigheid* (humility), as being *hoogmoedig* (arrogant), *opmaak* (haughty), *stiffy* (formal) or *braggerig* (bragging). 'If you say you're hungry a *hoogmoedige* person will tell you to wait outside or at the front door while they fetch bread for you. They'll make you eat it outside too', explained Attie and his brother, Raymond. Given that white South Africans invariably respond this way to 'beggars', and particularly to *bergies*, in the suburbs, their example offers a clear class and raced index to propriety.

In their emphasis on sociability and relationships, the residents' model of *ordentlikheid* is markedly different from that of the developers, who foregrounded aesthetics and individuality. The model that residents espouse is not particular to The Park. It is a core cultural trope in expressing the desires, aspirations and hard work of working-class Coloured people in the Western Cape. Writing of Manenberg in Cape Town, Elaine Salo notes that *ordentlikheid* is strongly gendered: 'ordentlikheid refers to the intense, lifelong social and physical work that women have to do to keep the natural order of the bos or the wilderness at bay' (2004 172). In a very old-fashioned anthropological formulation, and in very general terms, one might say that ordentlikheid stands in relation to the bos as culture does to nature.

The work of creating ordentlikheid involves not only caring for appearances but caring for persons – moulding relationships so that people will be considered moral beings. Yet we should not be misled into thinking of ordentlikheid only in terms of its positive attributes. Some social ideals are over-determined (see Ogden 1996) and their inculcation may be underpinned by violence. For some people, the forms of the appropriate behaviour glossed as ordentlikheid were learned through bitter experience. This was visible in practices of child care and socialisation, where children who did not behave in accord with social desires – even where their behaviour drew from and mapped onto standard forms and norms of adult interaction – were cruelly scolded and sometimes severely beaten (see Chapter Three and Henderson 1999). Adults complained a great deal about children's lack of respect without recognising that their own lifestyles and methods of socialisation were at least partly to blame.

Violence is ordentlikheid's shadow. One man, explaining to me how to behave with propriety and to recognise respectability in others, commented that he had learned proper form at the end of a sjambok (a rawhide whip) wielded by the farmer on whose wine-farm his father was employed. The sjambok here represents the hard edges of decency: he had been beaten for failing to show the appropriate forms of 'respect' (read subservience) to the farmer. The mode of comportment appropriate to some forms of respectability is not impartial. Drawing on models that have their historic roots in forms of capitalist labour practice – slavery and exploitation – ordentlikheid may be shot through with traces of violence and injustice.

Ordentlikheid governs mobility and visibility, marking some spaces as appropriate to women and some not. If violence erupts around those who break the tacit codes, as for example if a woman is attacked at a subeen, others are unlikely to intervene – 'she asked for it' is how their lack of intervention is justified. Women thus inhibit their behaviour both in order to conform to a model they value highly and in order to circumvent men's violence and its sanction in patriarchal custom.

Adam Phillips notes that such self-inhibition is also a form of cruelty, commenting that 'when we inhibit ourselves ... we are in fact choosing safety in preference to transgressive excitement' (2002: 62), and arguing that

> this great unkindness, this inventive cruelty to oneself always has one over-riding consequence; it renders a person apparently predictable to themselves.

... [W]hat is then occluded, what is concealed or even supposedly abolished, is the unpredictability of the self. (2002: 73)

It is precisely this unpredictability that ordentlikheid seeks to cover, so one might say that respectability estranges a certain kind of freedom.

In the instances I have described, where ordentlikheid is shadowed by baasskap (domination/mastery) and patriarchy, violence moulds submission and labels it 'respect'. Avoidance or conformity to the demands of the powerful, both of which are read by the latter as forms of respect, are the only ways to circumvent humiliation or violence in such contexts.[20]

Ordentlikheid may operate as a mask, particularly in relation to domestic violence. Let me give an example drawn from my fieldwork in late 1995, a time when the residents had just learned of the possibility that they would be able to access formal housing. This knowledge had generated several debates about marriage and forms of proper living (see Chapter 4), debates that had been further grounded in a warning given by the chairwoman of the settlement that those who failed to eschew violence and public misbehaviour would lose their access to housing. Her rhetoric urged residents to solve their domestic disputes in ways that did not involve neighbours or alert others to the problem. In other words, domestic disputes were to be kept private.

One effect was to make it difficult for children to escape situations of domestic violence. Whereas in the past children had sought refuge from fraught domestic circumstances with neighbours and kinsfolk, now they felt the strong social pressures to conform to the model of privatised domesticity, nuclear family form and domestic peace. This was brought home to me shockingly when one young girl explained that if she had run to a neighbour the previous evening when the adults in her home had fought, as she once might have done, she ran the risk of revealing the distress in her home.[21] She was deeply afraid that this would foreclose the opportunity for housing. Here, her actions indicate a sensibility to appearance; responsiveness to the implications of change; a willingness to shoulder responsibility, even at the expense of her own safety and coping routines: in short, an ethical orientation so often assumed by outsiders and sometimes even the residents themselves to be entirely lacking in residents of shack settlements.[22] The consequences may have been grave: in her determination not to jeopardise opportunity, she was exposed to physical and psychological dangers. She was not alone in her assessment that potential access to public material resources demanded forms of deception. Adults and children alike were concerned that their behaviour be seen to conform to the ideal, and at that time many people commented on the ways that they were adjusting relations to their perceptions of the new demands, including by attempting to hide episodes of violence or of material lack (Ross and Spiegel 2000). The liberal distinction between public and private is here revealed in its hollowness.

For the most part, then, in the period leading up to the move, residents of The Park described ordentlikheid as a disposition inculcated by environment. Although one is born ordentlik (that is, it is an essence – an essential attribute of being human), and can be socialised to remain that way, negative environmental factors are sufficient to precipitate its loss, and positive factors may restore the sense of personal will necessary to regenerate the social dimensions of ordentlikheid.

That so many residents identified ordentlikheid as an aspiration suggests the extent to which they had internalised the negative assessments made by more powerful others of their living circumstances and their persons. They hoped that accessing public funding and moving to formal houses would enable them to concretise their ideal social forms. For some, this transpired. For others, reduced material circumstances and individual ways of dealing with these continued to demand a form of life that lay beyond ordentlikheid. Some were considered merely unlucky, but others, particularly women who had more than one lover simultaneously or in too rapid a succession, and men who were involved in gangs, drug-smuggling and violence, were considered rou. Rou means 'raw' in the sense of being unfinished, incomplete, anti-social. There are echoes here of the symbolic distinction Levi-Strauss draws between the raw and the cooked in which he argues that life's rawness is transformed by and into culture. A similar model operates among the people with whom I worked, for whom rou people are lacking the basic elements of ordentlikheid. To be accused of being rou is to stand accused of being less than fully human. Sometimes people make exceptions for those who are 'wild'. Dina explained that Nico's insistence on making ablutions 'in the bush' long after he had moved into a house, and his inability to use the (free) electricity in his house was because 'he was born in the bush and he grew up in the bush. You can't change that, really. He doesn't know anything else'. Similarly, Clive, who described himself as 'wild' commented that it was the result of his upbringing:

If you grew up in the ghetto then you're like that. It's just the way you grew up .... I don't want to change while I'm living here (in The Park). Maybe in another place (a reference to The Village) but not here. You have to be tough because if you're going to roll over (klein speel – play small) and play dead then everyone will walk over you. You have to act tough around here, even if you're not that tough.

Like others, he believed that improved living conditions might enable a gentler self to emerge, as though from a shell.

Ordentlikheid makes weighty demands and some people, like Baby, were anxious that after the move to new houses they might be found wanting in relation to it:

[When we move] ... we'll just have to change. We can't stay the way we are [here] ... Every day we are deurmekaar. ... This will have to change when I move to the new place. I'll really have to change, once I move in there, my child.

Prompted as to how she felt she'd have to change, she commented,

I'd have to go to church and things like that. I'd have to stop being so loud and I'd probably also have to stop scolding people. Every night I go to bed with a headache, and in the morning I get up with a headache. Because of all this, I can't always make it to work. It's because of all this stress.[23]

New housing is here linked with transformations of lifeways. Baby anticipated changes in her behaviour (note the Protestant underpinnings to this model). She was not alone in her assessment. Wilma said,

Man, I'm looking forward to it. I'm probably looking forward to it too much. I don't know. But my man isn't looking forward to it. ... He thinks it's too small but I'm looking forward to the comfort of a house. You know, we'll have electricity, which we've never had. We've never plugged in anything ... (giggles). No, for me it's very exciting. I'll have the TV playing all day long ... (giggles). I've never had things like that, so I'm looking forward to it. I don't care how small it is, I'm still looking forward to it. ... I'll become a better person. I keep telling myself, 'My house will look like this or that' (giggles). I don't have any new things but that will all come later. I'll wangle it with the little I have. ... I told my husband that I want a nice, clean yard. Here, we can't do our washing every day because we have a problem with water. At the new place we'll have water and then we can do whatever we please. No, I really want to be a better person. (Emphasis added.)

Wilma's sentiment was common in the community, where it was widely held that formal housing would facilitate new kinds of social relations and change personal behaviours for the better.

The move

Eventually, the houses were built using casual labour drawn from The Park and other shantytowns. Square blocks of 27 m², each structure was supplied with a separate bathroom consisting of a flush toilet and shower, a sink, an electricity meter with three plugs, and internal water provision. There were no internal walls save for those enclosing the bathroom. Properties were approximately 100 m², and the houses were usually centrally placed on the sites. While the sites were substantially larger than the cramped spaces of The Park, the houses were much smaller than many of the shacks had been and some people lamented the fact that their furniture would not fit into them.

The residents were excited about the move. Many began carefully packing their goods weeks before the move was scheduled. In July 2001, flatbed trucks ferried goods and laughing children from The Park to the Village, accompanied by the proud new occupants. By the end of April 2002, less than five months after the last residents were moved, most properties in The Village boasted fences and gardens, often with concrete paths and flower beds marked out in the dusty, unforgiving ground. Marigolds, cannas and gazanias dominated. A few people planted trees. Some residents asked Rastafari men to collect indigenous plants for them from the mountains: bright orange watsonias were a popular choice. Several people built elaborate gates and fancy bridges along the paths to their front doors. Raymond planted a 'health and waterwise garden', stocked with marigolds to keep away the flies and mosquitoes, and *vetplante* (succulents) that need little water. Neels divided his yard in two, planting a tree and a gazania-lined lawn in one half and a food garden with tomatoes and potatoes and carrots in the other. Five people planted food gardens and some of the Rastafari even dared grow marijuana plants discreetly on their plots. Some people added decorative touches – a painting of a candle and bible on one house, a Lion of Judah protecting the entrance to another, a brass door knocker, adhesive numbers, welcome signs. Some people plastered the bare concrete walls inside before painting. One woman detailed window and door frames in blue, painting the edges of her kitchen furniture and room-divider to match. She became legendary in The Village for her house-pride. So delighted was she with her new house that she spent hours every day after work decorating and rearranging the furniture. She was so busy that one of her neighbours warned her that she ran the risk of being ostracised for being 'hoity-toity'.

Almost all houses have net curtains hanging in their windows and most people have separated living and sleeping areas, if not with walls or furniture, then with curtains. Furniture appeared from storage with friends, employers and relatives, and even in the houses of the poorest people there was at least one table covered in knick-knacks and framed photographs. For the first time, children had safe spaces to play and when school came out, cul-de-sacs echoed with the sounds of boys playing cricket and soccer. Although still visibly inhabited by poor people, the new site was a far cry from the squalor of the shack settlement.

Yet uncertainty remained one of the core features of everyday life, uncertainty about whether people could live up to their ideals and about their health and incomes and relationships. Unaccompanied by changes in people's economic circumstances, the material improvements in their shelter have not, by themselves, been able to effect the almost miraculous universal transformation to 'decency' that the residents anticipated. Given the extraordinary importance of ordentlikheid in both residents' and developers' imaginations, it is not surprising that people should comment bitterly on those who, in the new settlement, do not match up to expectations of decency. Their judgement is harsh. It is difficult to live up to ideals when material circumstances are so constrained, when violence is pervasive and is given justification in gender and class ideologies that hold one in thrall. At times, people are fully aware of the forms of violence that are hidden within ideals. Sometimes the ideal world is unattainable, despite people's best efforts. And sometimes the material means with which to attain social ideals are not within one's grasp, rendering one still more vulnerable.

Social tensions simmer between those who are read as having made the transition into ordentlikheid and those whom they consider to have failed to do so. One of the harshest insults that can be levelled is the accusation, 'Hy/sy het die bos saamgebring' (s/he brought the bush with her/him). People who behave in ways that call this epithet upon themselves are a harsh reminder of the rawness and ugliness of life and relations in the shack settlement. They are considered shameful in the sense of shame proposed by anthropologist Michael Jackson (2002: 187): 'Shame is a transgression, deliberate or inadvertent, that causes one to stand out from the crowd, a sore thumb, a misfit, an undesired reminder of something collectively repressed, an object of the gaze of others, arrested and ostracised, possessing no will or reality of one's own'. Many people find it humiliating to be faced with this expression of what their lives had been and very often remained, albeit disguised by the newly acquired privacy offered by private property.

'Nothing has changed around here'

By 2002, the erstwhile leader of the settlement described the experiment in 'moral living' as a failure. 'The reason why they gave us this land was because we promised to be a model community. ... But we ended up not being a model community', she said. 'Nothing has changed' is how several people have described their living conditions, despite the manifestly better state of their housing and residential surrounds. They go on to cite material poverty and the behaviour of neighbours that is deemed disrespectful – public arguing or fighting, noisy drunkenness and sexual profligacy or inappropriate sexual relations usually figure prominently in their accounts, as does a lack of community sentiment. Drugs, alcohol and violence also play their part. Leaders state that teenage pregnancy is on the rise (although there is no evidence to support their claims) and the reason they offer is that the new houses afford the privacy for romance. 'I always say that if we still had to live in [The Park] I wouldn't have been a grandmother today. Lots of parents say the same thing', said one woman (herself a teenaged mother twenty years previously).

> I think it's because there's more space and more privacy. I mean, in [The Park] we could hear and see everything. Look, the bush was our toilet and they couldn't exactly do things like that (have sex) in the bush, because it would have meant doing it in the toilet .... You see, we didn't have these facilities in the squatter camp ... to be romantic. We were so shocked when we started having these teenage pregnancies ... [24]

The new houses are also blamed for illness and death: 'Didn't you hear how people died when we first moved in here? People were saying that the houses were the cause of it', said one woman (see Chapter Six). Another said that so many people had died when they first moved that the site was widely believed to have been cursed.[25] Unemployment, always high, increased during the early period in the new houses. The new settlement was too far away to walk to the 'job corner' where men waited for casual work and as a result 'piece money' did not come in. Residents believed that the churches no longer assisted, that casual employment had become scarce and that they were poorer. Their assessments were not altogether incorrect. Builders' holidays shortly after the move meant that fewer casual labourers were required over the festive period. In 2002, many people who usually worked as casual labourers on the farms during the harvest season were not employed. Farmers said that too many people from The Park the previous year had 'made trouble' by being drunk at work. The new settlement was further from town and residents accustomed to walking to work now had to pay for transport. Taxi fares increased, as did school fees and the costs of school transport. Despite a growing national economy, the basic cost of living has increased every year with devastating effects on the poor.

While residents are aware of the effects of neo-liberal market principles on their pockets and prospects, their conversations suggest that the emotional experience of economic hardship is felt in terms of a loss of community. Women were particularly vocal. 'God knows what's going on here now. We're living past each other …', said Baby. Her sentiment was repeated often, Tanya said,

We were very close but now everyone seems to be doing their own thing. We greet each other but that bond we used to share is no longer there … I think these *vrot* (rotten) houses may also have something to do with it.

Sandra concurred: 'We've been "dumped,"' she said. Heibrey told a journalist, 'In the old place, the informal settlement, everybody stood together. I don't know what has changed, whether the houses are changing people' (*Cape Times* Life supplement, 11 December 2007, p. 3) and Chrisna told Janine:

Since we've moved to the new houses, things have changed completely. Look, how can I say this? We're not living so close to each other any more and nothing's like it used to be. People pass each other without looking at one another. If you greet someone they don't greet you back. We live like enemies.

Asked 'Why do you think it's like that?', she replied:

Look, they think that because they're living in these houses … look, we can also live in houses now. They've forgotten where they came from … But we have to remember how we used to struggle. If times are good then we have to enjoy them, but when they are, we think we're high and mighty. But when we fall and we've come to get some bread on the ground, then we run into the very person we didn't want to greet or look at in the street!

Clive commented that 'I don't know if it's the *muurhuise* with electricity that are making people haughty, or what …' 'Or their own yards', added Carmen. 'Everyone's on their own now: there's no such thing as community any more', finished Clive sadly.

Some people blamed the new formations of space – houses that look alike, former neighbours parted, straight streets and demarcated properties – for the changes in sociability (see Chapter Three). Loraine's assessment was contradictory. On the one hand, she claimed that 'It's very much like it used to be when we were living down there (The Park). We stay together all the time.' But she quickly countered this:

The only thing is that we lived close to our friends down there but now we're spread all over the place. So as a result we don't visit each other anymore because the one lives over here and the other lives over there. So that's why I just sit here at home … [I]t's better to sit in your house than to walk around (rond te loop; Loraine's usage implies rondlopery, aimless wandering and time-wasting. It is considered un-ordentlik and when young women do it, they are suspected of 'looking for a man', that is, soliciting).

Some people blamed the absence of communal institutions, especially a church and community hall. Others blamed newcomers who (illegally) purchased houses from residents. Some argued that a new subeen was responsible for a breakdown in sociality, others said that new drugs were entering the community. 'Hoopies' (cliques) formed once more, breaking 'the community' into small groups. 'Life in this new (place) is all about jealousy', said Chrisna.

Zolani Ngwane (2003) calls for an understanding of social forms as the manifestations of desire and imagination. Ordentlikheid marks one form of desire and the move to houses offered a potential space for its expression. The ideal, however, founders on the reality of material differentiation and lack. Even within the category of the 'poorest of the poor', the effect of the move to formal houses has been to distinguish the extremely poor and destitute from those with more reliable incomes. The latter invest in houses and appliances and the material accoutrements of ordentlikheid (see Chapter Five). The former cannot, and look on their neighbours resentfully. A discourse of envy now accompanies an older one of interpersonal jealousy (see Chapters Three and Six). Whereas in The Park difference was largely masked by the unsightly appearance of shacks, with new opportunities to invest in appearances, the similarity has disappeared. With the end of the struggle for houses some of the social glue that held people together 'in community' has dissolved. People's explanations for their feelings of loss have in common a concern with the permeability of boundaries, a paradoxical sense that 'the community' was both more isolated than before and yet more vulnerable to fracture and to the social pollution that outsiders bring. The erstwhile sense of community is resurrected in conversations that differentiate 'us' from 'them' – people who live outside The Village, newcomers, visitors.

Writing of propriety in Lyons, France, Pierre Mayol describes it as a compromise in which, through

knowing how to 'behave', to be 'proper' […], the dweller becomes a partner in a social contract that he or she consents to respect so that everyday life is possible. 'Possible' is to be understood in the most banal sense of the term: not to make life 'hell' with an abusive rupture of the implicit contract on which the neighbourhood's coexistence is based. The compensation of this coercion for the dweller is the certitude of being recognised, 'well thought of' by those around one, and of thus founding an advantageous relationship of forces in diverse trajectories that he or she covers. (1998: 8–9)

Negotiating propriety in everyday life involves a careful balance between adherence to social rules, even where these go against individual desires, and 'singularisation' (Mayol 1998: 113), the process of making the neighbourhood – or, as it is locally rendered, 'the community'[26] – and the relations that characterise it one's own. Erring too far on the side of propriety renders one 'hoity toity', 'posh', which creates the risk of social alienation. Alienation is also the punishment for those who have erred too far on the other side as well. They earn the racialised epithet 'bosman', which, for residents, implies lacking civilisation and civility. Both categories suggest being unable to be properly social, to live up to the terms of the (sometimes implicit, sometimes explicit) social agreement about the need for and forms of decency. The next chapter explores some of these dynamics.

Mapping the sites

"You must use condoms for your own health because you cannot trust men, men here sleep around." – Teenage girl

ROAD – CONTROLLED USE

PEOPLE AFRAID OF RASTAS

Woman

corruption

TB

FEEL-GOOD MUSIC

RASTA CAMP

conflict

FREEDOM OF SPEECH

"GOOD FENCES MAKE GOOD NEIGHBOURS"

BIG FAMILIES

Substance Abuse

AMSTEL LAGER

SHEBEENS

VERY POOR

i'm fed up with my husband

HAND WASHING

GOSSIP

fighting

DISABILITY

DRINKING ALCOHOL ON TRACKS

MARTELL

SPOUSAL ABUSE

RAILWAY TRAC

SMOKING GANJA

FIREWOOD

Maps are generally assumed to offer neutral and objective representations of the world, but they actually elide as much as they reveal. After the difficulties I encountered in mapping The Park (see Chapter 3), I asked my research assistant, Janine, and some of the children to draw their own maps. Janine's map, conventional in form, seeks to depict the 'mood' and particularities of The Park. It is an intimate representation, based on her social and emotional experiences, her knowledge of people's relationships, speech acts and activities.

Janine's map of the mood and particularities of The Park.

ABOVE **Liesl returning to The Park after collecting firewood, 1991.**

RIGHT **Ponkies and Liesl, frustrated by my mapping efforts, 2000.**

BELOW **Gladys, delighted at the prospects of her new life in The Village, 2001.**

OPPOSITE ABOVE **The neatest portion of my attempt at a map of The Park.**

OPPOSITE BELOW **Portion of the municipal map of The Village.**

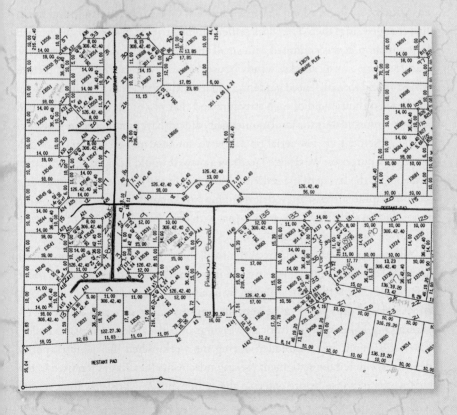

3

Sense-scapes:
senses and emotion in the making of place

Beginning with a map

Late in 2000, I asked Ponkies to accompany me through The Park to introduce me to people who had arrived since my last period of work there and to find old acquaintances after my long absence. I had last worked there in 1995, and much had changed since then. The shack settlement had tripled in size and quadrupled in population. It was crammed with small and large shacks, varying in formality: lean-tos, large sturdy shacks, 'wendy houses', shacks with pitched roofs, picture windows and formal, fenced gardens. Ponkies and I decided to identify on a map the heads of household of each structure and that way to trace the people I had known. Unfortunately, the local municipality did not have a graphic representation of the settlement. Its few aerial photos were outdated and taken from too high to suit my purposes. We decided to draw a map. It would help me re-familiarise myself with the layout of the settlement and would assist students in conducting a demographic survey. I knew that mapping would not be straightforward owing to residential shifts, but I was certain that with care, mapping The Park would be a relatively quick and easy task.

Although perfectly visible from the road, the settlement had a curious air of seeming somehow slightly secretive and impermeable to non-residents. To those driving past, the settlement whipped by in a blur of zinc, plastic and cardboard, an occasional glimpse of a person, an impression of dirt and squalor. Few passing would know of the intricate weavings of paths and named places inside, fewer still would enter unbidden during the week. When the *speurders* (police detectives) entered the settlement seeking miscreants they always reported to the chairwoman's house before entering the settlement. At Christmas time several local churches held parties for the children and weddings and funerals were held in the *saal* (community hall) built in 1993. Only occasionally did one see young white men smoking a zol[1] and being educated in the ways of the Rastafari, and sometimes NGOs ran interventions (such as leadership schools and crèches) there. Over weekends, more visitors came – friends and family from elsewhere, people seeking the liveliness of the settlement's nightlife, and, for a time, various church groups which held services in the *saal*.

The hall was one of several public spaces in the settlement. The water tanks were another, and clearings in the settlement afforded people an opportunity to congregate around a fire and chat. There were several *subeens* and *smokkies*. Four of the former offered seats, encouraging people to 'stay for a bit'. Bernie's 'shop' was frequented by her neighbours, mostly people formerly from Aberdeen and the Karoo. Bernie was considered both *ordentlik* and hospitable, and women liked to sit on the benches that ringed the room and tarry over a drink and a chat. In later years she had a television which ran off a car battery. Select women were invited to come and watch soap operas in her lounge. 'Security's', named after the owner,[2] was bright pink with a wide verandah, big entertainment area, a neon-coloured jukebox loaded with *kwaito* and pop, and a pool table. It was usually managed by his wife and cousin and was a favourite afternoon and evening haunt of the younger people and of men, who played pool and jived while older men sat drinking on the verandah. Mitha's 'place' was smaller than the others and was frequented mostly by neighbours, who popped in for a drink or to make small purchases throughout the day. They were tended by Mitha or her niece Tasha who worked there from early childhood because she was 'good with numbers'. Stanley's *subeen*, which he and his wife ran, boasted chairs and tables. It occasionally sold *umqombothi* (Xhosa traditional beer), as well as wine, commercially produced beer and brandy. It was usually frequented by Xhosa-speakers and was busiest over weekends when people came from neighbouring settlements to visit.

There were other, less formal sites of public interaction. Shacks eddied around four or five cleared spaces which were the site of much activity. Early in the morning fires were lit and women made coffee while men smoked themselves awake in preparation for the day. Throughout the day, women collected around these spaces to do their washing and prepare meals while chatting. Children darted among them. At night, men gathered around the fires to talk and drink as they waited for meals. One area was used solely by Rastafari who shared a zol, talked and reasoned. Another was regularly used for prayer meetings hosted by Bru Patrick, a lay minister.

Residents considered the railway line dirty and throughout the period of my association with The Park the area banking the line was where refuse was thrown and where children defecated. A dirt road, used mostly by men, ran along its length. Between the road and the railway line ran a small stream and alongside it, for about two-thirds of the length of the settlement ran an unnamed 'road', a wide path. Cross-cutting this were two other 'roads' and a wide shallow stream that seldom ran. The two cross-cutting roads were named. 'Main Road' was where the two community leaders lived, and 'Aberdeen Street' was named after a town from whence the first residents hailed. Narrow paths that wound into and through The Park were not named. When I lived there in 1991–2, everyday speech recorded sites in relation to features in the immediate landscape – 'by die sloot' (at the stream), 'langsaan die pad' (alongside the road), 'naby die lyn' (near the railway line), 'onder die bome' (beneath the trees), and so on. Some sections of The Park were named: there was 'Pick and Pay', an area west of Main Street, where destitute residents lived, some of whom had previously slept under the bridge at the nearby shopping centre for which the area was named. It was also sometimes referred to as 'the hospital' in recognition of the fact that many of its occupants were ill. An area in the south-eastern corner of The Park was, in the early 1990s, known locally as 'Crossroads', an echo of its counterpart on the city's edge, a site where some of the most famous struggles against the apartheid state for urban residence were conducted. Here, Xhosa-speaking arrivals to The Park were sent to live. I was told that this was to enable them to keep cattle close to grazing lands, but their relegation to the outer perimeter of the settlement also owes something to apartheid's racial classification and modes of separation.

Michael Jackson (1998: 175) observes that 'A place name is ... the trace of a story, the story about how a name came to be given'. He argues that by bringing the external world into our experience 'we go some way toward closing the gap between subjectivity and objectivity' (ibid.). In the names given its sectors and features, The Park incorporated and assimilated other spaces, bringing the elsewhere into its ambit. The names operated as reminders of other places, of the routes that brought residents to their present abodes. In so doing, they marked both the otherness of the residents and also helped to domesticate the landscape. Residents thus made the area their own in defiance of apartheid laws (particularly the Prevention of Illegal Squatting Act), yet in ways that continued to reflect the segregation imposed by the state.

So, beginning the map-making, I planned that Ponkies and I would walk the roads and paths along the gridded outline I had fixed in my mind, that is, in terms of my cognitive map. As we walked, I sketched the layout on sheets of A4 paper that I would later stick together. Remembering that the settlement became more densely populated from the centre to the eastern parts, I carefully recorded the number of each house that I drew, using the numbers allocated by the municipality and community committee. That was not as straight-forward as it sounds. In the preceding years there had been a number of surveys of the settlement and there was sometimes more than one number per shack, or the numbers painted on houses predated the most recent renumbering, so that external signs did not necessarily correlate with current knowledge. In addition, some structures had been subdivided and the numbers that people 'knew' to be their numbers did not necessarily coincide with the numbers painted onto wood and plastic walls or doors. In other instances, lodgers who were eligible for housing subsidies counted themselves as separate from the households which 'owned' the structures they were sharing, so subdivisions of properties into 'a' and 'b' and even 'c' abounded. Realising this, I wrote down the names of persons living in the houses so that I could orient the map properly when I stuck it together. I numbered each page consecutively and included on each new page the last house marked on the previous page. That way, I anticipated that all I would have to do would be to put the pages in their numeric order, matching up the houses as a check, and apply Sellotape.

Mapping was relatively simple at the narrow end of The Park. Ponkies and I walked, I drew, we stopped at each house to (re)introduce me to residents. But as we came closer to her house, at the base of what had been known as Main Street, things became more complicated. There had been several fires in The Park in the period that had elapsed since my last research, and people had taken advantage of the opportunity to reorganise their domestic arrangements (see Bank 2001). There had been an influx of people into The Park as it had secured recognition as an informal settlement from the local authorities. Some of the residents had become relatively prosperous and had expanded their houses into the area that used to be a street. Some people had built additional shacks to house children or lodgers, making enumeration still more difficult. For others, leaner times were reflected in the contraction of their living spaces, the shrinkage making space for newcomers to build small adjoining shacks. Recent homes had been built more closely together, jostling the paths that I remembered. New paths wound tightly against houses, cutting through fenced-off gardens, creating clusters of shelters that seemed to eddy against what I recalled as 'streets'. The old names of areas in The Park were no longer in use, and the road which had been Main Street no longer existed. Two huge water tanks and a large subeen headed the area that used to be the beginning of Aberdeen Street, and people now referred to it as the Water Place or Security's, named after Security's bright pink subeen.

Soon, I began to realise I had lost track. I could not work out our location in relation to what I had drawn. We kept walking, entering some houses and greeting people, all the while trying to draw. It became more and more confusing. I could not assess how the paths we were following intersected one another. Ponkies could not understand my puzzlement or why I was using the paths as identification rather than the people we were meeting and the houses we were so carefully drawing and recording. I insisted that we walk the settlement in a grid formation. She pointed out that the grid did not exist. The map became higgledy-piggledy. Her attempts to point out the (much changed) houses of people I knew did not help much. I could not orient myself in the absence of the paths I recalled from earlier fieldwork and I could not understand how Ponkies was orienting us in the small settlement.

We tried hard to make sense of our joint attempts to plot our movements. She could not understand why my map, drawn en route, seemed not to correspond with her knowledge of The Park or our current location. Initially we found my confusion funny, but she began to grow frustrated with my incompetence. The mapping and introductory process, which I had anticipated would take us a day, took four to complete. At times I found myself in the settlement easily, aligned to roads, the small stream, the larger stream that intersected it, a house that I recognised. At other times I could not understand how we had come to be where we were at a given time and my carefully drawn and annotated map did not help in the least. I felt foolish. It is a small space and ridiculous to be 'lost' in, especially when the railway line and road were only a hundred metres in either direction and could easily be found by orienting oneself in relation to the wider landscape – the mountains where the Rastafari go to meditate and to collect herbs on one side, the forested windbreak of a wine farm on the other. My sense of being lost was thus clearly not geographic – I could orient myself in relation to the wider geography of the landscape quite easily – but cognitive and emotional. I was disoriented as the familiar slipped past me.

The sense of disorientation I have described here has physical, emotional and cognitive components: coming to know a space was not the product solely of a visual relation with a landscape but an embodied one. The incident speaks to changes in emotional and intersubjective experience over time, to an interrupted sense of bodily placement in relation to features in a landscape, and to a puzzle about the relation of the senses to the modes and products of categorisation and classification. The very fact of the emotional disturbance that resulted for both Ponkies and me, and the ways that it produced a sense of 'disorientation' for us both, suggest that ethnographers need to pay careful attention to the roles and effects of emotion on recognition, way-finding and emplacement.

Of route-finding, relationships and representations

Maps are often assumed to be transparent and neutral, reflections of 'what is there'. Yet, as Edward Soja (1989) has shown, space is never neutral, and as the history of South Africa's racially exclusive spatial planning demonstrates, spatiality is profoundly ideological. Michel de Certeau (1988) argues that understanding – 'reading' – a space has much to do with one's own position in it. The views from 'above' and those from 'on the move' differ in important ways (see also Pandolfo 1997).[3]

De Certeau draws on Linde and Labov's distinction between 'maps' and 'tours' (1975, cited in De Certeau 1988: 119). As cartographic representations, maps offer an objective and distant perspective, while tours tend to be site-oriented and immediate. De Certeau envisages maps as schematic representations and tours as speech acts, and argues that the former rests on seeing – thus prioritising vision and the ocular – while the latter draws on action, going, moving, speaking. I would add to these two terms a third – route-finding – which engages a sense of moving through space, navigating relationships, a careful weaving between the known and unknown. Drawing on these concepts, one might say that the confusion in the mapping process I have described above is the result of a confusion of activities associated with specific conceptual frameworks. In this case, Ponkies and I were 'going to see'. The phrasing here implies a temporal dimension that has anticipation at its core. Anticipation is oriented to the future. It implies cognition, emotion and action, and contains both a sense of the expected (that is, predictable) and of the uncertain. This complex sense of temporality was belied by the actual intent of the task at hand – to produce an immediate and clear representation.

There were multiple layers of misunderstanding in the map-making exercise. Both Ponkies and I were engaged in re-accustomising me to a place and its residents—she through orienting me to her social space, me through abstracting that social space into a representation in which I was outside and beyond. During map-making, we were walking her everyday paths to friends and the sites of her occasional work in The Park. Her speech was a clue to our emplacement on her route: her language and style were informal when we met people she knew, but reserved and distant when we visited people with whom she did not have friendships or reciprocal relations. She pointed out the houses occupied by people she interacted with regularly and bypassed with silence or a short gesture and brief words those whose occupants were not part of her social circle. My map was a formal and distanced representation, modelled on street maps; hers an intimate and immediate representation, modelled on social relations. She was giving me a tour of The Park based on her routes through it, while I was drawing a map. She anticipated that her tour would serve as an introduction or reintroduction to relationships, I that it would give rise to a representation. She was introducing me to her space as a subject, and I was attempting to absorb it and render it an object. In so doing, the possibilities that were opened through walking and talking – possibilities of relationship – were reduced to representation.

Relationships imply work over time, a duration that stretches from the past into the future. Cartographic representations imply immediacy, the present tense,[4] and an abstraction from the routines of everyday life.[5] A map's presentness is achieved by eliding the temporal relations engaged in its production. In this fold, one can intuit how the objective might be produced from the subjective, a theme to which I return.

Initially I felt foolish for having anticipated that my abstracted knowledge of maps and the city would necessarily coincide with Ponkies' as we walked the paths of her home. I am, after all, an anthropologist, with a commitment to local knowledge, who therefore ought to have anticipated that her representation would reflect her own locatedness in the immediate context. And besides, I am often the butt of friends' jokes because I cannot easily orient myself by the cardinal points or by street names, preferring to refer to features in a landscape to find my way. In other words, in my own social life, my orientation is intimate and particular, not abstract and universalist. But it was not far-fetched to assume that Ponkies and I would operate with a similar conception of mapping. She is schooled, lives in a city, navigates it in the same ways as I do, that is, by familiarity and in terms of representations that rest on abstraction and gridding as both principle and expression. This might suggest that the difference was one of context not culture, that is, that the difference in our ways of understanding space rests on a history of activity within a landscape. Encountering the unfamiliar, Ponkies and I would likely both use an abstracted model,[6] but in familiar terrains, the modes of engagement and emplotment rest on rhythms and routines, patterns of social interaction.

Sociality, mobility and the gendering of space

Sociality relies on movement – we visit friends, hug those close to us, etc. Our bodies are expansive and motility is productive of our social worlds (see Merleau-Ponty 1964; Jackson 1995; Casey 1996; Mayol 1998; Ingold 2002; Massumi 2002). Yet, movement is constrained by ideas about properness, about the appropriate distribution of persons in space. Colonialism and apartheid produced racially and ethnically segregated spatialities and a distinction between places of 'work' and 'home', places of familiarity and those to avoid. We should not forget that these are legally enforced, sometimes violently.

Examined more closely, other factors come into play too: men and women, young and old, do not occupy space in the same ways – their movements are moulded by (implicit) social rules of age and gender. Some of these dimensions are addressed in Women and Space, in which Shirley Ardener and her co-contributors articulate the links between gender and space; the 'principles of order' (Ardener 1993: 5) that underpin and shape social life. Describing the hidden components of the relation between sociality and spatiality, the book reveals the gendered rules of how spaces are inhabited and how spatial practices reinforce or challenge gender norms. Missing from these normative accounts is the experiential and the emotional.

De Certeau writes, 'To walk is to lack a place. It is the indefinite process of being absent and in search of a proper' (1988: 103).[7] By 'proper', here, he refers to rules governing the distribution of elements in a field. For De Certeau, a place 'is the order ... in accord with which elements are distributed in relations of co-existence. ... The law of the "proper" rules in the place'.[8] 'Knowing one's place', that injunction so firmly embedded in colonial society, and against which postcolonial societies must struggle, is an instruction to adhere to the implicit law of the proper – the rules of hierarchy through which power is expressed and maintained. A class structure is at stake in the injunction, as, to a lesser extent, are age and gender statuses. Small wonder that, as I have described in early chapters, some residents are angered by others' apparent failure to behave in an ordentlike fashion in the new site. Their attempts to secure appearances in South Africa's cruel hierarchies are undermined by those who not only do not 'know their place' but wilfully disregard it and in so doing cast doubt on the status of other residents as decent people.

De Certeau's notion of the proper is also useful in relation to how people engaged with terrains outside of The Park. Take for example 'shortcuts' between the town centre and the settlement, which circumvent established and authoritative routes. They may eventually become established as routes but do not necessarily acquire formal status and will not necessarily be recognised in official representations of an area. Shortcuts may not be used by all equally. For example, women resident in The Park and Village avoided shortcuts for fear of attack and rape. They did not collect wood from the forests alone, were anxious when performing ablutions in the forest, and spoke of frightening episodes where women and children had been violently attacked in the surrounding agricultural and forested areas. Identifying dangers as masculine and – sometimes erroneously – as external to their community, women accompanied one another on excursions. In this way, the remedy to the possibility of male attack was female friendship. Here, danger is set aside by friendship, and sociability works to ease fear.

Gendered spatial rules are further embedded in local conceptions of respectability and manifested in gossip and sanctions linked to women's visibility and mobility. Ordentlike women stayed close to home. Those considered to 'rondloop' were stigmatised. Women developed standard routines and patterns of movement that included visits to neighbours and family, to the water tank and to the tuckshops and subeens. Movement outside of these established routines was frowned on by community leaders and most residents. Judgement was not made only by men: women were cruel in their assessments and kept minute account of one another's behaviour and demeanour. For the most part, ordentlike women were identified on the basis that they kept to themselves, kept their homes neat and tidy, catered to the needs of their menfolk and, when they ventured outdoors, walked decorously along established paths to close friends and kin. Here is Lien, married and a mother of two, who was at the time of research terribly ill, describing the sites and routines of movement: 'Ek ga' kliniek toe, hospitaal toe, huis toe. Ek stap nie rond nie.' (I go to the clinic, to the hospital, come home. I don't walk around.) Indeed, I never saw her anywhere in the settlement but in the immediate vicinity of her home. Neighbours collected water for her from the tanks outside her home. Her husband assisted a subeen owner with collections and deliveries and was given food. He moved about the settlement and between The Park, neighbouring shack settlements and nearby urban centres.[9] If Lien was not in the hospital or resting at her mother's home, she was always to be found near her home, inside, sleeping or cleaning, or sitting on the verandah, hidden from view by the wooden fence, or sitting on the concrete surrounds of the tanks. Lien was known by community members to be HIV positive, a status she shared with her husband and child. Residents spoke approvingly of her stay-at-home tendencies, describing her as a 'decent' woman, one about whom they would not gossip.

Different modes of occupying space imply different modalities of sociality and sociability. Women who walked around The Park with no discernable reason were considered immoral. Rondlopery implies aimlessness. It is thought to have to do with visiting a lover, purchasing drugs or 'making trouble' by minding gossip. It engages a specific bodily comportment – 'los' – a term that implies wantonness. To describe a woman as los implies that she is amoral, promiscuous. Women are afraid of being identified in this way. Stigma attaches easily, drawing blame, scandal and sometimes violence to its bearer. Scandal and gossip give rise to shame, humiliation and anger. These emotions work to make people conform with or reject the (often implicit) social rules that govern how things should seem. A women considered los receives little help or sympathy if she is beaten or raped because 'she was asking for it'. That is, the relation of comportment, speech, emotion and violence has manifest consequences in the spatial distribution of persons. Space, language and emotion are mutually constituted and constituting.

I want to explore this further by paying attention to how the model of *ordentlikheid* considered appropriate to adult women is instilled in younger women. Here, spatial practices express social norms and cultural conventions in relation to individual life-cycle processes. Young girls were frequently warned not to *rondloop*, and on one occasion I was taken aside and warned that my habit of striding boldly along the paths and roads of the two settlements as I went about my anthropological business was disconcerting to women residents and might be construed as inviting to men.

Drawn by passion, cajoled or coerced into sexual relations, young women are made to leave school when their sexual activities become public knowledge, something that happens quickly in such a small place. *'Jy kanie skool toe gaa'nie as jy 'n man het'* (You can't go to school if you've got a man), I was repeatedly told. The local model of childhood is such that book learning and sexual learning are incompatible. Girls in sexual relations are considered 'grown' and are expected to follow the same conventions of *ordentlike* sociality, including the spatial practices described above, as are older women. Failure to do so carries severe physical and social sanctions. In one case, two unrelated young women, Mem and Donna, friends, who continued to behave 'like children' (by disobeying spatial and social strictures appropriate to 'women' and continuing to go to school) while having affairs with men in The Park, were severely chastised. Community leaders imposed a spatial punishment: the two girls and Donna's mother (with whom Mem boarded) were made to stay near their home. They were not permitted to use the main road or to walk through the settlement but were made to walk its edge, alongside the railway line, past the piles of rubbish, drinkers and scavenging dogs, crossing the paths of those going to and from their ablutions in the nearby bush. Donna's mother was afraid to go out in public and sent neighbours or children to collect water from the tanks alongside the road. Held responsible for the girls' inappropriate conduct, she was particularly upset about being held accountable for Mem's failure to adhere to norms of respectability, saying 'She is not even my child'. No similar sanction was brought to bear on any of the male protagonists.

The punishment of spatial restriction was standard, usually meted out by powerful women. It was enforced through threats of physical punishment and fear, through 'skellery' (harsh scolding, a standard form of public chastisement and discipline in the settlement) and coarse taunts, and, sometimes, through physical violence. No man has ever spoken to me of these forms of sanction, although women frequently did. It is as though women's social impropriety is contagious, its effects intimately affecting the women around. In the case described above, inclusion in a new social categorisation – the result of community acknowledgement of individual passion – involves re-emplacement in space.

Mem and Donna did not conform to local conventions, and the sanction they suffered suggests a correspondence theory of classification: the girls were to be publicly invisible or to occupy the septic edges of the settlement. Like the dirt along the railway lines, they were matter out of place, to invoke Mary Douglas's famous phrase, and their banishment was intended to convey this to them in a spatialised and embodied form.

There are echoes in the treatment of Mem, Donna and Donna's mother with the principles that govern the appearance of respectability in The Park. Local models of decency are manifest not only in the distribution of persons in space but also in the spatial distribution of objects and in people's demeanour (see Chapter Two). The attempts to confine Mem, Donna and her mother parallel these patterns, suggesting that they were being subjected to the same rules as govern objects in codes of respectability that rest on appearances. Part of their punishment thus had to do with objectification, with making subjects and their social relations the site of forms of surveillance and activity associated with things.

This discussion sheds further light on the complexities of map-making and experience that I described in the first section of the chapter. The route that Ponkies took mapped one moment in an idiosyncratic knowledge of The Park, but idiosyncrasy does not mean the absence of social rules. One might say that idiosyncrasy is how one inhabits culture and makes it one's own. Ponkies tried to re-introduce me to The Park and its residents in terms of her social relationships and in ways that respected local gender conventions as these were spatially manifest. Her routes were both particular and constrained by established age and gender norms that govern movement and visibility. Her contribution to the mapping was an attempt to predicate subjective relations rather than objective ones, an attempt undermined in my insistence on cartographic representation. Given that objectification is a standard punishment for violation of gendered rules in The Park, it is not surprising that Ponkies was discomforted by the mapping process.

It should now be apparent that part of the difference between our experiences of The Park as we mapped is in fact socio-cultural – it rests on local ways of knowing and moving through an environment, and is embedded in linguistic conventions, sensory and emotional experience over time.

Sensory experience and locatedness

Shirley Ardener observes: 'Aida Hawile once tellingly remarked that the boundary between the "public" and the "private" may, in some contexts and under some conditions, be measured primarily by earshot' (1993: 12). Ardener adds: 'We see from this remark that a map of significant spaces identified by gaze might not coincide with a map of significant sound zones' (ibid.). Tom Rice comments that 'Hearing and the interpretation of sounds are ... understood to be vital in a social, as well as a material and spatial sense' (2003: 9). As I have described, in The Park, people frequently complained about noise. They desired from brick housing and formal housing estate a sense of respite from the sounds of their neighbours, from the noise of everyday life's intimate details to which they were constantly exposed in the close living of informal settlements. Some people, especially church-going women, commented that the settlement's noise 'worked on their nerves', making them sinuweeagtig. Others commented that people's chatter as they waited to collect water at the central water tanks was a central part of what gave the community a sense of itself as a community. That is, that sound offered a means through which reflexive categorisation and understanding occurred.

Let us take seriously the effects of noise on people's emotions and social relations. In addition to locating the effects of the sensate, recording a 'map' on the basis of sound and hearing would reveal a sense of the rhythmic in the everyday. Such maps would, of necessity, have to be located at a particular point. That is, each would have a point of view, reflective of a particular time and place. They would not be abstract and universalist, as are cartographic representations, but distinctly local. The daytime sounds that emanate from Security's subeen and fill the neighbourhood – jukebox music, the clunk and thud of pool balls, laughter, anger, the clink of bottles, the jingle of small change, the different voices requesting groceries – are quite different from those of the more deserted end of the settlement where houses are locked up when residents leave for work and where children seldom go to play. No two days sound alike, but there are patterns that emanate from the rhythms of ordinary routines, and interruptions to those rhythms could be marked. There would also be times when it would be difficult to differentiate between human and environmental sounds.

Philosopher Alphonso Lingis (1994: 69–105) argues that such 'difficulties' are themselves the product of attempts to separate human sociality from its environments. A sound-scape taken with Security's subeen as its source would reveal certain routines of the day as they impacted on activity at his shop. Mornings, when all is quiet save for the occasional request for tea or coffee or sugar and the knock of dominoes as the domino players meet for their regular morning gamble-game. The 10 am and 2 pm opening of the water tanks, when a line of chatting women and children forms outside the subeen as people wait their turn to fill their containers and heave them back home. Clattering bottles at midday, when some of the more serious drinkers begin the day's intake. Crackle of tin roofs under the sun, or the thump of rain. Three o'clock in the afternoon, when the children return from school and are sent to purchase goods, or hang about the *subeen* waiting for excitement. Late afternoon: the sounds of television soap operas mingle with children playing. Night time, when young men play pool, watched admiringly by their girls, when the jukebox blurts its songs of passion and beat, when children rush about purchasing goods for dinner, when the drinkers have settled in and tempers begin to flare, when the sale of alcohol outweighs the sale of foodstuffs. Late night, when the last drinkers have stumbled home and noise is dispersed. A sound-scape would create a sense and representation of the rhythm that characterises the settlement in relation to the landscape in which it is embedded.

Or, consider what a representation made on the basis of scent might reveal about people's routines. Early winter mornings with their smoky smell as the *gallyblikke* (charcoal drums) are heated. The smell of weak coffee – the morning's staple intake – and left-over food from the previous day before it is warmed for breakfast. Mid-morning: the scent of green soap as women wash their laundry. Midday, and the smell of inadequate waste disposal systems begins to waft in the heat. Evening: the smell of food preparation; samp and beans in the poorer section, cabbage and greens in the areas inhabited by Rastafari, meat simmering in the shacks of those who received government grant payouts or wages this week. The smell-scape would reveal rhythms of the day and of the week and time of year: at different times different foods are prepared, different activities take place outdoors. Midwinter: the smell of damp clothes, carpets and floor linings, the smell of rusting metal and soggy cardboard, the smell of wetness as the water table rises. High summer: the smell of dust and sweat and damp ground where the laundry water is thrown. These accounts reveal not only the surface (shacks, paths, natural features) and the social (commensality, etc.), but also the three-dimensionality of space and time: a rising and falling water table, heating and cooling air temperatures, and so on.

Our sense of space, then, is an intimate one. It rests on rhythm and deeply ingrained practices, themselves emotive and emotional. It is deeply resonant with the involvement of all our senses in pursuing the ordinary activities of everyday life. Little wonder then that when the move to formal houses was effected, people often commented with puzzlement about their sense of something being amiss. While delighted to be in 'proper houses', they described a sense of imbalance, both bodily and social. They found it difficult to express the source of their discomfort but they felt out of sorts with the landscape, oddly 'out of synch', surrounded by too much space, the houses too neatly laid out, The Village's gridded layout difficult to navigate. Some said that crime had increased (though there was no evidence to this effect), some blamed *subeens* for selling alcohol to children (although this was not uncommon in The Park), and some said that they missed their friends (although they all lived in the same 'community' and were well within walking distance). People described their previous neighbours as *versproei* (spread out, sprayed; the word is usually used to describe water from a hose). Evalyn said that Anne was too far away to visit, and Anne said the same of Evalyn. Their old friendship disintegrated and soon they knew little of one another's daily lives. Their complaints were echoed by others who no longer lived alongside old neighbours. Raymond said that Security's new *subeen* was too crowded with 'strangers' (although they were the same youth who had played pool there in The Park), and as a result he preferred to drink alone at home. Raymond knew that people frowned on solo-consumption – drinking at home is considered the sign of an alcoholic (rather than reliance on alcohol, quantities consumed or begging for money for booze) – but he would rather risk social disapproval than the emotional and physical sense of displacement he felt when drinking at the *subeen* with 'strangers'.

Some described their literal confusion about finding their way. Dina recalled:

> We even got lost around here! Sometimes we had to show people where their house was because they got lost. I was one of those people. I still can't tell you why we got lost. I often thought I was knocking at Vicky's door (her sister who lives two houses away) but when the door opened someone else was standing there. Then I had to say, 'Sorry!' One day I had to fetch Aunt Evalyn from the other side because she thought her house was over there (giggles). I don't know why that happened. What was that about? Before I had the building (extensions) done on my house, it looked just like every other house around here. So one day I thought I was walking into my house but when I got there I saw Oom Price sitting inside. I had walked into his house which is next to mine, and I said: 'Sorry Oom Price, I thought this was my house' ... I don't know if it happened because all the houses looked the same or what ....

I was initially surprised by these experiences of displacement, not least because the new settlement was formally laid out: a grid of roads around a central square. And besides, the houses were numbered, neatly and consecutively. None of the complex numbering systems that had characterised the higgledy-piggledy former settlement. What could be easier to navigate? And then I recalled my own sense of being out of place in The Park, and the complex lessons in subject–object relations I had learned from Ponkies and my map-making.

Finding one's place in a new space where all the houses looked the same and where one's former neighbours were just that meant replacing relationship-based and multi-sensory navigation with other orienteering skills – at least until one could find one's way with ease and relationships once more took precedence in way-finding. This is not as simple as it sounds. Most of the sensory features of the old settlement had disappeared. The new site does not offer the same olfactory assaults. There is no sloot (stream), sometimes clean and crisp, sometimes sluggish and smelling. There is no railway line smelling of hot iron, urine, waste, dagga and oil. There is no main road with its residue of hot tar-smell and exhaust fumes. The smell of human waste at the settlement's edges has disappeared. Water is provided to the house, so that the typical wet smell of water on dust at the water tap is no longer part of one's associations with movement through the settlement or with a sense of community. People socialise mostly indoors, so the hum of conversation and the sound of distinctive voices is no longer. In the early days after the move, every person I spoke to commented on The Village's comparative silence: concrete houses whose roofs and walls do not rattle and hiss with every breath of air, no juke boxes, no radios blaring. The Village's silence and the fact that so many people died shortly after the move there earned it the epithet 'Ghost Town'.

One result of changed smells and sounds was to disorient people's sense of time. In the old settlement, my day, like everyone else's, began at about 5 am when I heard my neighbours gathering around an outdoors fire to make coffee and share its warmth. The whole settlement was roused early thanks to the habits of those who had work or children who attended school. In The Village, people no longer made communal fires. They drank coffee indoors or on their own properties and the old noises that marked the day's temporality fell away. One might say that time became privatised, internalised and that sound no longer marked communal activities.

The ground in The Village is flat and even with no ridges and hollows to trip the unwary. There are no trees providing contrasts in light and shade. The houses are uniform in shape and orientation to the street. The new environment is one largely deprived of old sense associations, and thus one in which the visual has had to take priority. Yet the visual clues – the shape and colour and texture of houses, for instance – are homogenous and the site, laid out in concentric squares, seems to replicate itself so that people report that they wander in circles. Small wonder people felt disoriented when first they moved: at least three of the senses through which they knew their immediate world had become redundant, at least initially.

People found it discomforting. Not only because the familiar had slipped away, but because in seeking it and in being lost, they felt themselves subject to the same object relations that had so annoyed Ponkies when we had made the map. The layout of the new settlement had the effect of objectifying people's circumstances and relationships, making places interchangeable and disorienting people's embodied 'maps' of affective relations and sensory connections. Cognitive maps replaced intimate knowledge until people once more 'knew' where they lived and could find their way – efficiently and appropriately – to the homes of those about whom they cared.

The age and gendered dimensions of route-finding in the new settlement were remarkable. When the new settlement was designed, a central square was envisaged as a soccer field – that is, the settlement was envisaged as centred on male activity. To the best of my knowledge, soccer matches did not happen there, but the space seemed unrecuperable, a vast stretch of sand and nothingness at the heart of 'the community'. Children seldom played there, preferring instead the tarmac roads and the spaces between houses. Some women crossed it hurriedly on their return from work, but most women followed the roads, whose edges they tended to hug, unlike men and children, who occupied the whole road. Women kept indoors more than in the past and, when work was done, congregated with close friends within fenced-off properties rather than in communal spaces. Many women described how they spent hours rearranging the furniture in their new houses and doing domestic chores. Some said they felt lonely doing so, others reported a sense of satisfaction at their orderly houses and lives.

The new settlement was a distance from the nearby town and men no longer reported at the roadside to seek casual work. Several muggings and rapes, including of children, occurred on the short-cut path to town and people ceased visiting the centre as often as before. Instead they shopped at spazas and a nearby convenience store – both more expensive than the discount supermarkets in town. When they did visit the town, they preferred to catch a taxi than to walk the hazardous and now lengthy route. Taxi fares are not cheap and visits to town became 'events' rather than an ordinary part of everyday life. The rhythms of daily life were completely altered.

Rhythms of the everyday

Everyday life is reliant on rhythm in ways we do not ordinarily consider. Rhythm in daily life is that which gives it its taken-for-granted nature, what patterns it in relation to time and convention. Rhythm is not the same as uniformity. Suggestive of regularity and predictability, it does not obviate the unexpected.

Henri Lefebvre (2004) argues that rhythm, spatiality and temporality are intimately linked. He writes, 'Everywhere there is an interaction between a place, a time and an expenditure of energy, there is rhythm' (2004: xv). He argues '[A]ll rhythms imply the relation of a time to a space, a localised time, or, if one prefers, a temporalised space. Rhythm is always linked to such and such a place ...' (2004: 89). Lefebvre proposes four categories of rhythm: secret, public, fictional and dominating (2004: 18). Secret rhythms are personal – physiological and psychological (the heartbeat, memories that return, patterned ways of engaging the world with the mind-body).

Public rhythms are social; into this category fit celebrations and ceremonies and also those aspects of the personal that are expressed and shared (the examples he gives are expressions of tiredness and digestion). Fictional rhythms are 'eloquence and verbal rhythms'; language and learned behaviours. Dominating rhythms are 'completely made up'; everyday, 'aiming for an effect that is beyond themselves' (ibid.). What Lefebvre describes here is a way of linking the body and its rhythms with the space and time and systems of meaning and power within which we live out our lives. He notes that different places have different rhythmic qualities, and that rhythm is relative: something is fast or slow, regular or syncopated only in relation to something else. In other words, understanding rhythms involves comparative and relational knowledge. He claims that 'When rhythms are lived, they cannot be analysed', adding 'In order to analyse a rhythm, one must get outside it' (2004: 88). Literary critic Al Alvarez would concur: he argues that rhythm is not a product of 'perceiving a pattern in something that is outside us, but our becoming patterned ourselves' (2005: 58). This implies the operation of rules that we do not originate but which shape our lives, thoughts, social institutions, the ways in which our time is filled, the ways in which we sense rhythm and create our own.

For residents of The Park, stability and the rhythms that attach to everyday life through routine and established ways of doing things were hard-won and precarious. Daily routines were important to people, and women in particular resented disruptions. In part this was because routine offered a way to secure stability in lives rendered precarious by poverty, and those with predictable routines were considered to be *ordentlik*. Yet the rhythms associated with decency were difficult to achieve in contexts where ordinary life is uncertain and dangerous. This was especially the case when people initially arrived to live in The Park. I remember very well the difficulties that my neighbour, Margie, faced in trying to learn how to cope with the inadequacies of her shack, the demands of her newborn, the vagaries of her husband's income, the lack of water and refuse collection, and the indignities of having to ask a female neighbour to accompany her to the forest so she could make her ablutions because it was too unsafe for women to go alone. She found it difficult to establish a routine to her days and slowly withdrew into herself, scarcely leaving her shack. Her neighbours were disparaging at her failure to conform to their rhythms – her failures to collect water timeously, to do her washing early enough, to prepare food in the early evenings, leaving time during the day to be social, were considered grave misdemeanours, an affront to local patterns of relationship. Knowledge of how to cope in such circumstances had to be painfully garnered.

Lefebvre counterposes two kinds of rhythm: rhythms of 'the other' are those of 'the public', the discourse, representation (for which, one might read authority, power), and those 'of the self', concerned with intimacy and self-consciousness (2004: 95). He issues a warning:

> When relations of power overcome relations of alliance, when rhythms of 'the other' make rhythms 'of the self' impossible, then total crisis breaks out, with the deregulation of all compromises, arrhythmia, the implosion-explosion of the town and the country. (2004: 99–100)

I suggest that part of social life in The Park and The Village was in fact a kind of arrhythmia. Once established, people found that their daily routines were easily disrupted, jarring the rhythms by which they got things done. Small changes in routines could have enormous effects. The illness of a household member might jeopardise income and thence food for the week; one's own illness rendered one's body unknown; disruptions to the ordinary running of school buses might mean that children did not attend school for weeks (as was the case in the beginning of 2004), and so on. So much more so for large events – deaths, physical assaults, addictions, arrival of kinsfolk, pregnancies, etc. Given the instabilities of income and routine, disruption was part of everyday life in The Park, but no easier to deal with for all that it was expected. People complained that daily life was unpredictable, that they could not find their footing, or, having found it, were unable to secure it for long.

One way of getting outside one's naturalised rhythms, or indeed arrhythms – as travellers, migrants and exiles have long known – is to move, to be confronted with new architectures, new placements that demand a new comportment. Lefebvre describes this process as 'the requirement of passing from one rhythm to another, as yet unknown – to be discovered' (2004: 97). Discovery is always edged with danger. Dina's experience of getting lost, echoed by others, suggests an unbalancing that was disconcerting not only because unexpected but because it replaced an intimate knowledge of place, built over time, with the experience of having to navigate by representation in an environment that presented itself as already built, already complete.

Most of the residents had come to the city from small towns and rural areas on its periphery and, once arrived, had to learn to navigate the world as it presented itself. But there are striking differences between those individual trajectories and the process of moving en masse that characterises the move to formal housing. When people come to the city, they usually stay with relatives or friends and learn its ways through the rhythms of their hosts. So, residents had come to know The Park through the mediation, rhythm and routines of others. Even though the relocation of 'the community' to The Village was to an improvement in housing and services, the experience of mass relocation was disjunctive. Informed by the experiences of people forcibly removed from their homes and communities under apartheid, community leaders and advisers anticipated the disorientation of the move and initially tried to offset it by telling people they could choose their neighbours. In fact that seldom happened: the gridded layout of the new site militated against the complex neighbourhoods that had characterised The Park, and people accustomed to living in close proximity with myriad others suddenly found themselves spread out along roads in neat squares with only one neighbour on each side. Some people were so discomforted by the process of seeking out old friends that they felt unable to make the effort.

Rebecca Solnit (2006) makes a strong case for getting lost. When you get lost, 'the world has become larger than your knowledge of it' (2006: 22), she notes. And yet, 'Never to get lost is not to live, not to know how to get lost brings you to destruction, and somewhere in the terra incognita in between lies a life of discovery' (2006: 14). The sense of loss of control, she implies, might lead one to search for new ways of being. She cites Thoreau: 'Not until we are lost, in other words, not until we have lost the world, do we begin to find ourselves and realise where we are and the infinite extent of our relations' (2006: 15). This was the case for residents of The Park. As Attie commented (see Chapter Two), one may know where one is in geographic terms but be lost in relation to prevailing social values: 'Like me, they [the residents] also lost their way once they started living here [in The Park]'. Living in The Park meant knowing where one was spatially but living in ways that did not conform to social ideals. He reminded me, 'But it's not too late for them (residents) to change'. And, as the discussion above and in the previous chapter suggests, living in The Village meant adhering to dominant social values at the cost of being spatially and socially lost.

The state of temporal and spatial displacement about which so many people commented was a clearly demarcated period, one in which people had time and space to sort out their relations, to work out who mattered and why and to reorganise their social lives and worlds. Sometimes this was experienced as positive, as when Sandra joyfully commented that now she could enjoy being in her home without people calling her stand-offish. Other times, it was negative, as when people lamented friendships lost. Yet all the time, new relationships were being formed, new connections made and new rhythms emerging. They drew on prior ways of being, refashioned.

In both familiar and unfamiliar terrain, we do not move as automatons but as lively, engaged social beings – as both agentive and constrained by convention. Our understandings of the landscape reflect our emplacement within it as social and phenomenal beings. This means that our knowledge of a (social) landscape is likely to change over time as routines change and relations alter, as life-cycle processes and the cultural conventions by which they are marked shape and produce the experience of sociability in place. It implies that individual 'maps' differ, and that there are overlaps and underlays. It suggests too that the roads and paths etched into a landscape do not necessarily engage an individual's knowledge of a place or ways of inhabiting it over time. In addition to revealing the structural components of everyday life – the unspoken rules (of age, class and gender) and taken-for-granted rhythms and routines that modulate the ordinary – a careful consideration of the ways that different categories of person engage and interact in space allows us to consider the relationships between the sensory and the emotional in the making of sociality and everyday rhythms in particular places.

With this in mind, I return to the mapping exercise with which I opened the chapter. An occasion in which a map's making became ambiguous and its production the site of confusion lends itself to consideration of subject-object relations and the occasions in which they emerge. It also suggests the moment at which an anthropological enterprise shifts between the exploration of others' worlds and Othering, a shift echoed in the abstraction of relationship into representation that the story of mapping both tells and anticipates. One might say that my efforts at mapping tripped on the intricacies and complexities of relationships and everyday life as lived rather than as represented.

Perhaps one might characterise this as stumbling on life.

On home

Ask Joe or Jane Typical in the elite suburbs of Cape Town to describe 'home', and what most often emerges is a description of a place and a set of relatively stable affective relations (frequently described in terms of the nuclear family), often tinged with nostalgia. Before their move to The Village, however, residents of The Park frequently used 'home' in the future tense, describing it as a zone yet to become. While everyday life was structured and cadenced around family and friends, work and leisure, few of the people with whom I worked recognised either their living arrangements or their material and social environments at the time as enabling 'proper homes', and they frequently lamented the gap between their actual and ideal worlds. The possibilities of social transformation offered by a move to formal housing threw their concerns into stark relief.

Mary Douglas offers a provocation to complacent notions of home. Her controversial point of commencement is that home is a place, rather than, say, a set of relationships. She states, 'Home is "here" or it is "not here"' (1991: 1) and argues that it cannot be defined by its functions. Resisting common (and thus culturally and historically specific) ideas of home, Douglas asks us to imagine home in structural terms, as a virtual community, a structure in time that contains the capacity for planning, differentiation, distributive justice and complex co-ordination. For her, home simultaneously enables and censors. Oriented in both space and time, it is a zone of structured domesticity, and, she implies, of regularity and order.

For Douglas, 'The question is not "How?" nor "Who?" nor "When?" but "Where is your home?"' (1991: 2). In South Africa, the ways that family and social life have been shaped over time, particularly by colonialism, capitalism and apartheid, make *all* of these questions germane. As an extensive literature (beautifully rendered in Zolani Ngwane's 2003 article 'Christmastime', on which I draw in Chapter Three) shows, processes of exclusion, migration and mobility render the question of home extremely complex for many South Africans.

Xhosa speakers generally offer three terms to describe home. *Umzi*, *indlu* and *ikhaya* carry different social and emotional resonances. *Umzi* is usually translated into English as 'homestead'. It is always used to describe rural modes and patterns of living, constellations of agnatic kin. The *umzi* is the place of communal living – a cluster of buildings that house kin. Ideally, it is constituted around a *kraal*, the cattle byre, the symbolic heart of the homestead. The *kraal*, the cattle that occupy it, the social relations that enable it, and the histories of rituals performed there, constitute the *umzi* and give material centre to weight of time and ritual obligation. It is here that one's umbilical cord is buried, that the ancestors are propitiated, and important ceremonies are conducted. These rituals both enable the present and rectify social relations. The *kraal* is a gendered site: women are considered to be pollutants and, save for in exceptional circumstances, should not enter it or tend to cattle.

Indlu means house. The term refers both to a physical structure and to the ranking of polygamous relations in an *umzi* (members of the Great House, for instance). It is not commonly used in urban areas and when I have heard it invoked it is usually to describe a secondary structure built onto a residence. Another term for this structure is *intanga*, traditionally used to refer to a room built for young men of courting age who have not yet formed their own homesteads.

The word most commonly used in everyday translation for the English term 'home' is *ikhaya* but there are important differences between the use of 'home' by English-speaking South Africans and the Xhosa term. Ntombizodumo Ngxabi (2003) notes that a child refers to the homestead as *ikhaya lethu* (our home), while the head of the household refers to the same homestead as *umzi wam*. The terms *ikhaya* and *umzi* thus also reference different generational relations and responsibilities towards the homestead.

Xhosa speakers, particularly migrants, in the Western Cape differentiate between going to one's house and going 'home'. The verb 'to go home', in the 'deep', symbolic sense of home described above, is '*ukugoduka*', and people who originate in the same geographic location are known as '*amagoduka*', a term usually translated into English as 'homeboys'. *Ndiyagoduka* (I am going home) is generally accepted as referring to the place of one's ancestral belonging: it carries implications of time traced through lineages and descent. This sense of home is also, at least at present, firmly geographically centred. All Xhosa speakers who participated in the study stated that 'home' is in the Eastern Cape, even if they had been born in Cape Town. When I remind them of the historical dimensions to the presence of (and efforts to confine) Xhosa speakers to the Eastern Cape – the *Mfecane*, colonial expansion and the 'frontier wars', migration, apartheid planning, forced removals, creation of the 'homelands' of Transkei and Ciskei, pass laws and the Coloured Labour Preference Area, skewed urbanisation patterns, and so on – nevertheless the response to the question 'Where is your home?' was always couched in terms of what one might name mythic time: the location of the ancestors, even where people professed doubt in the vitality of the latter.

Many Xhosa speakers draw a strong distinction between urban and rural, but the conception is not solely fixed to geography. Constance Yose (1999) argues that her informants consider shack areas to be like rural areas: residents engage in the same kinds of social relations in shack areas as are expected in rural areas, and their social relations change when they move to formal houses. Their taxonomy blurs neat distinctions between urban and rural areas. Ngxabi reports similar data, showing that among shack dwellers in Cape Town, complex social taxonomies that mark status have emerged. She focuses on the role of ritual in making homes, exploring the ways that ritual is modified or set aside by residents of shacks who move to state-subsidised houses. Hylton White (2001) approaches the question of home from a different angle. His work examines affinal rituals among Zulu speakers in Northern KwaZulu-Natal. He demonstrates the transformation of the spatial layouts of homesteads by capital penetration and their reworking in ritual contexts in order to enable ancestral recognition of the home. But it is not only in relation to ritual that homes are sites of contestation. Zolani Ngwane (2003) describes how at 'Christmastime' in the Eastern Cape in the 1970s, when male migrants returned to the homelands, ideological and practical conflicts between men and women over the form of the household and ideal conceptions of home emerged. Read together, these papers outline the contours of ideas about home that are vested in complex processes which mesh ancestors, capitalism, urbanisation and the post-apartheid state.

As we will see in the chapters that follow, the efforts of residents of The Park to remake home in the light of new social possibilities and their ideals challenge Douglas's distinction between place, people and temporalities. For many residents with whom I work, making and maintaining home has long been about determining 'when', 'who' and 'how', and is increasingly about using these criteria to fix relationships in time and space. Learning from residents of The Park, I have come to the conclusion that one might best consider home in terms of affective, imaginative and shifting clusters of relationships, often but not always coded in terms of kinship and affinity, and frequently made tangible in material form (such as through material investment or ritual action). The reason for this rather complex phrasing lies in the intricacy of social organisation in the settlement itself, as I show in the next chapter.

Relationships that count and how to count them

I was not the only one caught flat-footed by life in The Park. Residents also frequently expressed a sense of stumbling on the improvisational quality of relations as they unfolded. As we will see, this was particularly the case when it came to making and sustaining familial and household relationships and shaping them to fit established legal forms.

'Who's going to live in your new houses?' I asked Sandra and Ponkies one day in 1995 while we were visiting Sandra. The three of us were sitting on Sandra's double bed which doubled as a sofa. Sandra's reply was quick: 'my husband and my sons', she said. No visitors who overstayed their welcome, no kin who felt they could impose, no 'extra' people who needed caring for, just the nuclear family. Ponkies was equally sure: she and three of her four daughters. The fourth had recently set up her own home with her boyfriend, and Ponkies's husband was living in Cape Town. The discussion moved on to the difficulties of sustaining families in conditions of poverty, of caring properly for children, and of the complex webs of reciprocal care that knit neighbours together and the delicacy in managing social relations that these called for – a delicacy often undermined by the contingency of everyday life.

In order to move to The Village, residents had to qualify for state housing subsidies available to the poor as part of post-apartheid social reforms. The state's definitions of eligibility were broad and flexible but the already-complex household and familial relations in The Park were compounded by the need to move as 'a community', even where individuals did not qualify for subsidies and therefore would not qualify for housing. For residents, questions of eligibility hinged on relationships rather than biological relatedness, and turned legal questions of entitlement into moral and ethical questions of community-making.

When I spoke with residents between 1995 and 2000 about their expectations of new housing, many spoke of their desires to create nuclear families or, more realistically, to stabilise two-generational female-headed households – a far cry from the extremely fluid social relationships that typified many households at that time. Many planned to formalise existing relations through marriage. Their ideals of stability, nucleation and marriage contradicted the reality of domestic life in The Park where mobility between households was high, children were often dispersed between households and across geographic space, and few couples were married.

Counting relationships

The move to new houses precipitated concerns amongst residents and developers about what kinds of relationships 'count' and how to count them. The stakes were high and differences between the perspectives of residents, developers and the state had to be negotiated before residents qualified to move to The Village.

From the perspective of the developers, residents obtained houses by being recognised as members of the community (a point to which I return towards the end of the chapter) and by applying for and being granted state housing subsidies. Initially, developers anticipated that each 'structure', as the shacks had come to be known, housed a single family, and constituted a household, an unambiguous domestic unit. They therefore assumed that there was a neat correspondence between the number of structures and the number of families in The Park, anticipated that each household would qualify for a subsidy, and planned accordingly. They were soon to discover that their model of a neat overlap between family and household was too simple.

The post-apartheid state was considerably less naïve than the developers. Family life in South Africa has been deeply shaped by the region's political-economic relations: among other features, colonialism's discriminatory work and migration processes and the apartheid system of Separate Development.[1] The exclusion of Africans from cities gave rise to massive regional, seasonal, gendered migration and the sundering and reworking of kinship ties.[2] Well aware of this complexity, the state made its housing subsidies of between R9 000 and R18 000 (between USD1 500 and USD3 000) available to adult South Africans who qualified on the basis of a means test and dependency relations. The specific relationship between applicant and dependants is not completely defined. The application form devised by the National Housing Board states:

Applicants for subsidies should either –

- be married (in terms of the Civil Law or of a customary union) or be cohabiting habitually with another person as if they are husband and wife; in all of which cases the applicant's husband or wife or partner in cohabitation is referred to as the 'Spouse', or
- have one or more dependants,[3] in which case the applicant could be widowed, divorced or single.

The definitions of dependence do not necessarily imply a moral dimension to eligibility: the emphasis is on legal and economic relations. They are, on the surface, sufficiently broad and flexible to accommodate the diverse forms of relationship that historical processes have engendered. Nevertheless, even granted that completing official forms is always complex, some residents of The Park faced considerable decision-making about who 'counted' and how.[4] The process of applying for subsidies highlighted differences between the state's definitions and those held by residents. In part this is because the former, while recognising the complexity of 'dependency', assumes that there is a temporal coherence to being a dependant. The state's definition of 'dependant' also rests on assumptions about the nature and duration of kin and affinal relationships. These did not have a taken-for-granted character in The Park.

Facts and fictions of kinship

Relationships came under close scrutiny when people discussed who would live with them in The Village. Residents describe kinship primarily in biological terms, but biological relationships may be expressed in a variety of ways. Alongside the taken-for-granted mother-child dyad, and the recognition of fathers, only some of whom acknowledge their offspring and take responsibility for them, there lies a range of relationships expressed in biological terms and containing elements of surprise. Take the common situation in which a child born to a 'blood relative' is taken in by kin. For example, Raymond's wife bore their son. Shortly thereafter, Raymond's wife's mother gave birth to a daughter, a *laatlammetjie*. The term literally means a lamb born late in the season, and thus one in need of special care in the face of the threat that encroaching winter offers. Raymond and his wife felt that the older woman would not cope with a baby so late in her life and decided to take the baby in and treat her as theirs. So, she was brought up as their 'daughter', their son's sister, although by standard biological reckoning – one way that residents reflect on relatedness – she is Raymond's wife's sister, his son's aunt. The different modes of classification are not considered contradictory, merely context dependent.

Most of the adult women in The Park bore their first child while teenaged. The trend continues among their own children. It is uncommon for a woman to reach her early twenties without having been pregnant. Sometimes the fathers of children born to teenaged mothers acknowledged their children but more often young progenitors did not acknowledge, support or participate in the daily lives of children for long, particularly if the men did not reside or have blood relatives in The Park/Village. As we have already seen, the beginning of sexual activity marks the ending of girlhood and the passage to forms of adulthood that are usually marked by leaving school. Sometimes the new mother returns to school, but more often she seeks work outside the household or, if there is sufficient income, stays home to help care for the baby.

Very often a child born to a teenaged mother is brought up by the teenager's mother as though the child were her own offspring. While people in the neighbourhood are aware that the (grand)'mother' was not pregnant, the child is socially recognised as the son or daughter of his or her biological grandparents, and the biological mother's sibling.[5] Hence, a fiction of sorts: a social pact not to acknowledge the 'facts' of biology that people generally consider to be the basis of kinship. The biological is overwritten with a kind of 'secret' that some know and some do not. It is a generational and therefore hierarchical secret, one that the biological mother and grandparents know, and sometimes seem to forget, and one about which younger siblings may not even be aware. The latter is particularly interesting because siblings are usually keenly conscious of how they are related. Mothers are taken as given in children's lifeworlds (see also Bray et al., forthcoming): it is children's relationships with fathers that exercise them, and siblings measure their relationships to one another on the basis of whether they were fathered by the same man. Thus Donna could write of her mother's partner that 'Hy is nie tevrede oor ons nie. Ons is vyf kinder; hy wil nie vir twee kinder sorg nie … Hy wil ons uit die huis sit' (He isn't satisfied with us. We are five children but he will not care for two children …. He wants to throw us out of the house). Those two were herself and her brother, both borne of Donna's mother's relationship with another man. I shall return to the issue of how and whether men acknowledge children, and with what implications for the children and their mothers.

A biological relationship previously disguised may be revealed to the child later in life. One woman's son learned that she was his biological mother when he was about ten. Until then he had lived with his maternal grandmother whom he called mother. He came to live with his 'biological' mother (ware ma – true mother), her husband and 'half'-siblings when he was a teenager, in order to attend High School nearby. The disclosure involved telling the other children that they had a brother and the husband that his wife had a son from a prior relationship.[6] Shortly thereafter, the woman's third child was sent to complete her education in the small town where her mother was born. There the girl lived with her grandmother, whom she called grandmother, and her sister, whom she called sister – the same people who her 'half'-brother had called mother and aunt. Kinship may thus embed surprise and children in the same generation born to the same woman may at different times have entirely different classifications for their surrounding kin.

There is no guarantee that children will necessarily enter the familial genealogies of those who bear or those who care for them. Where the mother's relationship with her own kin group is not stable, the child may be abandoned (uit gesit, uit geskop, weg gegooi; put out, thrown out, 'thrown away' – abandoned). Young people thought to be sexually active and thus 'adults' even if technically well below the legal age of adulthood are also sometimes abandoned. I knew of several such instances in The Park. In one case, described in more detail in Chapter Seven, a teenaged youth was abandoned by both of his parents. His father was ill and left the settlement to be cared for elsewhere and his mother left the settlement altogether with her new lover. The latter refused to accept her son into his household and the boy was left to his own devices.

The refusal is not uncommon. A man entering a relationship with a woman who already has children does not necessarily take up the role of 'father' in relation to them, even where the children have no contact with their progenitors. Children call the relationship accurately: 'Hy's my ma se man' (he's my mother's man/boyfriend) and often try to avoid addressing the man directly, circumventing the emotional and social complexity of naming. If a man acknowledges a woman's child from a prior relationship, the child may be permitted to become part of the household and may even call the man Pa (Dad), or women may be allowed to send remittances to those who care for her children elsewhere.

What enables a child to be taken as a relative therefore seems to have to do with men's preparedness to acknowledge a woman's sexual and reproductive past. Where such acknowledgement is not forthcoming, women must choose between giving the care of their children over to others, abandoning them or engaging in subterfuge to support them. It is a desperate choice, particularly for women without work who sustain themselves and others only through their vat en sit (see below) or sexual affiliations (see Ramphele 1988 and below). So, as with women who work as childminders for the rich at the expense of caring for their own children (see Cock 1980), or migrants who can sustain rural households only by sending remittances earned in urban areas (Murray 1981), poor women may have to sustain their children by moving away from them, by sending them away and/ or by disguising their relationships to them.

Sometimes children whose usual carers have left them (*weggooi kinders* – thrown away, abandoned children) are taken in by other adults who are not related biologically and whose social links to the child may initially have been slim. Such children are known as *grootmaak kinders* (lit. 'make big' children; children being 'grown up'). *Grootmaak kinders* sometimes held the same rights in households over time as did biological children. Meitjie's experiences offer an illustration. Her parents separated shortly after Meitjie's birth and her father and his family played little role in the child's life. Susan, Meitjie's mother, had sole responsibility for her. When Susan moved in with Price, Meitjie accompanied her. Susan and Price lived together for a few years and because Price was good to her, Meitjie grew up calling him 'Pa'. When Susan and Price separated, Susan left Meitjie behind in The Park. At this point, Meitjie was potentially a *weggooi kind*. Price's sister, Baby, took the child in and cared for her. '*Sy het haar grootgemaak*' – 'she grew her up' – as they say locally. *Grootmaak* is a common social institution; a manifestation of care rendered as taking responsibility for the life of another. Meitjie grew up calling Baby 'Ouma' (Grandma) and Price 'Pa', although she is not a biological relation to either.[7]

A decade later, Price applied for a government subsidy for a house, listing Meitjie as his dependant. When the houses were built, Meitjie continued to live with Baby. Shortly after moving to The Village, Price's 'lady friend' moved into his house and continued to live there after he died, although it was widely felt in the community that Meitjie ought to inherit it, and legally, as his listed dependant, was entitled to do so. Meitjie meanwhile had dropped out of school and was hanging out with a *rof* (rough) crowd. She had taken to drinking and smoking *dagga* and after warning her repeatedly, Baby sadly said that Meitjie was behaving like an adult and was therefore responsible for herself.

While she was alive, there was debate over who had greater rights to residence in Price's house – Meitjie, listed as his dependant, or Price's lover, who had no legal rights over the house but was considered both responsible and *ordentlik*. The case was made more complex still by the arrival in the settlement of Meitjie's biological father, Michael, whose sister owned a house there. He asserted a claim to Price's house on the grounds that Price brought up his child, that she ought to inherit the property and that as her father he was entitled to manage her estate.

Meanwhile, Meitjie had left the village. She was brutally murdered in 2004.

In other instances rights dissolved, and with them access to basic material and emotional resources. In such cases, children were cast upon their own ingenuity and social networks in finding new homes and creating new forms of relationship.[8] I illustrate this with the life experiences of another child, Mem. When I met her in 1991, Mem was living with her mother Jeanette and her *ma se man* (Anthony), with whom Jeanette had borne two children. Sometime in the mid-1990s, she left him and moved back to her parents' home on the West Coast. The two younger children were left with Anthony's parents, but Mem was not considered part of his family, and so was not included in the arrangement. Ponkies, the mother of one of Mem's close friends, took her in for a while, saying that she would not watch a child being thrown away (weg gegooi), but her own material circumstances were so tenuous that she could not care for Mem for long. Mem moved between the homes of several of her friends in The Park and was eventually listed as the dependant of an old blind man who had taken over the property her mother and Anthony had vacated. She lived with him for a while and then set up home with her lover.

Marriage and respectability

Marriage was another site in which complexities arose as people tried to make sense of their relationships in terms of their interpretations of subsidy definitions and their own understandings of propriety. There was no neat overlap between the terms used by the state, no matter how broadly defined and flexible, and those in common currency in the settlement, where couples are acknowledged as 'habitually co-resident' (in local terms, as man en vrou – man and wife) when their relationship is considered stable, enduring and decent. When I began research, only two couples were formally married. Church weddings or ceremonies conducted before priests are immediately recognised as creating marriages. Elaborate and costly affairs, they have great prestige and those few who have had such weddings usually display large framed wedding photos prominently in their houses. Ceremonies conducted before a magistrate do not have either the moral weight or prestige of church weddings, and are seldom entered into.[9] Less stable relationships are described in terms of vat en sit ('grab and sit' – living together) or, less pejoratively as man en meisie (man and girlfriend).[10] These relationships are not recognised by residents in the community as having much moral or legal weight, although children may arise from them and property may be obtained. They are considered 'make do' relationships. As one woman inelegantly but succinctly put it to me: 'Ons vry nou. Saambly voor jy afkak', (We're making out now. Living together before the shit hits the fan).[11]

Between 1991 and 1993 – the first phase of my research in The Park – no marriages took place in the settlement, although several new co-habitational relationships were established. Such relationships had no formal legal standing and women did not accrue property rights from them. By 1995, when the possibilities of funding for new housing first became known, conversations frequently circled around the question of marriages as people began to consider their relationships with an eye to obtaining housing rights. It was widely held that only those who were married would be entitled to housing, an idea that has its base largely in local conceptions of decency, and also derived from the facts that a Christian minister had recently taken up the cause of housing for residents, and that churches had promised funding.

Marriage emerged as central to women's imaginings of the kinds of relationships they desired and which they thought appropriate to 'proper houses'. A strong gender ideology holds that decent women are married women, and marriages should be solemnised in white weddings.[12] I recall a conversation in 1995 in The Park with Lenie, a woman in her fifties who, learning that housing might soon be available, planned to marry her long-time partner, Fanie. She proudly showed me the dress she planned to wear for her wedding. An elegant Matric gown, it was apricot-coloured, satin and organza, slim-strapped and slinky. It hung behind the door in a plastic cover to protect it from the dust and mud that plagued their wood, zinc and plastic shack in The Park. In Lenie's opinion, marriage was apposite to formal housing, to the propriety that housing might offer, to her vision of herself as an *ordentlike* woman. Fanie was much less keen. Throughout the latter part of 1995 they bickered constantly about it, often in public, precipitating much discussion on the topic of marriage, relationships and gender roles and their relation to the improved living prospects that beckoned on the horizon.

These discussions were given additional heat by the marriages in 1995 of the community leader, her deputy, a member of the community committee, the settlement's 'ANC representative' and the *subeen* owner (that is, all the people who held positions of power in The Park). All were Christian weddings. I attended two: those of the deputy chairwoman and 'the ANC representative'. The latter, Gerald, was resplendent in his black suit, white shirt and green satin bowtie. Lien, his betrothed, smiled shyly from beneath her white veil. It had taken three of us two hours to dress her in her flowing white gown at her aunt's house in a nearby suburb, all the time laughing and joking with friends, family and neighbours who 'popped in' to wish the bride well, while a small bottle of brandy did the rounds 'to calm the nerves'. As the couple took their vows, they were surrounded by an entourage of bridesmaids and groomsboys, one of whom was their son. Two toddlers, children of residents in The Park, took the roles of 'miniature bridesmaid and groom'. Many years later, one of the first things that Lien did when she moved into their house in The Village was to hang a framed photograph of her wedding day in pride of place and ask me to take a photo of her sitting beneath it with her two sons.

Sandra, the deputy chairwoman, and Tella were married in a church in Eerste River, accompanied by some family and friends. Tella was sartorial in grey coattails, his beautiful dreadlocks loosely tied. Accompanied by his Rastafari friends and three sons, he chatted quietly until the ceremony began. Sandra was effervescent. Elegantly attired, she was accompanied by her matron of honour, the chairwoman of the settlement, herself recently married in a Christian ceremony to her long-time Rastafari partner. The wedding entourage was stylish. Her parents and some relatives attended the ceremony. Afterwards, they returned to The Park where lunch was served to all who wished to partake. The party lasted the whole afternoon and well into evening.

These formal, white weddings were carefully wrought and costly. Ceremonies were conducted by a Christian minister, wedding dresses and suits were hired, cars arranged, parents approached for permission for children to take part in the wedding procession, white table cloths and decorations set out, 'fancies' (cakes and finger food) organised, food cooked, drinks purchased, wedding cakes selected, and so on. It was customary for the whole community to share the celebrations, particularly the meal, usually curry and rice followed by custard and fruit for pudding, and accompanied by soft drinks, beer or wine. Meals had to be prepared and served, drinks poured, dishes washed up and set out again ready for the next round of visitors. Organising weddings mobilised large networks of people, sometimes re-establishing kinship relations that had been dormant for lengthy periods. Holding such celebrations required that someone had a job and savings (extremely uncommon in the settlement, where few people had bank accounts) or the calling in of what one might call 'social debts' that exist through networks of reciprocity. I return to some of these in Chapter Five.

A remarkable feature of the five marriages contracted in the latter part of 1995 is that three were of Rasta men who had previously told me that they eschewed marriage as 'a thing of Babylon'. I was curious about how and why they had married. The men usually shrugged in response, saying that marriage was merely instrumental, a way to secure housing, but the chairwoman of The Park said in response to my queries that she had felt embarrassed seeking funds for housing from an international Christian community when she herself was co-habiting ('living in sin', as she described it) with the Rastafari father of some of her children. 'I must set an example for my people', she said.

Marriage and its anticipated relation to housing acquisition prompted something of a moral panic among residents, precipitating much discussion and dissent on the topic of relationships and gender roles. Not everyone found the idea of marriage attractive. In response to a rather heated discussion about Lenie's wedding dress, Lenie's neighbour, Gladys, a young woman then in her late twenties, explained that she did not intend to marry her son's father with whom she had lived in a *man en meisie* relationship for at least seven years. She anticipated that marriage would undermine her social support network, claiming that as a married woman she would no longer have the right to 'run home' to her mother for protection when her husband beat her. Her concern was well-founded: local conceptions of gender relations in marriage formalised women's subservience, often rendering them extremely vulnerable to male violence, assumed to be naturally the result of men's excessive passion and jealousy and women's lack of probity and virtue.

Gladys's concerns seemed prophetic. She left her man when he began beating her more frequently. She found a job as a casual labourer on an apple farm in Grabouw, some thirty kilometres away, and, when the farmer offered her work as a butcher's assistant in the Free State province, decided not to return to The Park. She worked in Senekal for fifteen months, then moved to Maitland in Cape Town, where she continued to work in a butchery owned by the same farmer. (I take up some of these issues of mobility within the workforce again in Chapter Five.)

When her mother had a stroke, Gladys returned to The Park to care for her. At the same time, Gladys tried to have her son return to live with her. His father, Lammies, instituted action against her at the local Welfare offices, claiming that she was an unfit mother. Distraught, she pointed out to me that he was a habitual drug user who did not provide for his son (men are not expected to participate in childcare but 'a good man' gives material support for his children and those of his girlfriend or wife), but she did not lay counter claims with Welfare. In June 2001, Lammies left The Park, leaving Adrian, now a teenager, alone in the house.

Meanwhile, Gladys had met and moved in with Xolela. Initially a vat en sit relationship, they lived together for two years. When I visited Gladys in The Village in December 2001, she was seated outside her new house, dressed in the finery of a makhoti, a newly married woman. She explained excitedly that she had been married a month earlier, in a traditional Xhosa ceremony conducted in the Eastern Cape. She was learning to speak Xhosa and was pregnant. She exclaimed, 'Fiona, I used to be Coloured but now I am Xhosa!'

Her happiness did not last. She miscarried. Xolela lost his job. He began drinking heavily. He also began beating her. She became very depressed. She also began drinking heavily. By 2004 she had left Xolela and entered a vat en sit relationship with another man in a nearby resort town. Within a few years, she was pregnant again but again miscarried. The relationship failed and she was evicted. So began a period of moving around the city trying desperately to establish relationships and consolidate her living arrangements.

This pattern of attaching oneself to a man was common among impoverished women in the Cape (see Ramphele 1988). For many women in The Park and surrounds, it was often a desperate attempt to secure some semblance of respect, protection and material security. The gendered terrain on which relationships are built is extremely uneven. Men have little compunction in rejecting women whom they feel are not 'good women', which often seems to mean 'are not sufficiently subservient'. They also reject women when they grow bored or find a new girlfriend. Many men 'move on' when their girlfriends fall pregnant and a number of women I know had maintenance cases pending against the fathers of their children.[13]

Rejection hurts. Several women who had entered *vat en sit* relationships with the hopes that they might consolidate into *man en meisie* or even *man en vrou* relationships told me they felt scorned and believed (often correctly) that they were the subject of *skinder* (gossip). Young women were usually able to return to their maternal homes but for some this was impossible and then women were cast upon their own meagre resources and great ingenuity in making ends meet and crafting new lives for themselves. Sometimes they were successful but very often they were not. For example, Paula worked as a domestic worker but her new partner insisted that he was 'a good man' and would care for her and her children, one of whom was disabled. She gave up her job and in conforming to the local model of *ordentlikheid* also sundered many of her social ties with her previous 'crowd'. As a respectable woman, she spent her time at home but soon complained that she was bored and began to drink. Her partner 'threw her out' (*hy't haar uitgeskop*; lit. 'he kicked her out' as one would kick a football) and she was left destitute. Her parents were both dead, her brother in jail and she had sundered ties with the aunt who had brought her up, so she had no immediate kin to whom to turn. She was unable to find work and her drinking problem worsened. Rumour had it that she eventually ended up a *bergie* living on 'Busy Corner'. I have been unable to ascertain what happened to her children.

I do not wish to imply that all households were as chronically unstable as these case studies might suggest. Some people managed to secure relatively stable domestic units over time. One such was that of Sandra and Tella, who brought up three sons in an extremely stable home. In the years that I knew them, they were also able to extend a welcome to two other people who lived with them for lengthy periods: Tella's uncle and a young boy whom they took in for several years before he won a sporting scholarship to attend a school in Johannesburg. Sandra valued stability – both social and economic (a point to which I return in Chapter Five) – and sought to inculcate it as a value in her children. She was deeply upset when her oldest son, the first child in The Park to complete a Matric (i.e. the senior school exit exam), quit his first job as a cabinet maker because it was 'boring'. 'How will he be stable enough to be a good husband?' she fretted. By

2007, all of her children were employed as artisans – one as a cabinet maker, one as a tiler and one in a printing works. The two youngest were already fathers and had taken responsibility for their children.

The descriptions I have offered here begin to suggest the complexity of householding arrangements in The Park. I turn now to a closer examination of these in order to explore further the contradictions between state policy, development practice and residents' ideals.

Households and relationships

Developers' middle-class notions of a stable domestic unit housing a nuclear family soon foundered on the complexity of householding and familial relations in The Park. Let me illustrate, drawing from material from my earliest period of research which focused on the difficulties of defining households in contexts of dire poverty.

Baby's domestic unit is one I have analysed before (Ross 1995: 55–64 and Ross 1996: 61–4). Throughout the period of my early research, Baby reported herself as living alone. As is apparent from Table 4.1, however, a large number of people generated rights in and access to her domestic unit over a short period of time. In trying to understand the composition of the 'household', I sought to isolate some of its functions and to ascertain the relationships that were generated. Table 4.1 shows that over a short period, different people ate and slept at Baby's. That is, commensal (i.e. consumption) and caring (reproductive) patterns did not neatly mesh with 'the household'. In Table 4.1, a resident is considered someone who undertook all household functions within the same geographic space – that is, someone who produced and consumed for and in the unit. Eaters are commensal members: they did not sleep at Baby's, but ate meals there with varying degrees of regularity. (In Table 4.1, *italics* indicate those who ate intermittently and did not necessarily contribute to the costs of meals; **bold** identifies those who contributed cash to the household and plain text indicates those who produced for the household in other ways, such as through doing housework, collecting firewood and water – that is, through contributing their labour.) The column entitled 'income' identifies changes in income to the 'domestic unit' resulting from the contributions of various personnel moving across the boundaries of the domestic 'unit'.

The table summarises enormously complex relationships across and within Baby's shack and the social functions that it housed. One might say that Baby's home was one of several nodal points in The Park. The table shows the entrance of Meitjie

Table 4.1. Summary of residential and commensal relationships in Baby's shack, November 1991–July 1992

MONTH	RESIDENTS	SLEEPERS	EATERS	INCOME R/M
November	Baby	Ponkies's daughter, Thelma	None	R400
December	Baby	Thelma	None	R400
January	Baby	Thelma	Anthony (family friend)	R400
February	Baby Baby's brother's ex-partner (Susan) and child (Meitjie)	Thelma	Anthony Price (Baby's brother) Raymond & Johannah (Baby's neighbours)	R400
March	As above	(Thelma leaves)	As above	R400
April	Baby Meitjie Lenie & Fanie ('home-people' from Aberdeen) (Susan leaves, but continues to eat at Baby's)		Anthony Price Susan Thelma II & Korporal (Baby's friends)	R500
May	Baby Meitjie Jemima, a recent arrival from Aberdeen who stayed for three weeks and left		Price Thelma II & Korporal Raymond & Johannah	R500
June	Baby Baby's adult daughter (stayed for several weeks then established her own shack) Thelma & Korporal (Meitjie leaves, but continues to eat at Baby's) **Ou Rose (an old friend who previously lived nearby. She stayed several weeks then moved back to her own house)**		Price Anthony Meitjie Raymond **Blankie (a single man living nearby)**	R580
July	Baby		Price Anthony Raymond Thelma & Korporal	R530

into Baby's domestic world: as we have seen, she was to become Baby's *grootmaak kind*. We have also met Lenie and Fanie who stayed at Baby's until they established themselves in The Park, and some of the others listed here appear throughout the book. Householding relationships were complex and neighbours were tied to one another over time by relationships of indebtedness and reciprocity.

The resultant relationships carried their own emotional intensities which cannot be described in a table. For example, 'Meitjie drove me mad' recalled Baby, who tried hard to *skel* (scold) the girl into *ordentlike* behaviour to little avail, 'But I had such a soft spot for her; I loved her'. Ou Rose and Anna could talk all night and when Raymond was around with his quick wit and riposte, time passed quickly in a haze of hilarity. Lenie and Fanie moved out of The Park long before the move to the Village. They still keep in touch with Baby and Raymond. In other words, the relationships associated with householding are not only about material support, but may create rich and deep emotional ties. These may be positive, as in the instances described above, or negative, as when people remained materially indebted to others, causing smouldering resentment and anger that could burst into physical violence or *wreed* (cruel) words, or was expressed in long periods of cold, hard withdrawal.

The 'household', then, is an analytic category, a way that social relationships of a particular kind can be envisaged and measured, a means by which certain forms of analysis (usually policy-related and often predicated on economic criteria), can be undertaken and the consequences of specific social relations revealed (for example, households headed by women tend to be poorer than those headed by men). What the 'household' conventionally measures are productive, reproductive and consumption relations. The household is a view of social relations from outside and beyond them, an abstraction of relationship into relations in much the same way as a map is an abstraction and objectification. What is left out of such analyses is the emotional experience and social ties, the effort that goes into creating relationships and the complexity of sustaining these over time. It is for this reason that I prefer to think of 'nodal points', shifting sites of emergent complexity and unfolding relationship.

Critiques of the household concept dating from the 1980s (see, for example, Murray 1981; Guyer and Peters 1987) have long noted the contingency of domestic arrangements in both the short and the long term (see Smith and Wallerstein 1992). Jane Guyer, for example, points out that underlying the concept is an assumption that it is homogenous and governed by laws of economics such that the household 'control[s] resources and [makes] joint decisions about their allocation' (Guyer and Peters 1987: 98). In fact, decisions are often the site of considerable tension and gender differentials. Guyer and Peters (1987) point out that incomes may not be equally distributed within households and women's coping strategies in such contexts link people in relationships across household boundaries. Their work demonstrates that 'the household' is both a porous construct and one that disguises diverse and often conflict-filled relationships.

Zolani Ngwane (2003) builds on these insights. His account of 'Christmas time' in the 1970s in Cancele, Eastern Cape, offers a lively description of the tensions that emerged when male migrants returned to rural homesteads. Men sought to re-establish and assert their power while women attempted to hold onto the autonomy they had created when men were away. The end of the year crystallised interpersonal struggles about the ideal form of domestic arrangements and the routes to achieving them. He notes,

> the household never quite attained the status of a unit, but merely existed as a site of struggle over an imagined form of the household, a form whose realization was perpetually deferred in practice owing to a combination of historical transformations (regional political instabilities in the nineteenth century, the rise of oscillating migrancy and the demographics of segregation) and attendant internal structural fluidities (for instance, constant movements of large sections of people, circulation of dependants across kin circles, and adaptation to new physical and cultural environments). (Ngwane 2003: 688)

Ngwane calls for an understanding of social formations as the materialisations of desire and imagination (2003: 635) and implies that 'householding' is a chronically unfinished project, one subject to ongoing reinterpretation and conflict as different parties seek to enact their visions. His argument, perhaps more germane to 'home' or 'homestead' than 'household' per se, urges a consideration of how social organisations are produced through imagination, material effort, conflict and co-operation in relation to desired goals which may not be uniform over time, and indeed may be regularly punctuated by events (such as 'Christmas time') that bring differing ideals into conflict.

Ngwane's important point of departure is that the household represents an ideal towards which people strive and in relation to which efforts may succeed or fail over time. Such analyses pose important challenges to much social science theorising which has attempted to distil from the flow of experience specific social forms, often at the expense of an understanding of temporality and of the ways that time and social relationships intersect to produce social forms and institutions (see debates in Amaoteng and Heaton 2007, for example). Ngwane demonstrates that those who work towards achieving a social unit do not necessarily share the same ideals, and that their strategies may differ, converge and conflict. He describes the 'unit' as a 'self-articulating collective in which hegemony is, at least momentarily, complete' (2003: 688, footnote 49), and notes that in terms of that definition, 'the household has remained an ideal rather than a real social unit' (2003: 699).

As ideals, however, concepts have a reality in that things are done in their name. At specific moments, constellations of events occur such that people are able to give concerted attention to these projects. They may also come closer to actualising them than they have before. In The Park, the possibility of housing represented one such moment, in which, over time, a variety of social concerns arose as residents sought to rework their relationships into forms that more closely fit their ideals of 'family life' as well as the legal requirements for subsidies, and at the same time to safeguard 'the community'.

Some of the complexity that resulted is caused by specific political and economic configurations (for example, influx control laws under apartheid regulated who could be legally resident and thus shaped familial relations in the city; poverty renders relationships precarious and contributes to the dispersal of children; sexual relationships are often unstable). As the piece On Home (p.74) intimates, some of the complexity might be characterised as 'cultural', and some is the product of specific attempts, improvisational in character, to deal with social and emotional issues at hand. People seldom attempt to form 'households' per se. Our efforts are directed at creating and consolidating relationships, at making home, stabilising domestic relations, ensuring the continuities of homesteads, securing genealogical relations over time, and so on. We love, lust, fight, create and dissolve relationships, resolve differences. Our attempts are directed towards relationship: we try, through a variety of means and in accord with diverse conventions, to create enduring associations, sets of relations that are both material and affective. That is, they entail practised emotional and material investment over time.

What this actually meant in The Park was that domestic relations were enormously complex and diffuse. In Houses Without Doors (Ross 1995), an early study, I showed how residents' domestic relationships, while not necessarily stable or robust, were sufficiently flexible to meet short-term material and social needs, something that is also demonstrated in Table 4.1. In my early study, I noted the separation of domestic functions concerning production, reproduction and consumption. These, I suggested, were in large measure products both of poverty and of apartheid legislation regarding residential, family and labour matters. In conditions of extreme poverty and uncertainty, the functions usually associated with households were separated and spread over a variety of social configurations. I characterised such relations as 'diffused domesticity'. Spiegel (1996) calls the phenomenon 'domestic fluidity'.

My study concluded that,

> [some] residents of a Western Cape squatter settlement created extensive, but
> short-lived networks of support which stretched across and beyond the settlement,
> linking individuals into complex and extremely fluid social interactions. So rapidly
> changing were these compounded knots of interacting individuals that they often
> appeared to have no boundaries save those imposed with situational immediacy.
> I have shown that although some people lived in stable domestic units which
> were the loci of specific relationships of consumption and (re)production over the
> research period, many of the residents of [The Park] were not part of such stable
> sets. Fluidity and change characterised ... social relationships ... (Ross 1995: 95)

Yet, even in the conditions of rapid social change that characterised life in The
Park, there were clear patterns in how domesticity was diffused. Residents worked
with ideas about responsibility, caring and what anthropologists call 'delayed
reciprocity' to generate rights in households and to their products. For example,
Thelma II in Table 4.1 regularly cleaned Baby's house while the latter was at work,
and Korporal collected firewood for her. This work generated rights to a meal
and later enabled them to claim a bed in Baby's domestic unit when their own
shack was being rebuilt after a fire. Exchanging labour or money for food was
common, particularly among young adults.

People usually approached friends or acquaintances for short-term material
assistance before approaching their kinsfolk in the settlement. In *Houses Without
Doors*, I suggested that these practices had to do with ideas about the moral density
of kin obligation. Using an analytic distinction between 'moral' and 'instrumental'
reciprocity, I showed that kinship was endowed with a morality that appears to
be more weighty and onerous than friendship. The result was that reciprocal
relationships with kin to meet short-term material needs were eschewed unless
circumstances were extreme. Such circumstances included setting up household
in The Park (as when Baby's daughter came to live with her) and when assistance
was sought for ritual purposes usually associated with the life cycle (funerals,
initiations, marriages, etc.).

The complexity of household relations was compounded by domestic
violence, which rendered relationships precarious and social institutions, such as
the family, vulnerable (Ross 1996), and caused considerable movement between
different units in the ghetto as women and children sought refuge.

The fluidity of domestic relations should not be read to indicate the collapse
of sociality as might otherwise be inferred. In fact, it may mean the opposite as
people seek novel ways to generate social links that can be activated both to meet

their needs in the absence of basic material requirements and to attain socially sanctioned goals over time. As a result, social relations, both positive and negative, are deep and networks of mutual obligation in the settlement were (and remain) wide-ranging. The depth and significance of these made it difficult to delimit both 'the household' and 'the community'.

Defining the community

The Consortium insisted that all people should be moved from the site. The residents wished to move 'as a community'. This sometimes produced a situation where the differing ideals of residents and developers conflicted with the social possibilities offered by the state.

One of the first difficulties lay in establishing the boundaries of 'the community'. In principle, this was not difficult: The Park occupied a clearly demarcated and easily identifiable space. Many of its residents had shared a long history of dispossession and resistance to eviction. They defined themselves as a community and felt themselves to have a strong sense of solidarity. However, houses were to be provided to applicants who fit the subsidy criteria, and not to 'a community'. The problem that then faced decision-makers was how to ensure the continuity of what already existed as 'a community' in the context of housing provision to units smaller than 'a community', where, as I've shown, householding relations stretched across relations in the settlement, producing and reinforcing a sense of community through reliance, affection, trust and social and economic debts.

As far as the developers were concerned, the core unit for measuring membership in The Park was not moral entitlement or social relations, however enduring they proved to be, but material structures. The requisite number of housing units was determined on the basis of the number of 'structures' in The Park. This seems practical, but was not as straightforward as it sounds, either. Over time, residents had taken in lodgers who were eligible for subsidies and thus constituted separate households in terms of the subsidy process but, as residents of a single structure, in the developers' eyes did not appear to be separate domestic units. The difficulties of measurement were compounded by the effects of two terrible fires, one late in 2000 and the other early in 2001, which razed swathes of shacks in the settlement. In total, some 100 shacks were burnt, some twice. In the fires' afterward, people rebuilt, some forging new householding relationships (see also Bank 2001). People who had previously been boarders built their own shacks and some young people moved away from their previous homes and built homes of their own. The developers several times expressed anxiety that newcomers had arrived and built shacks on the site, although the evidence for this is difficult to obtain and confirm orally. Nevertheless, the reworking of social relations caused by external circumstances and changes in the ordinary domestic life cycle (see Goody 1958; Ross 1995), the list of structures was an inadequate representation of the actualities of relationships in The Park.

Finally, not everyone who lived in The Park qualified for a subsidy. This gave rise to concerns that 'the community' would be lost, that people who were not eligible in terms of the state's legal criteria but who were long-time residents of The Park would not be able to move into the new houses. In the discourse of residents and developers, 'the community' became consolidated and operationalised as a conceptual term at precisely the moment that in terms of the state's definitions of eligibility, it lost its legal significance. Meshing multiple desires with material resources was, as one developer put it, 'a nightmare'.

For residents, what to do about moving 'the community' was a question that was framed in moral terms. Alongside it emerged others, such as how to accommodate those residents whose early, now failed, marriages had never been legally cancelled and whose legal allegiance now differed from their moral and emotional ties; how to ascertain whether kin who lived in separate 'structures' but shared resources constituted one unit or more. Community leaders were anxious to make provision for those who were ill and had no dependants. In several cases, ill people were registered as others' co-dependants in order to secure their place in The Village and to ensure that someone was available to care for them. Prior to the move, there was considerable debate about what to do about the placement of orphans whose parents had made applications for state grants but had died before the houses were built. These tragic events posed new questions: What were children's rights in relation to inheritance of potential subsidies that were tied into residential rights in a housing estate? What kinds of property could children inherit and under what circumstances? Who ought best to represent such children? In the event, ideals about ensuring that 'the community' remained intact often seemed to outweigh questions of inheritance and minors' rights.

The contradictions posed by the availability of subsidies for individuals and their dependants and the need to remain 'a community' were not all easily ironed out. Efforts to address the problem were often enormously complicated and confusing for people – such as planners – unaccustomed to the complexities of how people manage poverty. People familiar with bureaucratic processes thus found themselves unable to understand local contexts, while those familiar with local contexts struggled to give their relationships shape in terms of bureaucratic provisions.

The Park's committee determined that as far as possible, those who had established the settlement and lived there the longest should have priority in receiving houses, even where they did not qualify for subsidies. In several instances, the latter apparently lived alone (although as we have seen in Table 4.1, appearances may be deceptive). They often drew state pensions or disability grants. Lacking spouses or dependants, they did not qualify for subsidies although the disbursement of their grants within the settlement generated large networks of obligation and dependency. Take for example a friend of Baby's, Aunty Maggie, an old woman whose partner had died in 2000, shortly before the application process was finalised. She put the challenge succinctly:

> Must I marry to get a house? Must I find a dependant? Het ek gesê my man moet vrek? Ek wil in my huis alleen bly. (Did I say my man should die? I want to live alone in my house.) I don't want someone here telling me when to get up and what to do. If I don't get a house, then I'll stay here (in the shack area).

She elaborated her concerns to Janine:

> Boarding is not an option. You have to have your own place. Living with other people doesn't work out. I used to live with other people … but I promised myself, never again …. I want to live alone and then I'll have no reason to shout at (skel) anyone.

Recognising the difficulties that such cases posed, novel attempts were made to ensure that such people could qualify or at least would not lose their place in the community in the absence of a subsidy. The Park's committee factored in moral dimensions in which prior residence in The Park and quality of relationships were paramount in determining rights, above questions of formal eligibility for housing grants.

For example, the attempts made to secure a house for Price, whose complex 'familial' relations can be discerned in the discussion of Meitjie and the table depicting Baby's household. Price was 'one of the first people', a founding member of The Park. In 2000 when I returned to The Park, he was sickly and living alone, cared for by Meitjie, who still lived with Price's sister, Baby. Single and without formal dependants, he was not eligible for a housing subsidy, but he had been resident in the settlement for some thirteen years and the committee and community were adamant that he should be allocated a house. Meanwhile, as we have seen, Baby's domestic unit, like many others in The Park, had long been the node of intricate, rapidly changing householding arrangements. Meitjie was listed as Price's dependant. She had, at various times lived with him, cared for him, and called him 'Papa'.[14] Baby was also technically considered 'single' and therefore not eligible, but the problem was solved by registering her grandson as her dependant. She had long provided emotional and material care for the boy. His mother, who lived in the settlement, did not work. Her partner did not support the child (who was not his biological son) and Baby paid the school fees for and otherwise maintained her grandson who sometimes lived with her. The boy's mother qualified for a house on the basis that her domestic partner made the application, listing her and their biological child as his dependants. Thus, through careful reworking based on actual patterns of social relationship, three people who were considered morally entitled to move into houses but who did not easily formally qualify for subsidies – Baby, Price and Meitjie – were able to access housing. Relationships were moulded to resemble the law's requirements.

I offer below three more examples to demonstrate just how complex some of the decisions were.

Tyrone and Elise lived in The Park for about twelve years, having arrived there as man en meisie. Shortly before the subsidy applications were to be made, Tyrone fell in love with another woman, left Elise and married his new lover in a Christian wedding. The newlyweds applied for a house but were rejected because she had made an application with her previous partner, a man living in a shanty area nearby. Meanwhile, Elise made an application on the basis that the child born of Tyrone was her dependant. Her subsidy was granted and she and the child moved to The Village. Five months after the move, the child no longer lives with her but with family elsewhere and she rents out space to a lodger who had resided in The Park but had not obtained a house. The Park's residents and committee members were unanimous in their agreement that Elise deserved the house and had been ill-treated by Tyrone, and that, irrespective of the fact that he was now legally married, her claim to a house was greater than his. The result runs counter to planners' bourgeois values: in the community's reasoning, a single mother who sent her child away conforms more closely to local models of properness than does a married man.

Here is another instance. Neels and Monica arrived in The Park in about 1990, telling people that they were engaged. They did not marry, but this was not unusual and the long 'engagement' did not elicit much commentary. Neels, however, was already legally married to a woman he had left years before but never divorced. As a married man, he could only apply for a subsidy with his legal wife. The committee was faced with a conundrum: Neels and Monica were locally accepted as a couple, Neels's earlier marriage was recognised as legal but as having no bearing on his right to live in either The Park or The Village, Monica was widely liked, and both were considered to be part of the community. The solution, once found, was simple and elegant. Monica was to make the application, listing their child as a dependant, and when the house was built,

Neels would live with them. This duly happened. However, shortly after making the application, Monica fell in love with another man and when Neels became abusive she obtained a court interdict preventing him from setting foot on her property. Some residents were extremely angered by her behaviour, even though sympathetic to her suffering at Neels's hands. They argued that 'Neels made a way for Monica in the community' and that she had no moral right to exclude him from the community in which he had lived for so long. Nevertheless, she had the legal right to do so, and exercised it.

A third example: Paul had been married for five or six years. A jealous man, he frequently beat his wife when he thought she paid too much attention to other men. After a particularly brutal public confrontation, she left him and returned to her relatively well-to-do family, threatening revenge. When the time came, she refused to countersign the subsidy application as his legal spouse, and, despite Paul's pleas and those of several of the committee members and others in The Park, continued to refuse. Without her signature he was ineligible for a subsidy and thus would not be able to reside in the community he had lived in for several years. The committee tried to find other people who would be willing to register as his financial dependants, but, aware of his bad temper, people refused to consider living with him. Paul did not get access to a house and is now living 'like a bergie'. Occasionally he sleeps over in The Village with friends but for the most part is no longer considered a member of the community.

The last two cases are particularly interesting in that they demonstrate that women were able to make use of the subsidy and property processes to secure legal rights and to exact forms of revenge against men who maltreated them.

The complexities do not end with securing relationships so that people could apply for subsidies. The legal framework hardened fluid relationships into forms that the state recognises but that may not have ongoing salience in the local context, where relationships between people and property are open to various interpretations, including one's moral stature. The facts and fictions of relationship can cause complexities, especially where law and property are involved. Take for example the case of Tasha, who, at the age of five, went to live with Mitha, her great-aunt (her mother's mother's sister) who also lived in The Park. Until then she had been brought up by her ware ma and ma se man. Mitha's boyfriend, Quintin, had a son from a prior relationship who lived with his mother in a nearby town. Mitha and Quintin had no children of their own. When Quintin was murdered, his son, with whom he had had little contact over the years, came to claim his share of Quintin and Mitha's house. Mitha resisted his claims but as she sickened she became concerned to secure what she felt were Tasha's rights to the property. She found herself in a difficult position. She and Quintin had not married and he had left no will. His son claimed legal rights to inherit and argued that his rights as Quintin's 'ware seun' (true son) outweighed those of Tasha, whose ware ma lived nearby, even though Tasha is listed as a dependant on Quintin and Mitha's subsidy claim. The case polarised the community, with some siding with the youth, on the grounds that Tasha should eventually inherit her mother's house, and some with Mitha, on the grounds that as Quintin's long-term partner, she ought to have inherited the house outright and should be able to dispose of it as she chose, irrespective of kinship's claims and legal procedures. If the case went to court (which is highly unlikely), in the ordinary run of things the court would probably find that as Mitha and Quintin were not married, the law of intestate succession would apply and the son would inherit the property.[15] By the time I completed research the situation had not been resolved.

The materials I have presented in this chapter demonstrate that residents' efforts to actualise their ideal relationships were shot through with contradiction. Legal requirements for subsidies did not necessarily mesh easily with local conceptions of personhood or moral good or indeed with local patterns of making a living and getting by. The gap that opened between these two different levels of intervention – the state and the communal – presented itself as a moment in which people drew on existing cultural repertoires (both as ideals and practices) and imagination to facilitate solutions to social and moral problems.

There is no neat connection between ideals and realities. While residents embraced a normative model of respectability, the road to respectability sometimes required behaviour that is anything but. In the cases I have described above, the possibilities of accessing houses and with them, of actualising local models of ordentlikheid and desired family life, often rested on subterfuge, 'making a plan', as it is locally known. Reconfiguring and re-representing relationships to fit the requirements for subsidies is one example. It was a subterfuge that residents deemed necessary in order to actualise dreams of proper homes, and by some it was celebrated in terms of a Cape cultural model of trickery. Their tactics both adhere to and defy more conventional understandings of decency. In bringing great ingenuity to bear to address matters that were understood not as legal or material problems but as problems of morality and social obligation, residents reworked the authoritative with their own version of the ethical.

Ceremonies and celebrations

TOP Sandra and Tella's wedding procession at The Park, 1995.

RIGHT Holland and children fix the hall roof in preparation for the wedding

ABOVE Sandra's niece, Lauren, and nephew, Jonathon, were the miniature bride and groom in the wedding entourage.

ABOVE **Adrian and Mella** were the miniature bride and groom at Lien and Gerald's wedding.

ABOVE **Lien waits nervously to be taken to her groom's side in The Park.**

LEFT **Ponkies and Aubrey** asked me to take belated wedding pictures, ten years after their marriage.

ABOVE **Lien, Jerry and Jeremiah in their new home. The first pictures Lien put on the wall were her wedding photos and the image of Bob Marley.**

BELOW **Rowan was the first youth in The Park to obtain a Matric. Here he poses with (from left) Dina, his father, Tella, mother Sandra and his Matric Dance date, Dina's daughter Poppie.**

LEFT **Poppie**

5

'Just working for food':

making a living, making do and getting by

Clive: We don't get any jobs other than these, you see?
Carmen: Farm work ...
Clive: Do you know how my heart burns (brand my hart) for a decent (ordentlike) job? But we just can't get it. You only get season work[1] around here.
Janine: What to you is a decent job?
Clive: (getting very excited) Like in a restaurant or a factory where you know you can work for an employment company .... But here you can't.
Carmen: (also getting very excited) Kitchen work or something like that. Where you work for the rest of the year. If the job is finished then you must know that you can still go on working.
Clive: But here we just have to do season work and sometimes the season only lasts for two months and then it's harvest time. Then we're at home from April all the way until November.
Carmen: And then we have to wait again.
Clive: Until there's work again.

Friends, Clive and Carmen were in their early twenties when they had this conversation with Janine as part of a series of interviews about people's work experiences. Clive had grown up on a farm and he was accustomed to the work. From childhood, he had assisted his parents during the harvest. Child labour was widespread on farms in the Western Cape when he was a child, and although technically illegal, it continues today (see Waldman 1994; Levine 1999, 2006). Clive and Carmen were ambivalent about the farm work that, like many others in The Park, was their main source of employment in the year. On the one hand, it was nice to be working outdoors and relatively unsupervised, but on the other:

Clive: One would swear it's Pollsmoor (prison), because they treat us like prisoners (*bandiete*, convicts) ... The long hours we have to work ...

Carmen: [You] get sunburnt ....

Clive: And you get blotches from the poison. That's why I won't do that ever again.

Janine: You get blotches from the poison? So actually it's a dangerous job.[2]

Carmen: Yes, it is.

Clive: And you earn very little money. We get paid per patch of land[3] and sometimes the grapes don't hang in our favour. And when it rains then we only get to work two days a week, so we can't afford to buy things on credit (*skuld maak* – lit. make debt) and things like that .... We're basically just working for food.

Clive was bitter about 'just working for food' and being too poor even to 'make debt' at one of the *subeens*, let alone to purchase the accoutrements of *ordentlike* living through hire-purchase arrangements at stores in the city. The conversation illuminates the importance of the distinction between decent and seasonal work; the relation of debt and markers of social status; and the issue of temporality as it weaves through people's efforts to secure their well-being in the present and future.

Decency, durability and 'the poorest of the poor'

There aren't any people here with decent jobs ... you know, the kind of job that you can say they make a living from. (Janine S, aged 14)

Clive and Carmen's distinction between 'seasonal' work and 'decent' work was widely held. For Carmen, decent work is kitchen work,[4] factory work, working for a contractor. What is common to these is that they are regulated by labour laws and have the potential to last beyond a 'season'. It does not matter that such work might be shift work and might entail working at night. It is the guarantee of ongoing employment and the regularity and reliability of income that go with this that characterises 'decent' work. Most seasonal farm work was at best offered on a job-specific contract (for example, the completion of pruning or harvesting) or at worst on a 'piece work' basis in which people were paid by the day. As a general rule, casual workers were very poorly paid. (In 2000, one young woman reported working for R20 [less than USD3[5]] per day, after deductions for tools, protective clothing and debts incurred.) Minimum wage prescriptions for the domestic sector came into effect only in 2002 and for the agricultural sector in 2003.[6] 'Decent' work was thus work that was properly regulated by the state: work in which one received a proper wage, could anticipate working for more than a few months and qualified for Unemployment Insurance. These factors were important in offering security over time. In other words, in defining decency, durability matters.

In addition, as Carmen points out, one can 'make a living' from decent work rather than just getting by. Making a living implies being able to meet one's financial and social obligations, being comfortable and secure, able to indulge in the odd luxury without feeling pressed or guilty or having to forgo some household necessity such as food or school fees. The phrase also connotes respectability. Artisanal work is decent but *subeen* work is not, even if the owners could be considered *ordentlike mense* (decent people) in their own right and even if the proceeds from the *subeen* enable them to live comfortably. Casual labour on farms is not considered decent, partly for its lack of durability and partly for the structural and interpersonal violence that accompanies it (see below). Decent work thus also means having skills, working in a respected profession in a secure environment, with people who are *ordentlik*.

Very few of the residents of The Park/Village had either durable or 'decent' employment. Most workers were concentrated in the sector now designated 'elementary occupations' and that used to be referred to as unskilled or manual labour, and many worked intermittently in the year, irregularly in the week or for fewer hours weekly that qualified them to be registered for Unemployment Insurance. Leaders of the settlement habitually refer to residents as 'the poorest of the poor'. While somewhat hyperbolic, their usurpation of descriptive development discourse is not entirely inaccurate. The Park has always been home to poor people, although forms of employment have diversified over the last decade and reliance on state assistance has increased. Early residents made a living by casual work or begging. Over time, most of the early settlers subsequently found regular work as chars or gardeners, and one established a very successful *subeen*. Subsequent arrivals to The Park also found work mainly in the domestic employment sector (as chars and gardeners), as casual labourers in the building- and agro-industries, and increasingly in the informal sector (part of which entails the procurement and circulation of illegal goods and an illicit trade in drugs). Most employment within the formal sector is casual or part-time and jobs are concentrated in the lowest income brackets. Unemployment and underemployment rates are high. Several residents have prison records and find it difficult to find work.[7] In earlier years, Rastafari too found it difficult to find work: it was widely held that prospective employers would look askance at dreadlocked men.[8]

I offer a brief summary of employment patterns in the text that follows, making comparisons between the period of my earliest research (1991) and 2000 where data is available. Over this period, household incomes have dropped in real terms but pensions and other state grants have become more significant.

In 2000, the average weekly household income[9] was approximately R265 (about USD35, giving a per capita income of approximately USD10) during the peak pruning and harvest season when many residents, like Carmen and Clive, were employed as casual labourers on fruit farms. One-third of households subsisted on less than R200 (approximately USD25, or less than USD8 per person) per week. During the pruning and harvest period nine years earlier, average weekly household income was approximately R120: in real terms, incomes and purchasing power have dropped.

There has been a small decrease in unemployment rates since 1991, when the rate was twenty-five per cent, as compared with twenty-three per cent in 2000.

Of 345 adults of employable age, thirty-one per cent of those with jobs in 2000 were underemployed, working irregularly as chars and gardeners (n=102), in the building and related industries (n=39) and in seasonal agricultural employment (n=17). As in 1991, the bulk of employment remains in the domestic, construction and agricultural sectors. This does not imply that employment was stable or secure. Most people who described themselves as working in the agricultural sector were seasonally employed. Most domestic workers worked for more than one employer, and very few worked more than twenty-four hours a month and were therefore disqualified from UIF registration.[10] While some of the men working in the construction sector were skilled artisans, most were casual manual labourers on building sites. This form of employment is not reliable or regular: men are recruited on an *ad hoc* basis, often on only a day's contract. There are gendered patterns in employment: women generally found work as domestic workers, and although they were poorly paid, their incomes tended to be more reliable than men's over the year.

In 2000, the rate of state assistance among residents was one-and-a-half times greater than in 1991. This is a result of two factors: the extension of the state's welfare safety net[11] and an increase in the numbers of people who qualified for state assistance. The thirty-six people who received state assistance in 2000 – mainly disability grants and pensions – supported extensive networks of dependants[12] and also generated large debts at local *spaza* shops which allowed them to make purchases 'on tick' or '*op die boek*' (on the book). People with regular incomes, such as state grants, were able to use these as surety to purchase goods, usually food and alcohol, on credit from *spazas*. The form has its origins in stores run by farmers, at which people frequently ran up considerable debt and were unable to leave the farms until the debt was paid. Although there have been strenuous efforts on the part of the state, unions and NGOs to put a halt to such indebtedness, Elise commented of the shop on the farm on which her parents worked in 2004,

> [the farmer] gives people food on credit but then come Friday afternoon (i.e. pay day) those people have to give their entire week's pay to him. So then they have to go back to his shop and get some food again. I mean, they don't even have a chance to get their kids some clothes or things that they really need.

Clearly the practice of allowing workers to become deeply indebted continues on the farms in the region. It is not limited to farms; many residents had run up: considerable debt at the *spaza* shops in The Park/Village and had to hand over their entire wages or social grants to offset the debt. People who have regular incomes (*subeen* and *spaza* owners, some domestic and municipal workers, for example) hire the labour of other residents to perform household functions – collecting water, cleaning, shopping, washing and cooking. Children do odd jobs around the settlement in exchange for small amounts of cash.

There are several thousand unemployed people living in the area and competition for jobs is great. An industrial park abuts The Village. Developers expected that residents of The Park would find work in the newly opened factories and residential areas nearby. More than a thousand jobs were anticipated but to date few have materialised and most of those have been for women working as domestic workers in the new residential estates. As Clive put it:

> There are so many factories here. They (the developers) said that once we move here ... Look, we used to live on (land belonging to that) farm. There are big factories (there) now and they said that we'll get jobs there first, these people that are here now. But now other people are getting the jobs ... outside people, people who don't even live here. We just have to wait for the harvest, finish and *klaar* (finished. The phrase is redundant but emphatic: 'and that's that').

In asserting a claim to preferential employment based on prior residence, Clive is (perhaps unwittingly) reproducing the old discourse of job reservation, in which employment opportunities in the Cape were reserved for people classified as Coloured in terms of the Population Registration Act of 1950, a corner piece of apartheid legislation. On the basis of the declaration of the Eiselin Line in 1954, ferocious measures were put in place that limited 'African' migration to and presence in the Cape.[13] Although that legislation is now abolished, people are habituated to its provisions and, on occasion, tensions over work-seeking in The Park were expressed in racist terms. The process of housing was supposed to be a job creation scheme in which residents would be employed to build their homes. Owing to pressures of time, this did not happen: a few men were contracted from The Park but most of the builders were drawn from other sites because they were already trained. The tensions around job seeking were often expressed in ways resonant with apartheid and colonial discourses. For example, young Xhosa men spoke disparagingly of 'those Coloureds' who 'will not work'. 'They're just lazy', said one young man, echoing a very old racist discourse prevalent in the Cape. Meanwhile, Coloured men accused young Xhosa-speaking men of 'stealing' local jobs and sending their remittances 'to the land' (the former Transkei and Ciskei areas, now incorporated into the Eastern Cape) and out of the Western Cape, rather than investing locally.[14]

Poverty is increasingly being understood as more than just living below a minimum income level. Recent work documents a range of factors influencing poverty. Incomes are just one of them. Others include one's social networks and the ways that one may be able to activate these to access resources, including money, food, care and access to institutions (May 2000); one's 'capabilities' and capacities to mobilise these; and one's inclusion or exclusion from systems of power (such as patronage networks – see Du Toit 2004). A view of households over time reveals that some households move into and out of states of impoverishment whereas others are 'chronically impoverished'. That is, their social networks, individual skills and household relations are insufficient to allow the household as a whole or individuals within it to move out of poverty over time (see May 2000; Du Toit 2004; Adato et al., n.d.).

The recognition that poverty may be absolute and objective but also has subjective and experiential components (May 2000) is important because it highlights the role of meaning-making in day-to-day living. Some people give up hope of finding work, making a reasonable living, or even getting by. Others see themselves as relatively well-off compared with neighbours, while some compare themselves to a different strata of society and find themselves wanting. Yet what is common to all of these positions is that people try to make sense of them, to give them meaning. One way that residents of The Park/Village did so was by distinguishing between 'decent' work and its opposite, 'skarreling'. Negotiating one's way between these polar opposites required great social dexterity, as we will see.

Skarreling for a living[15]

Most people in The Park/Village did not have decent work and many only 'just got by' in trying circumstances. They did so through a mix of different kinds of work (formal and informal), loans, sharing and borrowing goods, and 'making a plan' – that is, improvising. Its temporality is oriented to the immediate present. Clive disparagingly calls this *skarreling* for a living. The verb means to rummage or scrabble, scuttle or scurry. It suggests a frantic search for life's basic necessities, the use of many tactics, a sense of haste and trickery. It involves living by one's wits. Its emotional and psychological consequences are that one becomes *senuweeagtig* and short-lived euphoria when one gets by temporarily. Some may take pride in *skarreling* but for others it is merely what must be done to survive. It is low in the 'hierarchy of dignity' (Lovell 2007: 324) of work and the lowest of all forms of *skarreling* is to be without regular shelter, eking a living by begging at Busy Corner or rummaging through rubbish bins.

Clive made ends meet by working as a casual labourer during the pruning and harvesting seasons on farms, doing piecework for residents in the settlement, claiming intermittent support from his mother, obtaining food and shelter from friends and occasionally engaging in male prostitution. His efforts to secure everyday needs thus traversed a range of relationships: he drew on friendship, kinship, formally contractual relations, illicit and illegal activities with strangers.

Carmen had concurred with his assessment of how one might makes ends meet but was shocked at his openness in revealing his prostitution to us, seeing it as an indiscretion that violated principles of *ordentlikheid* in speech acts (see Chapter Six). She chastised him, but Clive responded, 'No, it's the truth. Why do I have to hide it?' He held that *katte vang* (lit. catching cats; prostitution) was just one way among many of making use of the full range of tools at his disposal, including the sexual use of his body. He explained: 'Because of the poverty, we had to grow up very fast' (a term often euphemistically used to refer to early sexual experiences), and 'taking a man' was one avenue 'to give you another life, because there's no other income'. Working the streets is dangerous: violence is frequent and one's safety is always on the line. He traded sex for money, risking life to secure life. And he added, 'Dis *eintlik snaaks en* "otherwise"' (It's really strange and 'otherwise' – that is, unfair, unjust). Embedded in this throw-away comment is a deep understanding of a political economy in which some people find themselves so impoverished that poverty (*swaarkry*, hardship) forces them into prostitution.

While prostitution per se was widely decried, and I knew of only three people who had engaged in street work, it was not uncommon for young women to offer sexual relations and domestic labour to working men in return for a degree of physical and financial security, tenuous as these often were (see also Ramphele 1988). For women, these *vat en sit* (grab and stay) relationships, unsecured by marriage, were not considered *ordentlik*. Nevertheless, *vat en sit* was not considered to be prostitution. The two were differentiated on the grounds of the temporality and nature of the relationship. Prostitution is associated with once-off sexual relations with strangers, usually across racial lines, whereas *vat en sit* relations, even though often brittle and frequently abusive, heralded a single partner relationship with some hope of duration.

'Jobs are scarce' was a frequent refrain when people lived in The Park. It became even more pronounced after people had moved to The Village. Freddie told me that the new houses were too distant from the road and that trucks no longer stopped to collect casual labourers. Baby, a long-time resident in The Park, exclaimed,

> Oh, man! Jobs were even scarce when we lived in The Park. There are lots of young boys (*klonkies*) sitting around here without jobs. Look at these other children who matriculated: some of them are lucky enough to have a job at (a local supermarket; see below) and a few others are working in a factory in town. There aren't any other jobs so they have no choice but to go and work for that little money.

The forms of employment available to people with little education[16] were limited mainly to physically demanding work. Many women reported having done both farm and char or 'service' (live-in domestic) work. Of those who had done both, younger people preferred farm work even though the wages were generally lower and working conditions both less secure and more dangerous. They could be outdoors and share conversation and song (and, for some, a *dop*). The work, although strenuous, could be easily learned, and they felt they learned something – about nature, caring for plants, horticultural techniques, etc. Here is Chrisna, talking about her summer job on a farm.

> I liked it a lot because I learned a lot of things. I saw where bread and milk products came from and all kinds of other things. I saw where the fruit and vegetables come from and I know what kind of insecticides to use for vegetables and flowers.

She shares her new knowledge with neighbours, consolidating local social networks. 'The best thing about farm work is the work itself', said another woman.

But some did not like farm work. Petronella, who had worked on farms during pruning and harvest seasons since she was a young girl, said:

I don't want to work on a farm any more. I want to go and work in a boer (farmer; generic term for white person) kitchen. It's better. If you work on a farm you only get burnt by the sun. Jy brand swart en jy verdien nie lekker geld nie (You burn black and you earn very little money).

Verdien also means deserve or merit. Here Petronella implies that pay has an intrinsic relationship to personhood: a farm worker deserves little. Her comment 'Jy brand swart' implies more than sunburn, it indexes a racialised reflection on menial work.[7]

Elise, who grew up on a farm and started working there at the age of 14,[8] having completed Standard Three, said,

I didn't like it one bit. I told my husband, 'if you ever decide to go work on a farm again ...' (she left the threat hanging in the air). I don't think I'm up to doing farm work again because it wears you out. Yesterday I told my sister that I think the reason why I'm having problems with my back is because of the cold conditions we had to work in on the farm. We had to get up really early in the morning and we came home late at night. Sometimes we even had to work in the rain ....

Elise had suffered severe depression after miscarrying two pregnancies. She attributed the losses and her depression to her fears for her husband's safety after he had murdered another farm labourer who attacked him. Although the court found that he had acted in self-defence, the dead man's family threatened revenge and Elise and her husband believed that they would carry out their threats. They reported the threats to the police, who intervened. Although she received counselling, Elise remains traumatised by her losses and the events of violence she witnessed, she said.

I don't know how to describe it but my body is not the way it should be. I start to shiver and my stomach cramps (if I hear people fighting). If I hear something upsetting, then my stomach immediately starts to cramp. I have to take a tension tablet when I start to feel like this.

Here, experience has a visceral and incapacitating remainder. Elise is one of the many women who describe themselves as senuweeagtig (see Chapter Seven).

Violence – both structural and interpersonal – was endemic on farms.[19] Elise's work account documents three different kinds of violence. There is the structural violence of paternalism (see Du Toit 1993; Waldman 1994), verbal abuse by farmers and foremen, and interpersonal violence among workers on the farms.

Her account is not unusual: violence is endemic in farming communities. As Clive put it,

> Violence is everywhere, even in church. Yes, violence always happens during the harvest. It's all part of the harvest. It's nice to fight. There's always a fight in The Park ... The stories start at home but then they take it out at work. It's just part of The Park.

Janine pressed him: 'So these fights start as a result of gossip?' Clive replied:

> You'll always find gossip where there are lots of people. For example, if I pick more grapes than her, then she'll start a rumour, saying that I'm a thief or something like that. That's how it goes. It's jealousy. If I get paid more than her then they'll say, 'Oh, you're flirting with the foreman!'

Seasonal farm work was generally accessed in one of three ways: through networks of kin living on farms, through prior personal work histories on those farms, or simply by reporting timeously to the side of the road where labour contractors collected prospective workers. All of these might be characterised as forms of skarreling because of their ad hoc nature and because the individuals concerned were clearly identifiable as being desperate for work. Over time, labour contractors came to be more and more important in mediating access to work, especially on farms.[20] The effects for some people were devastating. Ponkies, for example, had worked on a farm near The Park. When the bulk of the farm was sold to urban development and the resident workers evicted, she continued to work there as a seasonal labourer. She introduced her daughters to farm labour and they joined her during the harvests. Later, however, a contractor was employed to recruit labour. The contractor did not know her or her history with the farm, and turned a deaf ear to her assertions of a right to work based on her past history and work experiences there. Her former 'social capital' (the networks that in this case enabled her to get work), based on her history of effort in a place and relationship with people, was no longer sufficient to secure her the job. The following year, the contractor employed only those people who had worked the year before. Ponkies was excluded.

People evaluated work in a variety of ways. Casual workers on farms reported enjoying learning new skills, such as shaping table grapes or pruning. Factory workers evaluated their jobs in terms of their physical toll and often valued more sedentary jobs over a higher wage. For example, Tania worked in a sock factory and preferred being a packer to a turner, a fitter or someone who managed the press machines and other machines: 'If you're a turner then you're on your feet all day long. It's really strenuous on your legs. If you were a packer then you could sit down. Other people preferred the press machine or some of the other machines but I think a packer was the best position to have.' Respect or its lack figured high in the accounts by women who had worked as domestic workers who applied their ideals of *ordentlikheid* to employers and often found them wanting. 'Hulle's *morsig*' (They're messy, untidy – i.e. no better than us) is how they often described their apparently genteel employers. Many complained that employers and their children treated them without dignity. A few women confronted their employers about their treatment. Baby recalled, 'I used to be very cheeky with the white people … Oh God! … No, back then I didn't tolerate any nonsense from a white person!' Knowing Baby's biting tongue and bravery, I can easily believe this to be the case, but for the most part speaking one's mind to employers is a luxury that few can afford, despite the new protections offered by labour legislation.

Very few residents had ever gone for a job interview. Few had curricula vitae (CVs), although some young people did approach me in 2004 to assist them with developing their CVs. Most jobs – domestic work, gardening jobs, manual labour in the construction industry, and even factory work – were accessed by word of mouth. For example, three young people found employment as packers and cashiers at a supermarket;—highly valued, *ordentlike* work. A woman working at the supermarket who had relatives in The Village visited the chairwoman of The Village and told her that the retailer was about to advertise posts. She helped four young people (all of whom had completed either Standard 9 or Matric) develop CVs and took them to the supervisor, explaining the poor circumstances of life in The Village. The supervisor prioritised the young people's interviews and three were employed.[21] Sandra's three sons tapped into her husband's networks in the building and related sectors and all were employed after leaving school. They were considered successful because their training meant that they would always be able to find work. Finding work thus meant establishing and maintaining the right kind of networks, including family, friends and acquaintances, and neighbourhood networks, through which one could be alerted to opportunities. Many of these networks were oiled through sharing of goods, alcohol and gossip.

Sometimes securing work involves 'making a plan', outwitting the powers that be, forms of trickery and *skarreling*. Here is Chrisna, talking about the difficulties of obtaining work. She had very little formal education but was a very quick learner:

Look, if I wanted a job, I had to fib (skiet 'n kaart) to get it. If they asked if I knew how to do something then I would say yes because I knew that I was a fast learner. Like, I just watched how they cut the vines once, and after that I knew how to do it. I'm a fast learner.

She also commented on the subterfuges necessary to secure one's job:

> If you don't go to work (for example, because you are sick), you send someone in your place who answers your name on the roll-call and then you pay them afterwards.

Several people mentioned to me that they had 'stood in' for others in this way and thereby earned a small wage.

People's work histories were fractured. Very few had worked for any length of time for a single employer.[22] Chrisna, for example, had worked on eight farms and held two jobs as a domestic worker, all by the age of twenty-two. Charmaine's employment history is typical of many women's. An only child, her mother died when she was nine years old. She was sent from Genadendal, a farming community in the Boland, to live with her uncle in Cape Town, where she looked after the children, cooked and cleaned the house in exchange for her keep. She reports having been 'terrorised' by the people she lived with. She hints at sexual abuse: 'I was raised as an adult', a common euphemism. At fifteen she stopped going to school. She refused to say why. Her uncle offered to send her back to school but she refused and sought assistance from the welfare office to return to her mother's family in Genadendal. There she moved from relative to relative, working on various farms and eventually finding a factory job through a *bekeerde* (converted) relative who put her name down for work. She worked a night shift, preparing cabbages and other vegetables for packing. She enjoyed the work, but a violent fight in which an obdurate foreman pulled a knife on her and she retaliated similarly ('I said, "a knife for a knife"', she reported) put paid to that job. By 2004 she was in her early thirties and had worked on farms in Genadendal and Paarl, in a factory, as an unpaid worker in her uncle's home, as a domestic worker and on a state-sponsored job-creation project, 'Working for Water' (or 'Fynbos' as it was locally known[23]) before bearing her first child.[24] Her daughter was born prematurely, a not uncommon experience in The Park.[25] Charmaine's health is poor (see Chapter Seven) and the various jobs she has held have exposed her to environmental risks.

Her daughter's father insisted that she stop working when the child was born: 'Oh no, you are going to stay at home until that child starts going to school', he said. His insistence maps a masculine model of decency in which men provide for their families; it is the opposite of *skarreling*. 'I told him that if I stop working, he has to give me everything I need', she recalled. He agreed. Although he lived in Cape Town and not in Genadendal with her, he supported her and the child with monthly groceries and a regular cash payment. After a little more than a year of this arrangement, she and the child moved to Cape Town to live with him. Shortly thereafter she became ill with a debilitating disease that has left her medically unfit to work. Throughout her life, she had been unable to save money and although her child's father supported the family, she felt her position to be precarious. She plans to apply for *ongeskikte geld*, a disability grant,[26] which, although small, will give her a degree of autonomy.

Charmaine's work history – a collation of unskilled jobs secured through personal networks – is marked both by a sense of contingency or happenstance and a sense of determined effort to overcome difficulties. In this it is similar to those of many others in The Park/Village. Most of the adults I came to know well could not easily count the number of jobs they had held in their lives, and there are no national data on average numbers of jobs held in this socio-economic stratum that would allow for either comparison against a larger sample, or extrapolation. A study completed in KwaZulu-Natal in 2001 (Adato et al. n.d.) made similar findings to these I report here and indicates that survey-based data collection on work and employment often misses the wide range of informal and formal economic activities in which people engage. As with the KwaZulu-Natal study which found that 'The employment stories of households told overwhelmingly of the brevity and interruptedness of so much of the work, both formal and informal' (Adato et al. n.d: 13), most people in my research reported having worked for many different employers, sometimes in the general vicinity of The Park but more often on farms surrounding Cape Town and its hinterland and in the suburbs of what is now the greater metropolitan area.

Once a couple had established themselves as more than *man en meisie* or *vrying* ('making out'; implies sexual relations with little commitment), or had children, it was unusual for more than one adult in a household to hold a job over an extended period. A strong gender ideology which holds that women belong at home was frequently activated when men had sufficient wherewithal to provide, and several women I know gave this as a reason for giving up jobs (although it must also be noted that there were no childcare facilities in The Park or nearby, and most women who did relinquish jobs did so only when pregnant or after having given birth). Indeed, an important part of the definition of a 'good man' is one who works for his partner. Masculine forms of decency are predicated in part on being able to provide for a wife who does not need to work, or worse, to *skarrel*.[27] Here, for example, are Clive and Carmen (who are friends, not a couple), talking about Carmen and her partner, a man who worked in the building sector as a painter:

Clive: Carmen ... has a boyfriend. She used to live with him in The Park. So then he said that she should come and live with him (in The Village) because she cooks for him. That makes her a housewife (*huisvrou*). So this way she doesn't have to come all the way from her mother's house to cook for him, you see.

Carmen: (agreeing) Mmmm.

Janine: Oh, I see.

Carmen: And we were already so used to living together.

Clive: And he's good to her. He works .... Yes, he's very good to her .... He also doesn't want her to work .... Now *that's* so beautiful (*mooi*: lit. pretty; nice).

Janine: Does he not want you to go to work?

Carmen: I wanted to go to work this morning ...

Clive: (interrupting) That's a big advantage: she's not *allowed* to work.

Carmen: But he didn't want me to go. He sent a message last night saying that the two of us made a deal last year that he'd work and I would stay at home.

Janine: And are you happy with that?

Carmen: I'd actually like to work with (i.e. and have) my own money, but that's what he said and so ... I feel happy and so on ...

Here a strongly valued cultural model that holds that a man should support his family works against an individual's personal desire, household economic security and potential upward mobility. Women's desires are contradictory: they desire autonomy and wish to conform to ideals of decency that entail dependence on men. And men's models of masculinity are similarly contradictory: they seek to create *ordentlike* relations and at the same time are frequently excluded from the material sources that would enable them to build sustainable households over time.

Locally, then, employment is gendered by sectoral availability, cultural norms and historical processes that have long excluded women from some portions of the employment market (such as permanent employment on farms) while ensconcing them in others (such as the textile industries in the City, or domestic work). Employment patterns are racialised too: the history of African exclusion from the city under apartheid, employment of Coloured women in the textiles industry, apartheid education's lasting legacies, and so on, mean that structured inequalities are written into the employment landscapes of the city and of 'the new South Africa' more generally.

Individuals' employment histories fluctuate both in the short term and over the duration of their lives. The fluctuations have many causes, including shifts in global economic relations and in national economic policies, changes in agro-industry production (including the introduction of legislation securing workers' rights, land redistribution policies, changes in technologies that make some kinds of workers redundant, etc.), and the demise of certain kinds of industry (some residents of The Park had previously worked in durable jobs in a canning factory that went bankrupt). Shifts in employment patterns also came about because of changes in peri-urban settlement and land-use patterns (in the case of The Park, gentrification of the peri-urban edge, the outward expansion of the city and the rezoning and sale of agricultural land for residential purposes with the consequent eviction of workers), the growth of a population of unskilled workers (thus expanding the available labour pool and decreasing individual opportunities to secure work), individual and social alienation, culturally informed patterns of gender relations, and so on. In short, there are many reasons that people in The Park, and others like them, are unable to secure work over the long term. Not all of the reasons I cite above impact individuals directly, but all of them are complicit in the making of a group of people marginalised from durable employment and categorised as 'available labour' (see Wolpe 1972; Auyero 2000; Robins 2005), and of causing gendered differentials within this category.

Short-term job-fluctuation and uncertainty can have major implications for household continuity and well-being. For example, as part of an early study in 1992, I asked five women to keep food logs for me. Erica's is typical and I reproduce it in Table 5.1. At the time, Erica and her partner Tol were unemployed. An ex-con, Tol had found it difficult to obtain regular work. He occasionally worked for neighbours in The Park and in town, and his sister sometimes gave him small amounts of money. Rumour had it that he smuggled drugs, but I cannot verify this. Erica was not formally employed and I never observed her doing other forms of work for people in the settlement. She was usually to be found at home, caring for her daughter Tassa, a toddler. (Tassa was later sent to live with another relative.) The log reflects Erica and Tol's food intake and to some extent Tassa's too. It reveals the extent of food insecurity in this household: during the seventeen-day period, no food was eaten on two of the days, and bread was the main sustenance on three days.

Table 5.1 Erica's Food Log, March–April 1992

DATE	TIME	FOOD
Tues 24 March	5 pm	Beans, rice, bones (stew made from waste bones obtained from the butchery – see Evalyn's recipe)
Wed 25 March	8.30 am	Previous night's food, warmed up
	12.30 pm	Bread, chips, warmed up left-overs
	6 pm	Rice & bones
Thurs 26 March	5.30 pm	Rice, potatoes, curry
Fri 27 March	7.30 pm	Bread & margarine

Sat 28 March	8.30 am	Bones & bread
Sun 29 March		Nothing to eat
Mon 30 March		Nothing to eat
Tues 31 March	6 pm	Pork & rice
Wed 1 April	7.30 pm	Packet (instant) soup & bread
Thurs 2 April	8.30 pm	Rice & mince
Fri 3 April	7.30 pm	Samp & beans
Sat 4 April	6 pm	Split pea soup
Sun 5 April	5.30 pm	Curry & rice
Mon 6 April		Coffee & bread
Tues 7 April		Meat & rice
Wed 8 April		Maize porridge & rice
Thurs 9 April	6.30 pm	Soup, potatoes & rice

When I discussed the log with Erica, it became clear that food was bought on an *ad hoc* basis, as money came into the house. The rest of the time the family made do with leftovers, or, as is evident from the log, with no food, or bread and other starches as the main meal. Erica could not always say what her child had eaten in the day—neighbours shared food with the little girl without telling her. On the basis of my observations, it is likely that the food Tassa received was sandwiches of refined white bread and polony. When money was available, the food of choice was take-away fish and chips. In general, as was the case in most households in The Park, the food consumed was high in fat and carbohydrates and low in nutritional value. Meat and dairy-based proteins were seldom available. Very few fresh fruits and vegetables were eaten in this and other households. The exceptions were households where Rastafari resided, where diets were, for the most part, vegetarian and low in protein.

I have included the food log because it offers an immediate illustration of the effects of inadequate, irregular and unpredictable incomes on nutritional intakes. Like many others in The Park, the family literally operated on a hand-to-mouth basis. 'We don't know what tomorrow will hold' is how people put it. The lack of certainty and reliability in incomes undermine people's sense of decency and make it extremely difficult to manage money effectively and plan for the future. It also creates wide-ranging networks of reciprocity and dependence among people in The Park.

Managing money: temporality and contingency

'Fiona, why are whites so rich and we are so poor?' asked Luzanne one day. A letter that appeared in the *Cape Times* on Friday 12 November 2004 (p. 4), written by Rodney T. Rhoda offers one common answer – an answer with which I disagree. In response to two articles the newspaper had run the previous week, asking why it is that Africa is growing poorer while the rest of the world gets richer, Rhoda argues that 'The role of cultural values cannot be ignored if we wish to solve the problem of poverty in Africa', and claims that:

> Different groups have the right to different values, but we must accept that cultural values affect a group's economic conditions. Some groups tend to emphasise enjoyment and social times while others emphasise sobriety and hard work. There is nothing morally wrong with either system, but the fact is that the latter is more likely to increase wealth. A high value on immediate 'fun', 'excitement', 'partying' and emotionalism has characterized the less successful groups. In a free society, individuals are at liberty to pursue their own values, including fun and excitement. But when a group does pursue such values, it can only do so by giving up the activities that might be more lucrative and they will tend to have lower incomes. All South Africans need to work harder, if we want to combat poverty.

In the anthropological literature, this is known as the 'culture of poverty' argument. It received its most famous form in Oscar Lewis's (1959) study of people living in a Mexican slum in the 1950s, and is a common explanation for disparities of income in capitalist economies. In essence, the argument posits that people are poor because once marginalised they perpetuate their poverty and alienation by socialising their children into the adaptations they have made to accommodate poverty. In Rhoda's rendition above, poor people opt for hedonism over hard work – that is, they choose to be poor. By this argument, being poor is an individual problem, but it becomes a larger problem because once they are poor, people perpetuate poverty by socialising their children into the same values – of enjoyment of life and of 'fun' – that they are said to hold. Poverty can only be eradicated by teaching these people the value of hard work, it is said, and by ensuring that these latter values are passed on to children. Such ideas are very common in capitalist societies, and South Africa's is no exception. They permeate even policy-making and development circles.[28] By this model, Luzanne's children will only become rich if they go to school and learn to work hard.

But there is an important critique of the culture of poverty thesis, which argues that poverty is not a choice and that marginalisation is central to capitalist economies in that it creates a pool of available labour that can be easily exploited.

A growing body of literature is concerned with casualisation and feminisation of labour as large industries divest of permanent workers and make increasing use of casual workers. I often hear middle-class people say 'they won't work' in relation to people living in impecunious circumstances. Too often people whose lives are cushioned by reliable incomes and decent work forget just how limited opportunities actually are, how precarious people's everyday lives are, and how historical processes of subjugation and marginalisation continue to structure and limit people's life opportunities. Individual social capital is precarious; it can erode or wither away if inadequately scaffolded.

It is not only the well-off who make disparaging claims. A pernicious stereotype of the lazy Coloured informs the perspectives of young Xhosa-speaking migrants who often have left their families in 'the land' (the former homelands, now the Eastern Cape) and have come to the city to seek work to build up their rural homesteads. During the construction of The Village, young migrant men who worked as manual labourers on the site spoke disparagingly of 'Coloureds' who did not find work on the project: 'They're just lazy', was the general sentiment. By contrast, some 'Coloured' men stated that it was so undignified to work for minimum wages that it would be better not to work at all than to compete with those scrambling for work at the bottom of the ranks. They weighed their models of proper masculinity against menial employment and settled for not looking for employment, to the detriment of their households. Denver, a plumber, one of the few artisans in The Village offers an example. Despite the rapid growth in the construction sector and the huge demand for skilled workers, in 2004 he was out of work. He blamed migrants, saying he had set his price for a day's wage and because 'the blacks will work for less', he can't find employment. The result, as we will see below, is that his wife, Big Anne, had to make ends meet for the family. The feeling of entitlement to jobs is widespread, and can generate tensions between migrants and those whose primary orientation is to The Park/Village. Differential geographic patterns of material and emotional investment, informed by the Cape's harsh history, are sedimented and naturalised in racial stereotypes – Africans as foreign to the Cape, Coloureds as lazy. These have little to do with people's everyday cross-racial interactions and much to do with racial stereotypes associated with apartheid.

'I can't even afford to save a two Rand (coin) because if I put it away today, I'll need it again tomorrow and that's how I always end up broke', said Freddie during a work history interview with Janine. Impoverishment raises the difficult question of how to plan for the future. Middle-class people often comment on what they see as a lack of financial and future planning in poor people's lives. Most of the residents of The Park do not have bank accounts. Some leave reliable jobs for reasons as simple as that they are bored. Some rely on casual work and favours to get by, or generate dependency and patronage relationships with those with reliable incomes. Until recently in South Africa, it was difficult for poor people even to open a bank account, should they have the means and desire to do so. One needed evidence of income, a fixed permanent address and proof of such, and to retain a minimum monthly balance. Bank costs are high. There are no ATMs in easy distance of The Park/Village. Many banks and other institutions would not accept a squatter camp as a legitimate address. Importantly, money in a bank cannot do the same kind of work as money available and at hand, which can purchase goods, soothe social relations, connect people into networks that have future use (see also Ferguson 1985). To characterise people as lacking financial astuteness is to underestimate the dexterous ways in which they do try to make ends meet.

There are a number of parallels in The Park/Village with what Robert Desjarlais (1997: 140–51) found among residents of a shelter for the homeless in Boston, USA, in the 1990s. There, he argued, two different economic sensibilities were in operation. Staff at the centre encouraged the forms of investment familiar in rationalist models of capitalism – that is, they encouraged residents to secure their futures through work and investment (1997: 150). Residents, on the other hand, 'focused more often than not on the day at hand', a characteristic that he argues is a result of a specific orientation to time that poverty induces, encouraging people to 'seize the moment'. He adds, 'Assuming that they would never be in a position to afford a comfortable standard of living, residents sometimes invested in moments of pseudoprosperity', including 'narcotic highs' (ibid.). Those moments were both self- and other-oriented residents treated themselves and shared their prosperity. What I would characterise as an economy of immediacy governed residents' relationships to money, tying them into the present tense, as against the desires of the staff at the centre, who sought to instil a rationalist economy of thriftiness and saving that has echoes of what Weber so famously called 'the Protestant work ethic'.

Desjarlais' account is important in that it recognises the different ways in which people might be oriented to time through economic relations: present versus future, investment in capital and goods versus speculation on the immediacies of feeling good and sharing that feeling with others, investment in the relatively distanced and abstract institutions of capitalist society – banks, annuities, policies and goods versus the immediacies of social relationships in the present of living in confined spaces. In short, reciprocal relations with others in one's immediate environs versus capitalist forms of investment. His account reminds us that these relationships are class-based, not 'cultural' or 'racial' as has so often been presumed in South Africa. Yet, it is important to recognise that what some might see as a lack of self-responsibility can also be understood as ensuring sociality over time through practices of generalised reciprocity. It is also important not to be drawn into an analysis that reduces all experience to rational modes of being. The implicit model that underpins most anthropological analyses of incomes and expenditures among poor people – and Desjarlais' otherwise sensitive account is no different in this respect – tends to demand of them that their behaviour must be more rational than the behaviours of the non-poor. Getting high, seeking additional stimulus or seeking to diminish the stimuli of exuberant or fragile everyday lives is as much part of being human as is rationally calculating towards tomorrow. Who among the middle-classes has not experienced the delight of splurging, the regret of a purchase rashly made, the excess emotion produced by the immediacy of spending? In fact, consumer society rests precisely on these: purchasing more than one needs, 'retail therapy', and so on. Capitalism in its present form administers to the delights of immediate gratification for those who can afford it. But poor people are judged not to be able to afford these 'luxuries', indeed, ought not to, and when they do succumb to allure, they are depicted as rash, careless, improvident, thoughtless, a drain on the state.

There is in this an interesting inversion of what Johannes Fabian (1983) calls 'the denial of co-evalness'. By this he means that anthropology conventionally depicted other peoples in the present tense, disallowing the possibility of change. This works to create a distance between 'us' and 'them', so that 'they' are always fixed on a scale lower than 'we' are, thus entrenching forms of 'othering'. In other words, the use of specific tenses can be ideological, working to make social divisions appear both natural and incontrovertible. Similarly, by assuming that poor people do not have a sense of the future, that they live entirely in and for the present, an economic elite is able to distance itself from the structural processes through which some people's opportunities are curtailed and others' enhanced.

In fact, it would be a mistake to assume that the impoverished residents of The Park live only in the present. While there is no doubt that many people find themselves unable to plan effectively for their financial futures and do spend their money in ways that those more puritan might consider improvident, people still have a sense of the future and worry about how it might unfold. One arena in which this is particularly clear is in relation to death. Although they may not have the means to pay school fees or transportation costs, or sometimes even food, many residents have fully paid-up funeral policies or are members of burial associations (Afrikaans: doodgenootskap, Xhosa: masincwabane).[29] These facts are clear indications of saving, of expanding reciprocal relations, and of an orientation to the future, albeit one in which they anticipate not being present.

'To budget is to choose', said Minister of Finance, Trevor Manuel in his budget Speech of 2006 (Manuel 2006: 4). But how one budgets, what one values and the choices one makes are shaped by cultural norms and ideals: anthropology has long shown that *homo economicus*, the economically rational man, is a cultural construct. In the Park/Village, managing money effectively is an attribute associated with *ordentlikheid*. This was made clear to me one day during a conversation with Bernie, who runs a shop owned by her husband Philip. We were talking and also listening to a conversation in the next room in which a woman was trying to explain to Philip how she would deal with the debt she had run up *op die boek* at the shop. The woman's husband had died unexpectedly, and with him, a grant that doubled their monthly income. On the strength of their joint incomes, they had run up debt in five different shops, some in The Village and some elsewhere in town. The problem now would be to manage the debts. Bernie commented disapprovingly that she could not understand how someone who had R1400 per month incoming from grants (that is, reliable money) should have allowed herself to be in a position to run up debt. She spoke about how she only bought for cash, and saved for the things she wanted. It takes effort and will, she said, not to simply open accounts in order to have the things one wants immediately, but the effort was compensated by the lack of worry about debt. One has to manage one's money, she said.

Some people were better able to do so than others. One such was Sandra, who, with her partner Tella, insisted that their three children attend school and who attempted to budget with meagre resources so that the key transition moments in their lives could be properly celebrated – their marriage, their sons' Matric dances, twenty-first birthdays and so on. Sandra commented to me that it was necessary to have a vision for the future so that one could plan towards it. 'It's important to dream for your children', she said, but noted that many people have had so little opportunity for themselves that they do not recognise it or make provision for it for their children. She began planning her sons' twenty-first birthday celebrations a year in advance. Each was a huge event. Each entailed the purchase of new clothes, the hiring of halls, tables, chairs, cutlery, crockery, table cloths. Flowers were bought, tables were decorated with 'fancies' (cupcakes and sweets) – blue for Rowan, green for Harold—meals were planned and baked. The events were memorialised in photographs and a video. Each of the boys received a symbolic gift – a key for Rowan, a trophy for Harold. All of these had to be planned for and purchased, and all occurred when Tella was out of work and when Sandra's jobs were intermittent. As a result, careful planning was necessary. She began by deciding on and ordering the fancies, paying for them when they were ready. This done, she could concentrate on paying off the food in preparation, and the hiring. Everything was carefully budgeted for and paid off over time. Even though both adults were frequently out of work during the period of the two celebrations, she managed to safeguard the events she dreamt of. She did so by activating kin and friendship networks. Her parents contributed to the events, a friend with a job paid the school fees and purchased uniforms and books for the boys, other friends helped with catering for the Matric dance, and so on. Making ends meet here involved creative accounting – massaging one's networks rather than one's savings account. Rational choice theory would suggest that she would have been materially better off by saving the money she spent, but she felt that it was important to celebrate life's accomplishments and to mark its cycles in culturally validated ways, which, rather like the classic anthropological example of the potlatch, involve forms of conspicuous consumption.

Still, as much as one dreams and plans, everyday realities of poverty, ill-health and lack of opportunity get in the way of actualising ideals. For instance, Attie envisaged retiring to his birthplace, Colesburg. There, he said, he would sit on the porch and smoke a pipe and have his grandchildren care for him. 'But', he sighed with wry realism, 'I probably won't be able to afford the *twak* (tobacco)!' His casual dismissal of hardship is characteristic of how people talk about their context and futures. '*Die lewe's swaar*' (Life's hard/heavy), he said, a comment with which everyone in The Park/Village concurred. Indeed, people usually use the word *swaarheid* (difficulty; heaviness) to describe poverty, rather than the technically more correct *armoede*. People *sukkel* (struggle) with the heaviness of everyday life and to achieve forms of decency that have cultural and social value. Struggle is part of daily life, something one expects. During a conversation between Ponkies, Sandra and I outside Sandra's back door one day in 2001, Sandra described how Tella recently lost his job. She said, 'It's okay if we have to *sukkel*. Sometimes that's life'. Ponkies agreed; '*Ons kry swaar*' (heaviness comes to us; life's hard). '*Daar's niks meer om te sê nie: ons moet net 'n plan maak*' (There's nothing more to be said; we just have to make a plan, cope). '*Die lewe behandel jou stief, maar jy moet maar gepaard gaan*' (Life treats you roughly but you must keep going).

It takes a certain kind of courage (*moed*), often easily dismissed, to live with the knowledge that life is heavy and unkind, that it is unlikely substantially to change and that one will be burdened with the effort of having always to cope or improvise.

Dexterity and 'making a plan'

'Making a plan' calls for ingenuity and skill. It also involves opening oneself to the potential humiliation of a request refused. Where incomes are unreliable, one is cast upon one's social skills in managing the relationships that facilitate getting by. A certain deftness is required, an adroit assessment of people and social circumstances. I characterise this as dexterity. Usually associated with skilled performance of manual labour, I use 'dexterity' here to describe the ways in which people, particularly women, attempt to draw on social skills and networks of relations to make ends meet in times of need. Given the happenstance nature of economic relations in everyday life, the term gives a descriptive dimension to the more usual use of the military terms 'strategies' and 'tactics' in the literatures dealing with how people cope. Michel de Certeau (1988) characterises strategies as bearing a formal relation to 'the proper'. They imply concerted action, enabled by rules, order and control over production, towards desired goals. They foreground place. Tactics, by contrast, have a quality of flexibility to the immediate context, and as such are oriented to time.

> The space of a tactic is the space of the other. Thus it must play on and within a terrain imposed on it and organized by the law of a foreign power. ... [I]t does not have ... the option of planning a general strategy .... It operates in isolated actions, blow by blow. It takes advantage of 'opportunities' and depends on them, being without any base where it could stockpile its winnings, build up its position .... What it wins, it cannot keep. This nowhere gives a tactic mobility, to be sure, but a mobility that must accept the chance offerings of the moment, and seize on the wing the possibilities that offer themselves at any given moment. It must vigilantly make use of the cracks that particular conjunctions open in the surveillance of the proprietary powers .... In short, a tactic is an art of the weak. (De Certeau 1988: 37)

For the powerless, properness is difficult to accomplish, even if desired. People navigate the everyday tactically rather than strategically. Because tactics are immediately responsive to the context at hand, they are not easily predictable or 'mappable' (see Chapter Three). They are reflective of the present even as they carry traces of the past (in people's knowledge of how to do what they do).

De Certeau is celebratory of the tactical in everyday life, seeing in it the way that ordinary people subvert the powers that oppress through their actions.[30] But it is worth noting that it is exhausting to be constantly tactical, unable to create or adhere to strategic action in the world, to act with direction and purpose towards desired goals. It is this sense of being adrift that people articulate when they speak of being senuweeagtig. Although most people in The Park had a very clear vision of how they would like to live, it was often not realistic or achievable. Very few had what might be called a strategy that could hold in the long term. Even those such as Sandra, who had a vision for their lives and tried carefully to secure it, are better described as users of tactics rather than as strategists. Most people might more aptly be characterised as opportunists. I do not mean this in the negative sense that the word often implies, but rather in the sense of having to be alert to possibilities, however slim, to make ends meet and get by.

In so doing they brought the strategic and the tactical into interesting relation. In attempting to accomplish *ordentlikheid* in materially and socially deprived contexts, people were attempting to achieve 'the proper' through impromptu activities. Thus, although they may be described as tactical, their activities were not necessarily subversive of the established order and might in fact have been directed towards supporting it.[31]

In her description of life in The Flats, in 'Jackson Harbour', Carol Stack (1973) notes a range of activities through which poor African American households make ends meet. These include borrowing and sharing, circulating material goods, 'swapping' in a meaningful system of reciprocity and exchange. As I have suggested in Chapter Four (see also Ross 1995), similar systems operated in The Park, where one might exchange cooking fuels for food or clean a house in exchange for rights to a bed. There is thus a quality of improvisation as people seek opportunities to make ends meet. A great deal of skill is involved – one cannot wear one's welcome thin.

The result of residents' efforts to meet material needs is a network of changing interactions that over time has brought many members of the settlement into co-operation and conflict with one another. As a result, affective relations, both positive and negative, are deep and networks of mutual obligation in the settlement were (and remain) wide-ranging. We have already seen the implications of this for how people envisage their relationships with and responsibilities towards others.

People's tactics to get by involve asking others for loans or *skrop werk* (lit. scrubbing; housework – particularly laundry – or odd jobs for people in the settlement), etc. They also require taking note of opportunities as they arise and acting quickly in response. All entail asking someone else to take a chance on one or to take pity on one or to recognise one's need and their possible links and connections to it. Refusal is experienced as a humiliation and people are careful to couch their requests in ways that will enable them to save face should a request not be granted. Friendships cannot easily withstand the anger and resentment that result when expected help is not forthcoming. Knowing who to approach and where to find funds involves knowing who has money when in the week or month – having created relationships sufficient that one can approach with a reasonable expectation of not being rebuffed – manipulating finances and finding one's way around institutions that may offer support. Take for example Anne, who received a R700/m disability grant. Big Anne, she was called. Extremely overweight, she suffered from high blood pressure and diabetes and was 'touched' with tuberculosis (TB) (see Chapter Seven). When the weather was hot, she said, her body swelled and her legs could not support her. The Cape's hot and dry summers were unendurable and she spent most of her time indoors at home or visiting close neighbours. Her man is the plumber I referred to earlier. In 2004, Denver was out of work. Anne said that he refused to work and he concurred, claiming that it was beneath his dignity to work for minimum wages. At the time, he was drinking heavily, to cope with the 'frustrations of life', he explained, adding that no one understood him so he drank for consolation. He often drank alone, which is usually read as a sign of alcoholism. In the week preceding our conversation he had worked for one day only and he and his friends used all the money except for R36 (about USD4), which he gave to Anne to pay for school transportation for their three children. The money covered less than half the cost: the children's transport alone was R75/week. Denver said that the children should stay away from school rather than incur debts on taxi charges. Anne was indignant about his suggestion that school was expendable. And besides, school fees were due. The fees, payable at the commencement of the year, were R700 for the eldest and R300 each for the two younger children. In addition, they had to buy books and uniforms. Anne had spent her disability grant that month purchasing school shoes for all of them, a new uniform for the youngest and books for the eldest, Emmerencia, a keen learner. 'While she still wants learn and isn't playing like an adult (i.e. engaged in sexual activity), she must to go to school', Anne said. I asked how she would find money for the taxi and the school fees and food and water and electricity and the other costs that go into operating a household of two adults and three youngsters. She shrugged. 'I'll make a plan', she said.

In the few households where there were two incomes, it was common that women's incomes were used to secure the household while men had more freedom in how they disposed of 'their' money. Although they are 'supposed' to give housekeeping money to their partners, most women complain that men spend the bulk of their money without consultation, usually on drink, gambling and activities associated with male camaraderie, and that little comes back into the household. Anne's case above is a good example: Denver felt he had a choice in how much money went into household coffers and what it should be used for, whereas Anne's entire disability grant was regularly absorbed into household expenses. A gendered differential arises, in which in practice the household is treated as consisting of women and children.

In trying to deal with the exigencies of her situation, Anne decided to approach the ACVV (Afrikaans Christelike Vroue Vereeniging; Afrikaans Christian Women's Association) to see whether the organisation could help her to secure a reduction in the school fees. Then she would see whether anyone in the community could help her by paying her to do odd jobs or laundry. She was dismayed at the prospect—it was baking hot and her feet and legs had swollen terribly. She wondered whether she should 'make a case' for child support through the Social

Welfare Office where one of the social workers is well known for her intransigent attitude to men who are recalcitrant with child support. Anne was sure that if she brought a case, the court would find in her favour and the Welfare offices would ensure that Denver made proper child support payments.

Anne's ideas were good, but each was demanding in a different way of her time, limited money and emotional resources. In deciding who to approach for skrop werk, careful judgement is called for, a close assessment of local relations and one's position within them. This was particularly complicated as she had recently held a position on the local governing structure of the settlement and some of the people she had antagonised with her forthright assessments and blunt tongue had been those whom she would ordinarily have called on for assistance. Getting to the ACVV involved borrowing money to make a phone call to set up an appointment, borrowing more money for a taxi fare and walking to the offices, making an application and returning in a few weeks' time to get the result. And her idea of laying charges against her partner required that she think carefully about the consequences for her relationship with him and his relationship with the children. Would he leave? How will one feel living with a man against whom one has laid charges? What forms of humiliation are potentially opened?

The costs, both emotional and social, of these efforts are high. One comes to rely on neighbourliness. To do so, one has to have held those relationships, nurtured them, responded appropriately to the requests of others so as to secure relations over time. One has to know who to approach, and also when not to approach. People are careful not to sound as if they are begging: begging is considered demeaning. It is part of a cluster of symbols that together are read to imply that one is a weggooi mens, a bergie, someone without dignity or social support networks – an isolate. Appropriate tones of voice and request terminology are called for, a phrasing that is not offensive. In some instances, this may involve 'straight-talk' – a clearly articulated request. In other cases, requests may be more elliptically expressed, a gentle circumnavigation of the topic which offers social cues to which the listener may choose to respond. Demands are made on listening. I return to these modes of engagement in Chapter Six.

For some, the avenues to daily material stability were more insecure still. Margaret did not work regularly and, unlike Big Anne, received no state support. At various times since I have known her, she did skrop werk for other women in the settlement for a small fee, and was once in charge of the crèche in The Park, for which she was paid a minimum wage. The Village, however, does not have a hall or central place where children can gather and as a result there is no crèche there. Consequently, her source of income fell away. She has four daughters, the youngest two of whom have children of their own. None of the children attended school – all dropped out when they became sexually active. One daughter lived with her partner who took on responsibility for her son, the baby's father never having provided child support. The other young mother continued to live at home with her mother although her baby's father offered some child support. The two older daughters also lived with her. Neither had regular work: both did occasional *skrop werk* in the community. One was drug dependent, possibly addicted to Mandrax, a drug widely used in the settlement. Her mother despaired of her and people referred to her with disdain. Her former boyfriend 'returned' her when she failed to keep house adequately and stole from him. Neither of the girls gave any of the occasional money they made to the household coffers. There was seldom spare money in the house, no chance to cover contingencies. When Margaret's estranged husband died in 2002, she was unable to raise the funds to secure him a proper burial and he was given a pauper's cremation in Cape Town. There was no funeral and there is no site to visit, to pay respects, on which to lay flowers. It was a cause of considerable sadness and great shame for her that she was unable to bury him properly.

By early 2004, her situation had improved somewhat: she met a man she cared about who worked and supported her. In return, she kept house for him although she continued to live in her own house. In addition, she did odd jobs around the settlement, receiving R25 for each large load of laundry that she washed by hand. Her first port of call for *skrop werk* was a neighbour who was widely considered *ordentlik*. Late in 2004, Margaret's *man* was involved in an accident and could not work for several weeks. As a result, she once more found herself without material support and was again required to find *skrop werk*. Pity and empathy moved some neighbours to offer her work. But one cannot rely on neighbours forever. Pity and empathy wear thin over time when people's resources are stretched and there is no sign of improvement in a person's circumstances. Margaret's *man* never really recovered and after he had spent time in seven hospitals in Cape Town, his family declared him mentally unsound and decided that he should return to the Eastern Cape to be cared for by relatives. Considered merely his 'town wife', Margaret's relationship with him was dismissed as both expedient and illegitimate. She was not consulted in the decision, nor did the family make any provision for her well-being. When she described her loss to me, she said she was 'worn out' from worry and too emotionally tired even to be anxious.

Where incomes are unreliable and times are challenging, people are cast upon their social skills in managing the relationships that enable daily life. A certain deftness is required, an adroit assessment of people and circumstances. Social dexterity rests on the personal. People must know not only the institutions that might be of assistance but also the name of a specific person within the institution who is reputed to be of assistance. Stories of assistance spread quickly through social networks, and individuals concerned are always named. Personality matters. Poor people experience institutions as fragmented and incoherent (see Henderson 1999), something both my research assistants, Janine and Robyn, have commented on in relation to The Park. In such contexts, it is important to be able to identify individuals who might pay attention. It causes great difficulty and distress to people seeking assistance when a person they know by name and repute is moved from an institution. New avenues have to be sought, new connections built.

It is clear that the context of impoverishment, replete with gendered differentials, has scope for considerable conflict and extraordinary social demands. A range of skills is necessary in order to secure a semblance of regularity and decency in everyday life. These are skills of social relationship; forms of social capital but without the hardiness that the term usually implies.

Concerns around decency again became important as people contemplated the move to The Village, their desires to have the objects that would signal their status as ordentlik, and their fears about the costs that this would involve. Ironically, in order to qualify for a house, one had to be poor, but aspirations and conceptions of decency meant that one had to disguise one's poverty once the houses were acquired. Having considered their actual experiences of work and poverty, I reflect now on their ambitions for respectability.

'Respectable people have nice houses'

If you've got a new house you must work. You see, when they were living in (The Park) they were lazy. They used to just sit around because they would get everything they needed. But they didn't take into account the fact that they were coming to live in houses (muurhuisies) where they have to pay for everything. But now they have to go out and find some work. Who do they think they are? They can't sit back like Madam and Eve![32]

So said Chrisna during an interview on employment, which rapidly turned to a conversation on getting by and particularly on the demands that decorating new houses made on skint pockets. The move to new houses opened the question of the relation between commodities and proper personhood. Residents made their new homes in The Village in the context of strong social pressures towards conformity, both aesthetic and legal. In addition to the model of dependancy that the state introduced, and the variety of models of relatedness in operation in 'the community' (see Chapter Four), enormous social pressures were brought to bear on conformity to *ordentlike* appearances. Material property counts in making respectable persons. Appearances matter and material investment – being seen to be proper – is an important component in people's imaginings of living decent lives. This includes pressures to invest in the material accoutrements that people associate with decent modern living – furniture and appliances (often purchased on hire purchase at high rates of interest and with high rates of default), fencing and gates, paint, and so on.

Expectations about how to furnish houses and pay for services caused considerable tension within households as people grappled with their desire to create homes that conformed to their ideals of *ordentlikheid*. Here is Antony, worrying about the costs he was about to incur with the new house:

> Well, (a house) costs you a fortune. If you invite someone to your home, you'd want it to look pretty. So, you'll have to spend some money if you want it to look that way. Then you also have to eat and you'll need some clothes. We'll have to pay for electricity and water and we won't have a choice because all those things are essential. Other expenses include buying furniture, bed linen, and so on, so this is what a house will do to you.

And Baby:

> If I could have some kind of furniture, it would be fine ... Maybe a nice table or something nice. I want my house to at least look like something. ... [You need] your tables, your chairs, a bed in your room and a dressing table (with a mirror). In your kitchen you have your pots and stuff like that, and probably a fridge. But I don't want a fridge because I can't afford one. No, I don't want that stuff ... because I don't have that kind of money! There's no money. Who's going to pay for it? I don't have a husband.

In a delightful turn of phrase, Michel de Certeau and Luce Giard describe homes as 'indiscreet', adding 'the home openly confesses the income level and social ambitions of its occupants. Everything about it always speaks too much' (1998: 146). Managing this excess of symbolic meaning is important; people considered 'hoity-toity', who put on airs and graces and make too much of their belongings are often socially ostracised (Bayi-Bayi, pers. comm. May 2000; see Yose 1999; Meintjies 2000). Social differentiation was carefully managed in The Park and residents (other than community leaders) were particular not to appear 'posh' by investing in material goods, both to avoid being accused by others of being unneighbourly and to avoid being asked for loans. Nevertheless, certain people – particularly the community leaders and church members – were expected to have 'nice' houses. In this respect, Sandra, a community leader, explained that she was a 'role model' for her community,

> We (she and her husband) know what to do with money, you see … it isn't like we bought a lot of food or we bought a lot of clothes … We bought something you can *see* (pointing out the TV unit, TV, video recorder, hi-fi, new lounge suite, fridge and stove in the shack). That's where our money goes.

In other words, local models of decency hold that where budgetary choice is possible, the correct approach is to invest in the trappings of a consumerist *ordentlikheid*. Where finances are limited, this raises complexities about how to allocate funds. For example, in 2000, Sandra had put a cupboard on lay-by at a nearby shop and had to pay for it by a certain date. If she did not she would lose both the cupboard and the payments already made. The trouble was that she had no extra money to pay the final instalment, and her sons' school fees, for which she had set money aside, were due. So she took the money that she had set aside for school fees and paid for the cupboard. She said she would either find someone to pay the fees or pay them off over the year. Here, a new cupboard is both the outcome of and a mask over the decision of whether to invest in a child's education by paying school fees or in social propriety by paying the hire-purchase costs on the cupboard. Family members outside The Park can be relied on or pressured to pay education costs, the costs of aesthetics can only be born by the household. In the event, a well-wisher paid school fees and the cupboard was duly installed. No sooner was this done than a visiting neighbour commented favourably on it, noting its neat appearance and functionality. Later, the proud owner commented to me, 'You see, I am a model for my community'. The episode was confirmation of our discussion during an earlier interview in which she had told me her vision for the community,

> My *visie* is ons moet bymekaar staan. Ons moet lief wees vir mekaar. (My vision is that we must stand together. We must be kind to each other.) And we must live like people who live in other places, like in wall houses, and so on … I think it's not useful for people to know … the finer details (about each other's lives).

'Living like people in other places' entails conforming to *ordentlike* standards of consumption and display; revealing oneself to be a modern person of substance. Thus while home interiors may reveal a great deal about the personalities of the occupants, as De Certeau, Giard and Mayol (1998) claim, they also reveal a great deal about prevailing social codes and people's ability to measure up to them. The kinds and distributions of furniture and ornaments within formal houses mark ordentlikheid or its lack. Public and private spaces were demarcated by either a wall or a curtain separating 'living' from 'sleeping' areas. Much energy went into decorating the house's public spaces. It was considered inappropriate for beds to be visible unless they were draped and dotted with cushions so as to double as sofas. Wall units and matching lounge suites were desirable furnishings. Where people could not afford to buy these on hire purchase, they used small tables cluttered with objects to make their displays. Wedding photographs were important accoutrements of ordentlikheid and were prominently displayed, as were china ornaments, photographs of family members, hi-fis and televisions (the bigger and flashier the better). Not necessarily intrinsically functional (as Helen Meintjes has noted in her important study of consumer goods in Soweto, Gauteng, where many of the objects on display were broken), they nevertheless have symbolic functionality: they signal a familiarity with the codes of modernist consumption and display.

Meintjes (2000 and 2001) shows that people make use of material artefacts such as electrical appliances in order to conform to local constructs of proper urban and modern living. Sometimes these conflict with generational interpretations of gender roles (Meintjes 2001). Young women desire mod-cons that demonstrate a familiarity and ease with modern living, whereas older women stress the importance of convention. Thus, for example, a washing machine becomes a symbol of modernity, and age-specific tensions to do with proper personhood are expressed in terms of whether it is seemly to have one's apparel washed by machine, or whether it is a woman's role to 'do the washing'.

Meintjes's argument is germane to investment events in The Village, where, given that income levels are extremely low and employment uncertain, financial strategies are fraught with complexity. A number of women in The Village reported that a 'proper' home should have a certain appearance – key items of furniture, net curtains, lace or crocheted antimacassars, etc. – and these ideals competed with already existent income and expenditure patterns. Some women reported feeling angry at the permeability of household boundaries and the pressures that the patterns of sharing and commensality described elsewhere brought to bear on meagre household incomes. These difficulties appear to be common in informal settlements. Students working on my project and researchers elsewhere indicate that social levelling mechanisms expressed through gossip and isolation are widespread in shanty areas. In shack settlements, gossip can cause ostracism and residents were careful not to flaunt goods lest they bear the brunt of local annoyance. While living in The Park, some people went so far as to keep goods with relatives elsewhere in anticipation of the move to formal houses and in order to circumvent 'talk'.

In her comparative study of formal and informal housing in the Milnerton area of Cape Town, Constance Yose (1999) found that Xhosa-speakers living in shanties make use of symbolic and linguistic associations that equate shacks with rural areas, and are thereby able to activate the kinds of social networks, obligations and forms of reciprocity considered appropriate to rural living. These have the effect of widening the social base on which to rely in harsh times. When people move to formal areas, the symbolic associations seem to fall away – often to the great bitterness of neighbours – and new forms of association, equating formal homes with nucleation and self-sustainability, begin to take their place. Residents of The Park/Village recognised this process and both welcomed and feared it. They sought the privacy that formal houses were thought to offer but were afraid that formalisation would lead to isolation. My first period of research in The Village suggests that their fears are not ill-founded: residents report that their previous patterns of sharing networks have not survived the move to formal housing, although they may well be re-instituted at a later stage.[33]

In contexts where incomes are unreliable and jobs scarce, people are reliant on more than just their manual skills or book learning to make ends meet. They draw on what I have characterised as dexterity, skills in cultivating networks and reading social situations. People with regular incomes (usually from state welfare grants) are able to live 'on the book', to 'make debt' at local *subeens*. Those who lack any form of stability in their incomes are forced to make ends meet in other ways, including through casual work outside the settlement, *skrop werk*, informal trading arrangements with other residents and other forms of reciprocity and social indebtedness. And almost every adult has some experience of *skarreling*, either for short periods between more formal work, or more often, as an ordinary mode of getting by. Most adults are unable to secure forms of work that conform to their image of decent employment, and ongoing forms of poverty and humiliation render them increasingly less likely to secure any formal work at all save for that concentrated in the lowest-paid, least regulated sectors. At the same time as they confront their ongoing impoverishment and the humiliations it offers every day, residents also have to deal with the fact that the forms of personhood they value and aspire to are heavily premised on consumer culture. People's anger and dismay at their experiences of failing to live up to consumerist ideals indicate the weight of conformity to appearances, the sheer burden of propriety.

Recipes

Dina's stewed cabbage à la Rastafari

Dina had to learn to cook vegetarian food for her Rasta man. The main ingredient to her Rastafari stew is cabbage, and you need a lot of it because it cooks down to nothing. It's best to get one of your older children to chop the cabbage: it's time consuming and quite boring, but children enjoy the responsibility. If they aren't old enough to manage a knife, call in a neighbour and chop together so that at least you have company and can enjoy a bit of a gossip while you prepare.

Dina and her daughter Poppie making bread

Cabbage is very high in fibre and so is very good for you, but you will need to find a good source of protein because nuts and eggs are expensive and Rastafari don't eat meat. Beans are good in this respect. Remember that Rastafari don't eat salt, so you need to find alternative flavourants.

You need: cabbage, water, oil, herbs. Onions are nice in this stew, and you can add beans for protein if you have them.

To make: Fry onions and cabbage in a little oil. Keep stirring while you do this because the cabbage tends to stick to pots and burn and it's hard work scrubbing them clean again. Add herbs. Keep the mixture moist by adding water if necessary.

Cabbage takes a long time to chop but cooks quicker than you think so don't try to multi-task while you make dinner.

The stew is best served with rice or bread, but if you haven't got these, *pap* will do.

Raymond's decorative flypapers

Flies and mosquitoes are a problem in the Cape's hot summers, and Raymond hated to be bothered by them, particularly when he was reading. But flypapers were ugly and drew attention to the problem even as they solved it. His solution was delightful: he hung bunches of fresh marigolds on strings from the ceiling. 'Flies and mosquitoes are repelled by the scent of calendula, and the flowers add a touch of surprise, brightness and homeliness', he said proudly.

Evelyn's 'Beef stew for lovers' or, 'A hungry man is an angry man ...'

Evelyn offered me this recipe for beef stew one day when we were discussing men's stomachs and their moods. It's a failsafe recipe, she assured me, guaranteed to make your lover happy and – she winked – lusty. It's a good recipe for when you know you've done something wrong and need to sweeten him up: a man with a full stomach can't be angry.

Barbara, Evalyn's daughter preparing dinner

You need: Beef pieces. For the best deal, wait at the supermarket butchery counter until the male butcher comes to the counter, and ask him for bones. If you smile sweetly and flirt a bit, he'll give you bones with extra meat on them. Better still, send Margie (an attractive neighbour) to buy bones for you.

You also need onions, water, salt, a stock cube if you have it, some lard. (If you don't have lard, oil will do but lard adds to the taste, especially if the butcher was mean and gave you dry bones.) You can add anything else you have to this; beans, stamp mielies, vegetables. It's best served with *pap* or rice.

To make: Fry meat and bones and onion pieces in lard till browned. Add water and salt and the stock cube. Cover and simmer. If you are cooking over a fire, start early and make sure that you keep the pot on the side so the contents don't cook too fast. Bear in mind that it can be quite difficult to make a good stew on a paraffin stove or gas two-plate because it's hard to control the heat setting.

If you are cooking *stamp mielies*, it's best to make them in a separate pot.

If you are making *pap*, heat the water, add a fistful of mealie-meal at a time, stirring gently, until the mixture bubbles and then stiffens. Leave it to steam.

The trick to the stew's efficacy lies in serving. When you serve the stew, give your man a deep, loving kiss. Guaranteed to produce results.

Veronica's stamp mielies and boontjies (samp and beans)

Veronica showed me how to make this staple meal. She cooked samp and beans on an open fire or on a paraffin stove left outdoors. She usually cooked it when she had to go and collect wood – once simmering, the meal can be taken off the fire and left virtually untended, although there is the risk of making stodge if the collection trip takes too long. If Veronica's day had commenced with an argument with her man, he ran the risk of getting stodgy stamp mielies for dinner, for spite.

Veronica and a friend preparing stamp mielies

It's best if you can find someone to keep an eye on the pot occasionally for you. In The Park, children were often left to do this if the pot was on an outside fire or in a *gallyblik*, and it was taken as a sign of maturity to be trusted to look after the meal, but it was risky to trust children. They might forget and go to play and you'd come back to a stodgy mess or, worse, a child who had been burnt.

Tasty *stamp mielies* and *boontjies* are a reflection of proper social relationships: they show that your humour has been good, that you've been able to complete your daily tasks and that you have enough social resources to draw on the assistance of others in watching your meal cook if you are not home.

You need: a packet of samp and beans, water. Some people like to fry up onions to add to the *stamp mielies* once they're cooked.

To make: boil water and add the required quantity of samp and beans. Simmer. If you are cooking on an open fire, move the pot to the side so that it doesn't get too hot. If you are cooking on a paraffin or gas stove, try to get the heat as low as possible. Ask someone to check that the meal is not burning; add water as necessary. If you need to leave, take the pot off the heat altogether.

Raymond's cockroach repellent

Raymond had offered to host weekly prayer meetings for members of his Apostolic Faith Community. After the first meeting, the pastor told him that his house was infested with cockroaches. He offered a cheap repellent recipe to deal with the problem:

> *Put a handful of dried chillis on a saucer on the floor. Close all the doors and windows and seal them from draughts. Light the chillis and let them smoulder. The smoke will suffocate the cockroaches. Those that don't die will have disliked the smell so much that they won't come back.*

Raymond and Queenie discussed the demerits of the recipe:

> *'It would take a long time to dry chillis out enough to burn them'*, Raymond offered.

> *'The smoke smell would stick to the curtains and make the house smell'*, Queenie said.

I asked Raymond how he had responded to the pastor's well-meant but rather patronising advice.

> *'Oh, I just told him I use Doom' (a commercial insecticide)*, he said.

Queenie's gingerbeer

Queenie gave me this recipe after I admired the tart, refreshing taste of her homemade gingerbeer one hot summer's day. Her brother, Raymond, cautioned me that it is best drunk immediately or within a few days – if you leave it a couple of weeks, he said, the fermentation produces effects that are delightful in the moment, but leave a nasty hangover. Queenie, a teetotaller, discovered this to her chagrin when, a few days into the New Year, she drank the remainder of the gingerbeer she'd prepared for the family's Christmas gathering, and found herself quite tipsy ….

Don't worry that no quantities are given here: Queenie told me 'A good cook doesn't follow a recipe, but goes by taste and inclination'. So, experiment to your taste.

You need: water; sugar; tartaric acid; wet yeast (about a square inch) warmed to room temperature so that it is liquid; lemon essence; Robertson's ground ginger. The secret is in the wet yeast. Dry yeast can be used but it produces a yeasty taste in the gingerbeer. Remember that wet yeast keeps in the freezer for a long time.

To make: Add sugar to water and dissolve. When yeast has liquefied, stir in tartaric acid, and add it to the sugar water mix. Add in ginger and lemon essence to taste. Bottle, cap and chill. Open it over a sink: sometimes there's extra fizz!

6

~~~

Truth, lies, *stories* and straight-talk:
on addressing another

*'Stories, stories, stories! I have never known for sure
if I am their prisoner or their jailer.'*

E. Valentine Daniel, 1996: 4

Language, like culture, offers a paradox: it is shared but must be made one's own. The way in which one inhabits it says much about prevailing social conditions and relations, about histories and norms, about idiosyncratic ways of being and saying and about struggles in the collective. What does attentiveness to ordinary talk reveal about people and everyday situations, particularly in contexts that are characterised by extraordinary ugliness, both environmental and social? The chapter is concerned with how people make and unmake social relations through speech. It explores the ways in which people talk to and about one another, and the effects of their speech in creating or undoing a sense of community.

Cape Flats Afrikaans (taal) is the lingua franca of The Park/Village. Wonderfully expressive, tonal, plastic and inventive, its quick singsong and tight gutturals are generally considered of low status compared to the slower forms of suiwer (pure) Afrikaans, ostensibly closer to Dutch, that was the language of power in apartheid South Africa.[1] Taal abounds with witticisms, metaphors, nifty circumlocutions, clever responses, vibrant metaphor, vigorous curses. People take delight in language and use it to great effect, both positively and negatively. Talk comes easily to some, though it may not necessarily be sensible or sensitive. As we will see, there are very clear unspoken codes that modulate tone, forms of address, demeanour, linguistic form and content. People on the Cape Flats often convey stories in magical realist ways, yeasting stories so that they haunt, cut, hint, tease. It is as though talking – hard talk, skelling (scolding), love stories, gossip, stories, tales of the fantastical – does more than simply convey information. And indeed it does: speech keeps relationships flowing (Johnson 1990), holding people together in what Dell Hymes has called 'speech communities'. Liveliness in speech facilitates acceptance and enables social relations. It also destroys them.

I learned some of this in my conversations with Raymond, a middle-aged man with a quick wit and passion for language, spoken and written. (Although most adults in The Park were functionally literate, few read anything other than a Bible regularly. I know of only one adult who belonged to the Public Library. Raymond and his brother Attie by contrast read voraciously: Attie described himself as 'n boekwurm, a bookworm.) One day when visiting Raymond, I noticed the pretty collection of rocks and pebbles – agates, jaspers, quartz and amethyst – neatly lined up on his kitchen shelf. I exclaimed over a particularly lovely agate, and he commented, 'Oh that, yes, I got that when I was in Alaska'. He had signed up for a year-long contract as a fish-packer, he said, but the cold and the smell and the salt in which the fish had to be packed had gotten to him and he had resigned after one season at the factory, ending his contract. He smelled so badly of salt and fish that no woman would have him, he explained, justifying his resignation. Because he had broken his contract, he had to pay his own airfare home, returning with nothing but stories and a lingering smell of fish to show for his time away. Or so he said.

I was not quite sure whether to believe him. Far-fetched as it may seem that a poor Coloured man in South Africa might have travelled as far as Alaska, his story had a ring of truth. For years, adverts offering high-paying jobs fish-packing in Alaska have appeared in the District Mail, the regional weekly newspaper, and people in The Park spoke often of the allure of large sums of money for work which seemed to them on a par with, if not more attractive than, work that was available at home.

A few days later, I asked about a beautiful piece of red jasper, one of my favourite stones. That, he told me, had come from Kenya, in the days when he had assisted the archaeologist, Sir Richard Leakey, with an excavation. Richard and he had become good friends, he recalled nostalgically, as he described for me the intricacies of an excavation: the long hours of brushing, the care that had to be taken with measurement, the excitement of finding an artefact, the curiosity of working with people who did not speak his language.

In fact, Raymond has never left South Africa. Like a cake or a good meal, a good story follows a recipe. Raymond knows it well. One needs all the ingredients beforehand: something to trigger the telling, an attentive audience, a playful mood, 'the tail end of a dop to oil the tongue' and then a judicious addition of spice—just enough to make the story piquant, not so much that it becomes unbelievable. The truth must be embellished, roughened with just enough of the fantastical to give it a hold on the listener's imagination so that easy sympathy is resisted and more attentive listening is demanded. And the fantastical must have just sufficient factuality to make it plausible, if not necessarily entirely believable.

This is clear in Raymond's effervescent telling. Yet, at the same time as his stories about his life and adventures entertain and invite, they are poignant. They point to what might have been, under different circumstances – a different time and place, and, significantly, different skin colour. It is not impossible to go to Alaska to pack fish, or to join an expedition to hunt for fossils. Unlikely, perhaps, but not impossible. Except for the fact of being classified as non-white in apartheid South Africa.

Truth, fantasy, lies and liveliness

What was the role of storytelling in Raymond's life, I wondered. My assistants Janine and Robyn asked him about the kinds of stories he had heard as a child. Stories about films, and the first and second world wars. And the stories his father told, which were sometimes very long. 'My father used to love telling us stories … but he would talk way into the night. He would talk us to sleep but I always made sure I didn't fall asleep', he said. It was not solely fascination with his father's stories that called for alertness: the children's wrongdoings were punished by withholding supper. Raymond was a mischievous boy and often went hungry. To counter this, he had to stay awake through his father's interminable stories.

> You see, if I fell asleep then I couldn't steal anything. His stories were too long and sometimes I'd pretend to be asleep. Once he saw all of us sleeping, he would stop talking and go to bed. But I would still be awake because I needed to visit the pantry.

Raymond frequently fibbed about stealing food with the result that all the children were punished – by going without food – for his crime. Stories and sustenance ….

Stories and talking about them led us into ongoing conversations about the nature of truth and lies. If truth and fantasy are interwoven, how then might a listener differentiate between truth and lies, I asked. Raymond told me that the assumptions underlying my question were incorrect. He argued that what is important is not whether the tale is utterly factual or truthful, nor whether one can identify the point at which truth shades into lies, but whether the story is lively. Liveliness is a vital component of life and of making relationships. If people are entertained, they will stand by you. If you can hold their attention with a good story, you have the basis for a relationship.

Raymond was good at relating to others and relating a story. He could greet people in any of the eleven official languages of South Africa, a skill that served him well, he twinkled. He explained this with an example: He would enter a bar, ears alert, and quickly identify the main language of conversation. People would be so delighted that he could greet them in their language that they would buy him drinks, he said, so that he never had to pay to get drunk when he was travelling.

Drink and talk are linked: an 'oiled tongue' is crucial to courting, for example. Raymond claimed to have begun to drink as a young man. Terribly shy, stuttering, he could not speak in mixed company, but a bit of wine or brandy loosened his tongue and he became eloquent and beautifully spoken. He had proven this when he wooed his wife: she had been seduced by his lyrical tongue. He said:

> I talk too much! I speak a few million words ... And my imagination runs wild! Jeez, I could talk about everything. I could talk about nature and plants ... It's true! It's very nice .... [And] I don't stutter when I have a drink .... If I'm sober then I have to think too much.

After their marriage, his wife had insisted that he give up alcohol, and his linguistic prowess had abandoned him. He would simply sit staring at her, tjoep stil (without making a peep), on the couch, unable to find words. His wife was distraught. Raymond's sister Queenie agreed: her own husband was a gentleman with words if he had had a drink, but stone-silent if sober. Her husband, sitting quietly in the corner of the sofa, nodded his agreement.

We should not be duped by an oiled tongue into accepting explanations at face value. There is a fine line between charm and abuse, the more so when alcohol is involved and, as I described in Chapter Two, many people, especially women, bore the horrifying effects of domestic abuse spurred by its effects. Nevertheless, it is widely accepted in The Park that the capacity to speak well – by which is meant engagingly and persuasively – is valued, and reveals something essential about a person's innermost self, even if that self can only be revealed when alcohol takes hold.

"'Homo fabula'": We are story-telling beings', writes the novelist Ben Okri (1993: 24). Stories offer an invitation. The peppered-up version of his life that Raymond had offered at various points in our discussions (including one riotous conversation in which he described joining the apartheid state's airforce so that he could parachute out of a plane over Bloemfontein in order to escape the irate family of a young woman he had impregnated while living in his hometown of Colesburg), led me to ask if we could record his life-story. I anticipated that the recorded version would capture the fantastical element in his narrating that I found so delightful, and might offer an avenue into the workings of imagination. We agreed that Janine and Robyn would work with him. He insisted that we set up a formal appointment, an 'interview', so that he would remain sober for it, but, he winked, not too sober. One hot afternoon in January 2004, the two young women interviewed him. He entertained them for more than three hours and still claimed only to have completed one-quarter of his life-story. They left his house in The Village charmed, promising to return to complete the work, and full of exclamations about his wit and humour.

Yet, when the interview was transcribed, the life-story bore little resemblance to the delightful stories he had told me. Instead, it consisted of descriptions of abandoned relationships and inadequate schooling, and a series of descriptions of a range of jobs held over the years – on a chicken farm, as a bricklayer, working as a casual labourer during the grape harvests, a gardener. His life-story revealed all the fractures that a poor man's life under apartheid might be expected to reveal: discontinuities in work histories, illnesses, relationships marred by an inability to provide materially for them, movements around the country – Colesburg, Bloemfontein, Rawsonville, Cape Town – as he sought work opportunities in factories, on wine farms, in construction, in the homes of the white elite. Abstracted from the contexts of its telling and absent the humorous and ironic tone that tinged his explanations, the expressive gestures that shaped his communications, the life-story was dry and fractured, a summation of events with little to mark it as uniquely his.

When I took the interview transcript back to give him, he waved it away impatiently, saying that he had been unhappy with his performance during the interview. He said that the story did not follow a proper narrative format but jumped about, from beginning to the end and then to the middle. It was not correctly ordered, he felt: life stories should begin at the beginning and end at the end.[2] A life-story, especially one for use in research, he said, should not be fantastical, nor straight-talking, but truth.

In this instance, truth meant conformity with a historical model of narration, based on fact and ordered chronologically. And this 'truth' in fact worked to disguise much, including individual desires and passions, the uniqueness of an individual's imagination and projection into the world. It was precisely their distance from usual modes of self-narration that entranced me in Raymond's stories about his life, but in the life-history interview, his characteristic mode of recounting emerges only sparsely – when he is lamenting his inability to stay with good employers ('I don't last long with the good ones. But with the sour ones! … I really work for them for a long time. Ai!!! I don't know why ….'), when he is describing the ease with which stolen goods can be sold (a radio exchanged for a *halfie wyn* – half a bottle of wine – in neighbouring informal settlements) and when he talks of his love for plants and learning (his favourite job was one in which his employer explained how to care for plants properly). A narrowed-down version of his life-story, the factual account that he thought would be proper, eliminated much of the liveliness of the telling. The formal account holds the listener at bay: a rendition that depicts a life as little more than a series of events that occur to a particular body and held together by time loses sight of the liveliness that enriches experience through imagination and relationships.

Genealogical methods and life histories have long been part of anthropology's research toolkit. They assist with locating each individual in relation to others in the present and past, and with understanding local norms, the patterns of social life and the ways in which individual lives fit into these and into time. Alphonso Lingis (1994: 116) argues that there are two 'entries into communication':

> the one by which one depersonalizes one's visions and insights, formulates them in the terms of the common rational discourse, and speaks as a representative, a spokesperson, equivalent and interchangeable with others, of what has to be said. The other entry into communication is that in which you find it is you, you saying something, that is essential.

The ways that life stories are often used in social research, as a means of identifying pattern and norm, while important, have the effect of making a teller into the 'representative' that Lingis describes, and the outcome the 'truth' of a narrative model. The choice to tell a story of one's life or experiences in terms that don't neatly reflect the prevailing norms of self-narration may be read as a warning not to lose sight of the individual in the more usual anthropological quest for pattern and regularity in social life. It is also simultaneously a withdrawal, a refusal to engage on the grounds of fact or chronology or other conventional modes through which the self is assumed to be narratable (Kerby 1991; Ochs and Capps 1996). Adam Philips notes that 'Modern self-disclosure is always a provocation: it asks us to assess the self, if we dare' (2002: 193). And Ben Okri reminds us, 'Stories are always a form of resistance' (1993: 34). Yet narrating one's life-story in conformity with standard autobiographical models may render one vulnerable to being judged by a listener. Disclosure invites a verdict. In narrating one's life in the standard chronological mode, which lends itself to comparison with others or with expected life trajectories, it is easy to be measured and found wanting. Raymond's work history narrated in the 'proper' mode lends itself to assessments such as 'fractured', 'impermanent', both of which are imbued with negative valence in a context that values permanence and stability. Yet the fantastical in his tales points to the idiosyncratic ways in which he occupied the role of worker, errant lover, traveller extraordinaire, and to his capacity to imbue a difficult life with elements of the fantastical that make rumination on life's hardships less painful.

This does not mean that there is no patterning in people's lives, or that history does not have an imprint in the social collectivity. It remains important to collect life histories as data that can reveal trends in the experiences and expectations of sectors of populations. But we must remember that as reflective and reflexive beings, people choose what to reveal of themselves, and they do so using a variety of different techniques, not all of which approximate 'truth' or 'veracity' as empiricist social scientists may understand them.[3] Sometimes this can be a deliberate strategy – a display of a wiliness that refuses to allow the individual to be captured in standardised representations. Sometimes people tell such stories because that mode of interaction is taken for granted in cultural life. Sometimes it is the product of discourses that limit or constrain.[4] And sometimes it is the product of individual creativity and imagination. To classify the fantastical stories that Raymond tells as 'lies' in relation to the 'truth' of his 'history' is to accept the model of veracity that holds that an individual is nothing more than the sum of his or her encounters with the material world, which can be objectively assessed. It is to lose out on the particularities that make each of us unique – personality, imagination, emotional dispositions – even as we may be shaped by the same historical, material and ideational forces.

Why then bother with the stories? Is Raymond not just telling tales to pass the time? Perhaps, but how people pass their time is important – it tells us about the values they hold, the kinds of relationships they seek to forge and the ways they do so. Story-telling and anecdotes have a place in social life, just as much as do ideals, norms, conventions and practices. Story-telling can be considered to have a function apart from entertainment. Some story-telling invites and cements relationships. Other kinds, such as gossip, rumour and accusation, establish and affirm norms and may undo some relationships, as we will see below. But stories are not the only mode of communication, and it is to others, particularly the relation of straight-talk and truth, that we now turn.

Straight-talk

Raymond and others differentiated between straight-talk and factual truth on the basis of the interpersonal qualities of the interactions these forms engage. Truth – *waarheid* – refers to something that has happened, something said and done. Its temporality is past. It is conventional, can be agreed upon, can be made factual and verifiable. This is not to say that it is not contested – people can and do argue about it. Anyone can tell it – although few do – but some are better at truth-telling than others. Anyone can hear it, though whether to act on it remains a choice. Waarheid is neutral – it exists independent of the tellers, who can only offer their perspectives on it.

Straight-talk, on the other hand, is not 'bluffing', as Raymond put it when I shared the contents of this chapter with him. It involves confrontation; it is an action that happens in the present, between people able to address one another. It is a face-to-face encounter, one that should not draw upon the face-saving conventions of 'I've heard through the grapevine' – the latter, a form of speech that is crucial to sociality in places where people live in close proximity, where desperate circumstances, alcohol and drugs mean that tempers run high. As Raymond put it, 'You must decide how to speak – Jesus gave you a brain. Other people mustn't come and tell you what to say'. Straight-talk 'might get you into trouble, if you are telling the truth'. Straight-talk is not necessarily waarheid: it is better understood as an encounter that exposes the self to another by revealing sites of need, hurt or anger. At its base, straight-talk raises questions about what it means to be in relation with others. Straight-talk is a mode of interpersonal honesty that reveals one's own and another's vulnerabilities.

There are many ways to confront someone, and people are judged on their abilities to assess how and when to engage in straight-talk. One of the committee leaders is widely feared because her mode is extremely confrontational. Angry words burst forth irrespective of whether one is in a public or private space. Indeed, she seems often to choose to stage straight-talk confrontations in public, an action that reinforces her power by humiliating those to whom she speaks. Another leader is respected for her calm approach. She usually takes one aside and tells one bluntly but in relative privacy about her complaint. Her approach does not reveal or debase, it is widely considered to be ordentlik and a sign of good interpersonal skills. Yet proper modes of interacting, as we have seen above, have a standardising effect; they are not revealing of one's true self. The second leader's approach, while valued for its ability to soothe difficult situations, is not necessarily regarded as good leadership. Confrontations couched in proper forms – forms of which marriage counsellors and conflict resolvers alike approve – are considered less than authentic and certainly less than effective: people value angry performances as reflecting the immediacy and urgency of the moment and motivating action, and many believe that the first leader is more effective than the second.

Straight-talk, more than truth, raises questions of address. In the local model, truth exists independent of its teller. We are reminded that this is one among many models by philosopher Michel Foucault (2001), who notes that in Ancient Greece, frank speech – truth – was intimately linked to the character of the teller. In order to speak truth to those in power, truth-tellers had to have specific moral qualities. They had to be brave: truth-telling required courage because it was dangerous to speak critically of power. They had to be citizens (which meant that they were free men since women and slaves could not be citizens) and they had to have a well-developed sense of duty and to be certain that they possessed truth. There was a narrow line between being a truth-teller and being a martyr: failed frank talk carried the penalty of exile. The ancient Athenian model of truth asks who it is who might speak frankly before power. The model of straight-talk in The Park/Village poses similar questions. What does it mean to address another? What are the conditions under which straight-talk is possible, required, anticipated? What tones of voice and bodily comportments are appropriate to the relationship that one desires to create through speech?

Questions of address raise other questions, such as those of how to recognise different status and modulate one's interactions accordingly. Deciding whom to address and how requires acts of judgement, and for residents of The Park/ Village such judgement is finely calibrated. Appropriate address matters. Failure to mould speech to status may render strategies unsuited, as for example when someone is begging in a tone of voice that renders the request a demand. Such a tone marks misrecognition of the status of the other. Without the expected tone of deferral, it is unlikely that the request will succeed in its desired ends. Women are expected to speak quietly and respectfully to men. When they do not, their status as decent women is in doubt, even if the man concerned is *rof* and *wreed*. Histories of oppression and violence have created a wide range of address. Strangers from whom one seeks assistance may be addressed in abject tones that may generate the desired response but run the risk of short responses or cruelty. Outsiders are received with guarded responses, distrusting silences or with violent words. Welcomes may be curtailed. Generous laughter is shared with one's familiars and not with strangers, where the mode of address is more likely to be primly respectful or stereotypic and self-undermining. Those of higher status are often addressed in ways that work to underscore the lower status of the speaker; speech is predicated on class, race, gendered and other social hierarchies that are marked in tone and linguistic form. Creating conversation between people as though they are equal is not straightforward.[5]

These data suggest that speaking is not simple: effective address – speech that achieves its objectives – must be carefully tailored to the characters and the occasion. This implicates judgement – of both the situation and the person to be addressed.

Lingis writes, 'To address someone is not simply to address a source of information; it is to address one who will answer and answer for his or her answer' (1994: 87). By this he means that to address someone is to call for and forth a responsibility in relation to the other. Ideally, then, an address is an invitation. He says,

The other turns to me and speaks; he or she asks something of me. Her words ...
ask for information and indications. They ask for a response that will be responsible
.... But they first greet me with an appeal for responsiveness. (1994: 131)

If this is indeed the case, then clearly speaking to someone involves far more than
simply allowing words forth: it calls for recognition and responsiveness, and is
risky in that it exposes one to another's possible refusal to respond. Story-telling
and laughter offset or deflect some of the risk in social encounters.

Like Raymond's stories above, people often relate stories – factual or fantastical
– in magical realist ways. The stories describe a desire that overcomes current
circumstances and a life constrained by limited opportunities. They invite
laughter, and laughter invites one into community. It passes time and creates
solidarities in contexts otherwise marred by hardship and boredom. People make
light of matters deadly serious, as though laughter might warn off danger.

Laughter bears on the experience of temporality, relieving the humdrum of tedious
days. Here, for example, is Clive, talking about how laughter offsets the boring and
physically demanding work undertaken by casual labourers during the grape harvest:

We make it fun for ourselves. We crack jokes with each other and that's how we
pass time. You see, our people like to crack jokes. Whenever we work together we
never leave each other in the lurch. One thing, we just stand together and things
like that. We just have fun with each other. It would just be us (people from The
Park), some people from Macassar and some other farm workers having fun.
And that's how the day passes.

His discussion moves quickly to an account of fighting on farms. Accounts of
violence and laughter both have a bearing on how people remember time. Violence
punctuates time fiercely.[6] Laughter, by contrast, seems to ease time, relieving
boredom in the moment and leaving little specific trace. People seldom remember
the details of what they laughed about, they know only that they did, and the recall
brings a shared sense of nostalgic pleasure.

Violence and laughter are not opposites. Laughter may have a cruel edge when
it is at another's expense. It may cut and sting.

Early in 2004, I popped in at Raymond's to drop off some formally posed
photographs I had taken for him to send his estranged adult son and grandchild
in Johannesburg. Baby chanced along and I gave her a photo I had taken of
her as she was returning home in a blustering south-easter, the Cape's summer
signature, a couple of days earlier. I had caught her in full *skel* and she looked a
sight in the pictures, wild-haired and wide-mouthed. Comparing photos with

Raymond she complained that he looked smart and she looked dreadful, a crazy woman. Raymond, ever quick, replied, 'Because good people photograph well and bad people don't. Character always reveals itself'. He added '*Ek's nie 'n kalkoen nie: ek's a tycoon*'. (I'm not a turkey; I'm a tycoon). His tone was light and convivial. We all laughed, including Baby, who seemed not to take offence at the cruel edge of his words. She and Raymond had been neighbours for many years. Perhaps one might see in her acceptance of his words a classic example of a joking relationship in which unkindness is excused on the grounds of familiarity. [7]

In laughing with rather than at someone, we allow ourselves to stand as if alongside them. This kind of laughter holds an element of empathy: a form of recognition of the other and of commonality. Anthropologist Michael Jackson says, 'Laughter catches us on the cusp of identification' (2002: 181). Laughter tests relations. What makes you laugh? Can we share this? Can we laugh alongside one another? Will your laughter be kind or edged with cruelty? In other words, are we alike? The question is an important one in a highly stratified society whose history and present are marked by radical inequality. Indeed, Justice Albie Sachs of South Africa's Constitutional Court holds that 'Humour is one of the great solvents of democracy', and 'an elixir of constitutional health' (Case CCT42/04, 2006 64).[8] He is not unaware of laughter's inherent ambiguity, noting that, 'Laughter ... has its context. It can be derisory and punitive, imposing indignity on the weak at the hands of the powerful. On the other hand, it can be consolatory, even subversive in the service of marginalised social critics' (ibid.).

It is wise to choose carefully how one laughs, at what and with whom. Adam Phillips writes,

> We are always reassured when people can, as we say, laugh at themselves. There is a violence we do to ourselves and others that is both enlivening and strangely consoling. There is the good mockery of everyday life that regulates our self-importance, and so relieves us of too much responsibility for the world. And there is the bad mockery that foists something upon us that we would rather, if we could choose, protect ourselves from. (2002: 40)

The laughter elicited by Raymond's wit and stories is wholesome because its tone is not self-deprecating or self-undermining but confident. Its quiet irony works against a local model of trickery and inversion in which turning the world upside-down does not always guarantee that one ends up on top. The Cape trickster model rests on humiliations acknowledged, as though to acknowledge something – even a stereotype or a lie – up-front might take the sting from it, though in claiming it, one masters it, or at least is able to tame its sting. This is a claim made by many theorists, Judith Butler among them (1997). But too often the strategy merely reinforces existing stereotypes: laughter levelled at someone transforms itself into cruelty. 'Laughing at someone is – like all real pleasure – a stolen pleasure. But when we laugh at someone they feel stolen from', writes Phillips (2002: 41). One might add here, 'and undermined', for he has already noted that 'When we laugh at someone else we violate, or simply disregard, their preferred image of themselves' (2002: 36). Phillips describes this as ridicule, noting its distancing effects: 'We only laugh at those with whom we feel we have an affinity that we must repudiate, that we feel threatened by. Ridicule, in other words, is a terror of sociability' (2002: 41). The boundary between belonging and exclusion is often marked by unkind jokes – stories at another's expense. South Africa abounds in racist cruelty couched as humour.

Raymond's stories encourage a different prepositional relationship: laughter with, alongside, rather than at. One might see in this the kind of democracy that Sachs has in mind. One is made a companion, rather than vanquished or elevated. Raymond's stories and others like them do not close down laughter's potential by curtailing it or edging it with bitterness or unkindness, but open up questions and playful possibilities about what could have been, might yet be. They invite the interlocutor into an imaginary world.

'The imagination is one of the highest gifts we have', writes Ben Okri (1993: 24). In the stories that Raymond tells, and others similar, imagination works to extend the self into other terrains. Such stories offer escape, a chance to reflect on one's circumstances at a distance but in company, to consider life as it may otherwise have been in different circumstances, a different place and time. Their telling is generous, a sharing of one's intimate self with others, drawing them towards one's own self. And one makes oneself a place of pleasure for others – one becomes hospitable in a context that is anything but.

Part of what has shaped that inhospitality is crude stereotype, in which crushing poverty is read as a failure of initiative or effort and attempts to hold suffering at bay through laughter, playfulness and substance abuse are interpreted by powerful others as moral failures – failures of the self. Small wonder that people thus humiliated find it difficult to speak to those they see as powerful. And small wonder that often people choose not to confront those more powerful than they, rather than demean themselves publicly.

'Sticks and stones may break my bones but words will never hurt me.' So went the playground chant. But of course it is untrue – as much or more so than sticks and stones, words carry the power to inflict pain. I was forcefully reminded of this one day at the beginning of the 2001 school year when Ponkies and I went to the local high school to arrange to pay off her daughters' school fees over time instead of paying them as a single lump sum. Ponkies was acutely uncomfortable by the time we arrived. She said she was ashamed of being poor, and that the feeling made her ill: 'Ek voelie so lekkerie' (I don't feel so good). She added, 'I always look around to see if anyone is watching or looking at me'. Although usually solid and self-assured in her presentation of self at home, confronted by the well-dressed and well-spoken staff at the fees office, her entire demeanour changed: her voice dropped and took on an ingratiating tone and her body seemed to curl in on itself. She appeared to become smaller, more abject. She turned to me and in a low voice beseeched me to speak on her behalf. She left me to do the negotiating and went to gaze at staff photos on the wall, her back to the transactions. Later, she said that part of the reason for her feeling of humiliation was that three of the staff members still teaching there had taught her, and that she was ashamed of her life, her drinking habit, and the fact that she could not afford to send her children to school. The everyday humiliations of poverty which are disguised in her home environment, where so many others grapple with the same realities as she, were here exposed, rendering her vulnerable to what she felt were the judgements of others. In the face of anticipated judgement, she was voiceless. The multitude of small humiliations built up so much tension that Ponkies quite literally felt herself unable to speak and feared that the particularities of her situation would not be heard. Her voice was swallowed in humiliation.

The fragility of speech is revealed in a conversation between two philosophers, Jean-Luc Nancy and Ann Smock (1993), who engage with Maurice Blanchot's comment, 'Il faut parler. Parler sans pouvoir' (It is necessary to talk, to talk without the power to do so). In exploring these dense phrases, Ann Smock unravels some of the web of meanings hidden within them. Here are some of her musings:

> The other who approaches speaks and asks you to make it so that he can speak …. In this situation there is nothing to start out from, nothing to base anything upon. You have to answer an utterance (an entreaty, a question, a command, who knows?) that you have never heard and that you won't have heard until you've answered …. You must speak just as the power to speak departs from you – just as the world wherein speaking is a possibility and a thing you can do recedes and leaves you face to face with the other as if you two were the sole vestiges of a world long over with. Yet this is the beginning, the start of the world where people can approach, can hear and answer one another, speaking together. The obligation that speaking initiates … must be the duty of vouching for this world – one where people recognize and acknowledge one another – when it is coming, precariously, unexpectedly, and implausibly, to be. (1993: 311)

Later in their conversation, Jean-Luc Nancy responds:

> Speaking comes by surprise. Or by chance, as a chance. Therefore, the best 'model' of speaking is the conversation, the loose conversation, where nobody knows what he or she will say before he or she has said it .... The contrary of the interview. (1993: 315)

Faced with another person, one is obliged to speak. Speech enacts recognition of the singularity of the person who approaches.[9] Lingis notes (1994: 88) that to enter into conversation is 'to expose oneself to the other, the outsider; and to lay oneself open to surprises, contestation, and inculpation'. Judith Butler makes a similar claim, arguing that it is only in making oneself vulnerable to the other that ethics is possible:

> ethics requires us to risk ourselves precisely at moments of unknowingness, when what forms us diverges from what lies before us, when our willingness to become undone in relation to others constitutes our chance of being human. (2005: 136)

The risks of that willingness are great in a context of grave hierarchy and stratification, such as that of South Africa, where one's vulnerability in speech may be met with anger, dismay or rejection.

In speaking, one extends oneself into the world and proffers an invitation. Finding one's voice is thus finding a place in language and in the world from which to speak authentically to another with an expectation of being heard. Alvarez (2005: 42) describes this kind of speech as being 'alive' and 'urgent', with 'a sense of the weight of the whole person behind the words'. But often hearing is circumscribed by preconceived ideas about the other; humiliation, stereotype, anger or dismay may cause a turning away, a refusal of the gesture of listening.

It takes courage to overcome these experiences. A conversation with Sandra one day in 2000 reminded me of this. An Afrikaans first-language speaker, and usually a fairly reserved person, she would not speak in English when I first met her in 1991, saying that it was too difficult and that she spoke it badly. By 2000, she spoke English fluently and idiomatically, but it had been hard to conquer her feelings of linguistic inadequacy. I asked what precipitated the change and she explained that she had had to 'claim' her voice in order to negotiate with local authorities on the community's behalf. Initially they did so in Afrikaans or not at all, allowing others to speak for them. Then, she said, 'Dina began to fight' for housing and social rights and so had to learn English. 'Then Dina spoke for the community and she spoke for me'. But Dina was appointed to Council and could no longer speak on behalf of the community alone. So she told Sandra, 'You must take your voice now', and Sandra learned to speak up, speak out and speak her mind. 'I found my voice', she said proudly.

Describing 'the writer's patient, exacting quest for a distinctive voice of his own' (2005: 76), Alvarez says that 'finding your own voice as a writer means – or is the equivalent of – feeling free in your own skin. It is a great liberation' (2005: 38). His words are apposite to the act of speaking in one's own voice – authentically – in South Africa.[10] Given the horrifying history of the relation of skin colour to freedom's lack, to feel free in one's own skin here is indeed liberation, and it is this sense of a body and voice integrated and speaking the language of power that, I think, gave such power to Sandra's claim over her voice. And yet it is ironic that in order to speak to be heard, Sandra had to speak in English, her second language, one in which the intimacies of mother tongue are absent, a tongue of new power.

'Language is by its very nature a communal thing; that is, it expresses never the exact thing, but a compromise – that which is common to you, me and everybody', notes the poet and critic T.E. Hulme (cited in Alvarez 2005: 36). For Hulme, expressing oneself involves 'a terrific struggle with language', resistance to 'ingrained habit' (ibid.: 37) in order to 'hold it fixed to your own purpose' (ibid.: 36). Finding one's voice in the circumstances I have described is more than simply speaking up – it entails resisting habituated patterns of speech and the power relations that shape them, learning how to make an address with confidence, having acquired grammatical skills and vocabulary, adjudged one's audience, tone and manner of speech, and overcome one's fear of being judged in ways that do injustice. In Sandra's case, it involved struggling to speak both in formal Afrikaans rather than the rhythmical, inflected, informal taal of everyday life and in English, her second language. Both are the languages of power in bureaucracies, and both are imbued with racialised, class and status hierarchies that present formidable barriers to many in working-class communities. South Africans are generally acute in their attention to linguistic codes. Hints carried in tone, gesture, intonation, vocabulary, forms of speech are read as indicative of a person's social rank and put downs consequent on the reading may be cruel.

Speaking anticipates an attentive and responsive listener. Responsiveness carries with it responsibilities. Perhaps this explains why people talk of and to one another in ways that are dismissive: the weight of responsibility for another may simply be too great to bear. It is easy to undo others in language, to dismiss them by failing to acknowledge their uniqueness and the pull that they have on one's obligations. Common phrases, 's/he is stubborn', or 'sy is mos so' (that's just how she is), are used as dismissals in situations where the speaker might ordinarily be expected to have taken action or to be morally responsible. For instance, Baby frequently yelled at other people, skelling at the top of her voice and using violent epithets. *Skel* is far harsher and uglier than its English translation (scold) implies. Shrill and ugly, it is language gone awry, violent in its insistence on asserting power. Women *skel*, usually at children or women of equal or lower status. Perhaps one might see in it the inability to make language habitable given the resources and constraints at hand. It echoes the ugliness of a dangerous world. It is particularly harsh on children (Henderson 1999). I know of some children who seldom found tenderness in the language or indeed presence of adults. They sought affection and comforting words from strangers and from their peers. Two in particular conceive of themselves as being like objects, their bodies available as tools for others' usage.

Skelling is dangerous: as public speech, it makes accusations that can do damage. For example, Carmen commented that she was not afraid of a woman she disliked and would outweigh her '*in 'n skel stuk*' (in a verbal fight): 'She'll end up second! *Ek sal haar dood skel* (I'll scold her dead) … especially about her *hoerdery*' (whoring; promiscuity). Although Carmen's words might not produce death directly, if the woman's husband were to hear the accusations of promiscuity, there is no doubt that he would beat her badly, and we all knew it.

When I told Baby that I was afraid of her sharp tongue she and her companions laughed. '*Ek's mos so*' (I'm just like that'), she explained. And that was that. When asked whether it was possible to get Liesl into a programme for her apparent drug-addiction, Margaret described her daughter as 'stubborn' (using the English word). In so saying, she exempted herself from acting in the girl's defence, whether by obliging her to go to hospital or enter a rehab programme or simply eat. Here are other instances: Queenie telling me that Irene had 'gone bonkers' and refused to administer her own medication for schizophrenia. 'She's just stubborn', Queenie said. Or Baby telling me that Meitjie had become a sex worker because she was stubborn and addicted to the high life. In each instance, dismissive language has resonances of *baasskap* relations – the humiliations of class and power structures, of racism and power structures written into linguistic forms that erode a sense of self and work against a sense of singularity. The words and their tone demean the subject and absolve the listener from responsibility for the other.

The humiliations of being treated as less than human are sometimes internalised, become so much part of self-identity that when people describe themselves and their lives they automatically use the vocabulary proper to animals. People describe themselves and their lives apparently unselfconsciously using words like *vrek* instead of *sterf* (to die), *vreet* instead of *eet* (to eat), *skarrel* (rummage, scrabble), *spuls* (horny, in heat), *vang kat* (cat-catcher – prostitute), and so on. Children internalise these expressions early. These commonplace usages suggest to me the extent to which the racist model of themselves as lacking or as less than human has been internalised in an everyday language that carries the trace of a vicious past. It was precisely against such forms of 'internal colonisation' that authors such as Fanon and Biko wrote with such passion.[11]

Finding an adequate listener may be difficult. The use of words appropriate to animal life suggests that even the self may be an inadequate listener. Sometimes the extension of self into other that stories offer is based not on fantasy but on experiential truth that is hard-edged, bitter and acrid. Sometimes the truth can be difficult to say, yet it may seek a home in another's attentiveness. Or, one may not desire to share experience, instead finding for it a home within oneself (Das 2000). Sometimes where sharing is a psychic or social necessity, the appropriate form in which to address another may be limited or lacking and alternatives must be sought within repertoires that are often constrained by circumstance. These can be both innovative and disturbing.

Writing proffers one possibility. Let me give two examples: one, an interaction between myself and Mem, a young teenager who resided in The Park with her mother, her mother's lover Antony and their two children; the other an account offered by Hendrik, my neighbour. In both instances, writing was addressed to me as a stranger in Georg Simmel's beautiful sense of 'the one who comes today and stays tomorrow' (1950: 402), who is always potentially about to leave, who receives 'the most surprising openness' and who attracts 'confidences which sometimes have the character of a confessional and which would be carefully withheld from a more closely related person'. For Mem and Hendrik, I was familiar enough but not too familiar.

One afternoon in 1995, Mem was not at school. When I asked if she wanted to come and join me in quiet reflection and writing, she hurried over. I asked if she was alright: she seemed more subdued than usual. She did not want to discuss the matter but, asking for a pen and notebook, she wrote, at first on her own and then, after I had read the initial writing, in response to my questions. She described domestic violence and its effects on her feelings about home life.

> On Fridays my father (Antony) fights with my mother. Then my mother runs away. When I ask my father for money he says no. Then when my mother comes home he takes her money. Then my mother goes to (the chairwoman) and she shouts at Antony.

I asked what she did when her parents fought. Mem wrote 'I cry'. I asked where she went when her parents fought. She wrote 'I'm in the house. Then [at night] I sleep in the [community] hall, I and Meitjie and Tassa'. When I asked, 'Where are your brother and sister when your parents fight?' she wrote that they went to their grandparents (Antony's mother and father who had recently taken up residence next door), but that she could not accompany them there 'because they don't like me because I am not Antony's (biological) child. This grieves me (*maak my artseer* (sic): makes my heart sore)'.

Here, the family fails a child. Spoken words, too, seem inadequate to the task of bearing the weight of her suffering. Sometimes, as is often the case in violent contexts, spoken words do not do full justice to experience. The voice flees from experience. Sometimes troubles can be too heavy for a voice to carry them.

Mem's was not the only instance I encountered in which experience sought a home in writing. As I was leaving at the end of my extended research in 1992, Hendrik, a neighbour in The Park, gave me a letter. Although an Afrikaans first-language speaker, he had written it in elaborate English, flowery and convoluted. It claimed that he was the subject of a witch-hunt, that community leaders said he supported apartheid because he worked as a security guard at the Tricameral Parliament and that they had threatened him with his life. When I returned, he and his family had left for one of the other informal settlements nearer the city. They did not return.

I do not know what, if anything, he hoped to achieve in his missive to me. Perhaps it was an attempt to get someone he deemed powerful to intervene with the committee on his behalf. And if so, that should give us pause for it is a real indication of the power disparities of apartheid South Africa that a young white woman, a foreigner, a student, could be seen to have more power to act efficaciously in the world than a mature man, employed, married, a father, Coloured. Perhaps the letter was an attempt to alert me to a situation grown intolerable, a warning. I can only surmise on the basis of partial communications, material traces that do not tell much of intention or will, only of the medium and the context.

Both Mem and Hendrik's writings created an opportunity for (a limited) sharing (see also Biehl 2005). Alvarez writes that 'the writer works to find or create a voice that will stretch out to the reader, make him prick his ears and attend' (2005: 16). Although he is describing literary works, there is no reason why his insight cannot be extended to the contexts I have described above. Jean-Luc Nancy says, 'The voice of a written text is not that of [its author]. It is a voice asking to be recognized ... as impossible to recognize. One has only to let it be' (1993: 315). By contrast, Joao Biehl (2005) insists that the writings of Catherina, a paralysed, 'mad' woman living in what he calls 'a zone of abandonment' carries a moral imperative to act, to investigate, to record, a point that E. Valentine Daniel (1996) also makes strongly.

Perhaps the writing afforded Mem and Hendrik a kind of catharsis, a sense of having found a home for their experience in another person. Perhaps the missives were instructions, calls for help, demands that someone take account of experience, do something. I am still not sure. I responded differently to the two writings. With Mem's permission I approached community leaders and raised the issue of creating safe spaces for children. It was agreed that the community hall would again be opened to children without question and that an adult would be on duty. Hendrik gave me his letter just as I was leaving The Park. By the time I returned, he and his family had left. Community leaders described their departure as 'choice' and would discuss it no further with me. The matter ended there but for its haunting presence in the letter, my fieldnotes, my memory and now here.[12]

For some, writing mediates experience, making it available to others without immediately implicating the self. For instance, one day Raymond and I were playing word games, in which I would have to guess at the meanings of the complex Afrikaans words he threw me, checking my accuracy in his dictionary. His nephew, Eric, who lived with him, interrupted to share some stories he had written in the back of an old, elegant A4 page-a-day diary. One was a parable, 'The Ugly Plaasman' (farm-dweller), about a labourer so ugly that he was shunned by all. After being falsely accused and found guilty of a crime he did not commit, the magistrate told him that if he could find someone who did not resent his face and could show that he was not a monster, the sentence would be retracted. The story unfolds as parable as the ugly plaasman seeks the person who might redeem his ugliness and reveal the humanity that lies beneath.

Here, parable works to describe forms of discrimination and hardships parallel to those of everyday life for residents of The Park/Village. A tale of the quest for belonging demonstrates that surfaces are deceptive and that one needs to look beneath them to find a person's true essence. The story resonates with a more pervasive despair in The Park/Village about the ways in which people are read through a class lens, as though they are little more than the sum of their surroundings or their accumulated and fractured histories. It is a calling to seek for a person's true self, not that immediately visible, and a reminder that appearances do not reflect inner essences. The tale is particularly ironic given the general emphasis on ordentlikheid as appearance in social discourse at the time.

Eric had written other stories too. One set was more explicitly linked to daily life in The Park/Village: he had transposed everyday experiences into the mythic structure of a Harry Potter tale. Friends and enemies in The Park/Village were likened to characters from the popular books: Muggles appeared, as did protective beings. Harry himself grew up with 'Uncle Scheepers', a Muggle of the worst kind, and so on. The stories are entertaining in themselves and also offer a way to approach the hardships of everyday life indirectly: truths are revealed without their having to be stated as such. I call this mode of speech 'elliptical talk'.

Such talk is common in conversations, particularly those that have to do with misfortune or evil, or which might attract violent responses. It is as though evil cannot and should not be approached directly. Michael Taussig notes of violence that in writing of it, one must approach it sideways, 'like the crab scuttling' (1999: 2).

In The Park/Village, and other places I have worked where violence lurks close to the surface, people approach dangerous topics obliquely. Posing questions about evil and asking for help from strangers are two of the more common contexts in which elliptical talk is used. These are contexts where one is vulnerable. Elliptical talk allows one to say what needs to be said or what one desires to have known without explicitly saying it. Therefore one cannot be held accountable for what is said, but something disturbing has nevertheless been alluded to or insinuated and, in so doing, identified, marked, brought into the open. Elliptical talk makes something available for discussion that was not previously discussed.

These modalities of speech are not particular to The Park/Village but permeate South African society. Elliptical talk allows much to be inferred without actually stating it. Such talk is demanding of a listener. For a start, one has to learn to hear metaphors and to trace their relation to everyday or recent events. To do so effectively, one needs to know much about the activities, interpersonal relations and histories of those to whom one listens. For example, Raymond described what he called 'the hidden "but"'. When you talk, he said, you begin with the good things. Then comes that 'hidden but'. Eric joined in: '"maar" is 'n bietjie gevaarlik' ('but' is a bit dangerous). For example, they offered, 'I forgive you' implies a 'but' and indicates the presence of other words – unspoken, implicit – such as 'hoekom?' (why?) or 'waarom?' (why?) that are usually questions about failures of moral responsibility. They do not need to be stated – they are implicit in the telling. And they subtly demand a response – usually of redress or remorse – from the other.[13]

Here is another example. A few days after a terrible fire in The Park, I went to visit a friend whose shack was close to the epicentre of the fire. She was not at home, but the woman who washed her laundry paused for a chat. She was circumspect at first – we did not know one another. But as it became clear that I knew other residents well, she became chattier and spoke of the different tensions manifesting in The Park at the time. I asked about the fire, which some had told me was the result of an accident with a candle or a paraffin stove, but which others had implied was caused by arson precipitated by tensions between the woman I'd come to visit and another resident. She paused. Then she appeared to sidetrack. She said that shortly before the fire she had come to the house to do the washing and just as she was about to enter, had stopped in horror. Close to the threshold was a huge crab. She was afraid but had overcome her fear, stepped over it and gone about her chores. During the course of the day, she had occasion to step over it several times. Later, the owner of the house came home and stepped over the crab, still on the threshold, before realising what it was and taking fright. The washer-woman recalled that she had been seized by terrible pains 'in her sex' that night, like a crab had 'pincered' her. Nothing eased the pain. The following day she went to the hospital but medical attention did not help. Then she prayed and in her prayers was told to abstain from food and drink and to pray. She recovered.

I was intrigued and not a little confused. I asked what she felt about the incident. She hesitated then explained that she believed that the crab was 'sent', intended to bring ill-luck to the woman of the house. The evil would be done when she stepped over it into the house, but she had come between the crab and its intended victim and its evil had befallen her.

There are a number of ways to read the incident, which is clearly about more than simply the wanderings of an unusually large and placid crab. On the surface, the story would seem entertaining or merely odd if one did not have knowledge of the local interpretations of illness and witchcraft, and how these might intersect with local gender ideologies. Conventionally, anthropologists might note the symbolic placement of the crab: thresholds are synonymous with ambiguity and with the dangers of moving across different spaces – public and private – that here are held to be differently gendered. We might note also the metaphoric association with sexual misdemeanour – 'crabs' designates STIs, an interpretation that receives some validation in the 'pincer-pain' experienced after walking over the crab. Its metaphor translates into a sexualised pain, pincering closed the body's vulnerable opening to pleasure and – through reproduction – the future. Behind the crab rests an accusation of infidelity and of risk, both to temporality and to the body. But the story is told locally to imply still more. It is related and understood as talk about witchcraft and power, and it intimates both communal tensions over women's place and appropriate activities, and individual conflicts and the forms of violence that have their power in their visible subterfuge. Witchcraft is powerful at least partly because it occupies a peculiar zone between the visible and invisible. The sender of evil may be suspected but is not known. The materia medica is sometimes visible and the consequences are always apparent. There is a peculiar directionality here – the invisible is made manifest, ill intent or anti-social belief has material consequences. (I note in passing that there are parallels here with writing, in which ideas receive a material form in legible words.) Accusations of witchcraft invite over-interpretation. The story hints of sexualities and other powers over the future misdirected, of fears of vulnerability and of uncertainty. What is noteworthy is that it emerged during a conversation about a fire, to which it makes no reference. The link between the two events – the crab's presence and the fire – is unstipulated, implied by tone and gesture, and by the very absence of reference to the event that prompted the story in the first place.

Listeners need to be alert to the unsaid that slips behind the saying, for part of what the story about the crab conveys is the danger or impossibility of talking about some kinds of experience or event. There are here, layers and layers of meaning and interpretation, alerting us to another dimension of speech – that saying and listening are interpretive and that meaning-making is the product of skilled attention and local knowledge. Elliptical talk merely refines the interpretive community, creating within its speech patterns, insiders and outsiders – those who are able to understand and those who are not. Writing of witchcraft, Jeanne Favret-Saada (1980: 11) notes, 'speaking to an ethnographer one is addressing either *a person supposed to be able ... or unable ...*', having earlier noted, 'In short, there is no neutral position with spoken words: in witchcraft, words wage war' (1980: 10; original emphasis).[14] While the case of witchcraft is perhaps extreme, nevertheless, the point she is making holds more generally – speech implicates the self and others in relations that are not only about knowledge but also about power.

For listeners (as opposed to the protagonists of the events-become-stories), elliptical talk is both duplicitous and generous. It is duplicitous in that it invites without explaining, drawing one in through allusion, hooking the imagination so that the listener is prompted to ask questions in order to clarify. Doing so obliges one to follow the explanation to its end, and that then creates responsibilities, as I discuss below. At the same time, however, it is a generous form of speech in that, unlike straight-talk (which begins from the premise that the listener is an interlocutor from the start), elliptical speech offers a listener the choice of whether to pursue the conversation by probing, unpacking, discussing. Doing so carries obligations: a story unfolded – like a letter – obliges its hearer to some action, even if that action is merely sympathy or greater understanding.

Ethnographic researchers are often advised to seek understanding and to listen sympathetically, but this has its dangers, for local models of sympathetic listening immediately imply an alliance, and alliances imply side-taking. Conversation, unlike census-taking, does not permit neutrality. In essence, listening to stories positions the listener, irrespective of the latter's own beliefs and intentions. I learned this one day during a time in which stories (harmful gossip) proliferated in the settlement. Dina accused me in a public confrontation of listening to and 'telling stories' about her. I denied the accusation of gossip – indeed, I had taken pride in the fact that I did not repeat stories or add my own. It was, however, hard not to hear stories that proliferated about her at that time, a time of great social change as people sought access to housing, the avenues to which she controlled. Dina responded to my defence by telling me a storie she feared that I had already heard which in fact I had not, one in which she figured as the embodiment of a trickster-witch figure.

The tale is hauntingly simple: A mutual friend of ours was dying and on her death-bed had decided to make an affidavit concerning the disposal of her property, already in dispute. She had called for Dina, who brought a policeman to help the dying woman make the affidavit. The storie that Dina accused me of listening to was that the woman had died before the affidavit could be signed, and that Dina had seized her dead hand and with it forged her signature.

There are many layers in this tale and its telling. The story reveals a literal understanding of signature – 'hand-writing' – and its relation to the law. The dead hand yet retained enough authenticity that its imprint would be considered binding – her handwriting, not Dina's hand, writing. It reveals also the powers of gossip and envy and spite. Yet, at the same time as the story lays bare some of the fault-lines of the community and positions the listener, its telling by the very person who appears as its main protagonist is also an act of power. Dina accused me of paying attention to those who circulated this tale (ironically, or perhaps intentionally, in this case, it was she herself), and giving others to believe that I believed it. In so doing, she felt that I was positioning myself against her in relation to an event and its polarising effects on the community. Telling a tale that cast her in a bad light had the effect of operating as a warning about her power and her willingness to use it. And its power is replete in the fact that I retell the story here.

Such stories allow other kinds of conflict to be aired – conflicts about how property ought to be disposed of, the power of specific people in the settlement, etc. In other words, they work to allow the unsaid to be heard. The power that underlies this is not physical or juridical force but lies beyond these, operating at the level of imputation and haunting, having its effect in what it implies not what it says. Its power lies in the interpretation, not in a literal reading of the material. Power does not always work through brute force and we are reminded to pay attention to the exertion of language on social forms.

Secrets, rumour and gossip

One of the most common ways that spoken words shape social forms is through secrets, rumour and gossip, all of which have the effect of creating in-groups and out-groups, regulating and reminding people of social norms, ideals and conventions.

Queenie loves to talk. 'I talk all day', she said. It is true, she does indeed love to talk, and flicks with ease between colloquial English and Afrikaans, all spoken at top speed and with scarcely a breath drawn. She is comfortable speaking, sharing her opinion and ideas with others. Her husband, by contrast, is a reticent man. Once, when we were discussing her extraordinary capacity for words, I wondered aloud whether she talked in her sleep. We laughed but it was a serious question. She was unsure: after all, she was asleep, so how would she know, she responded. There was a simple test, I told her – if her husband knew her secrets, then she must talk in her sleep. We all laughed, but he, wisely, said nothing, holding the question of her nocturnal activities open, keeping them secret, refusing to indulge our curiosity. Secrets nestled within secrets.

It is difficult to keep secrets when people live in close proximity. Secrets and privacy were often linked when people spoke about lives in The Park and their hopes for The Village. As Vicky put it,

When I have a decent roof over my head, I want to put my head out the door without knowing everyone's business. As long as I can open my door, not to throw out my water, but to admire the view, I'll be happy .... When I get my house, my business will be nobody else's but my own.

And Antony G, long-time resident in The Park said:

I'd like to live further apart because at the moment I can hear everybody's arguments. I don't want to listen to that all the time. I mean, if he coughs, then I hear him. The only time I won't hear anything is when they talk softly .... I wish for a lot of privacy.

And yet this model of a distinction between public and private is undone in everyday life, where circumstances demand close associations and extended networks of support. Here, a secretive person is thought to be lacking in sociability. Secretive people cannot be trusted – they belie their appearances. In part, this understanding underlay Dina's attack on me for listening to stories: in not repeating them, I had made myself opaque to others and laid myself open to accusation.

'Secrets' are revealed in gossip – a form of communication that absolves the teller from responsibility for the accuracy of the information. Widely disparaged as feminine modes of communication, skinder (gossip), stories (harmful gossip) and skandaal (scandal) nevertheless abound and are not particular to women. Their consequences are seldom seen as positive. As Maggie put it, 'These days you only hear stories more than anything else .... People gossip about each other and they always end up being mad at each other'. Or, as Fiela explained, 'You can't say anything because if you make a little mistake, trouble will be heading your way. They never get to all the facts, but they just come at you, scolding'. 'You know, people talk about each other a lot around here', said Johanna, 'You can say that these people are very busy' (besig – busy; a polite rendition, indicative of both her own ordentlike manners and suggestive of her interlocutor's. She might otherwise have said in colloquial terms: hulle krap; they scratch [in other people's affairs]). People were critical of those who told 'stories' – at the same time as doing so themselves.

There is a fine line between skinder and rumour, one that is often breached. Gossip, which is often thought of as harmless, can spill over into rumour, which Veena Das describes as 'a voice that was unattributed, unassigned and yet anchored to the images of self and other that had been circulating' (2007: 117). Skinder rests on intimate knowledge of individual behaviours evaluated in the light of external norms, and reported on 'as fact'. 'Rumour occupies a region of language with the potential to make us experience events, not simply by pointing to them as to something external, but rather by producing them in the very act of telling' (Das 2007: 108). Das adds that it is not that language makes these events 'out of nothing', 'but rather that memories that might have lain inert come to life in the form of rumours ... [that] become part and parcel of scenes of devastating local violence' (2007: 109). (To some extent one can see this at work in the ways illness narratives circulated in the settlements [see Chapter Seven], in which rumours of illness were concretised by actual events and resulted in eviction of some sick people from the body social.) Das characterises rumour as marked by 'the withdrawal of trust from normally functioning words' (2007: 117), the effect of which is to give force to a form of death rather than a form of life (2007: 132). I explore this further in Chapter Seven.

Gossip is an unruly form of speech. Because locally skinder is understood as having the potential to spill over into rumour, and because rumour can be annihilating, moderating it is important in face-to-face communities. People are chastised for 'telling stories', and that chastisement may take the form of physical punishment: violence is meted out by individuals in an effort to prevent rumour's contagion and its potential to mobilise groups into mass violence.[15] At the same time, however, when they stop short of rumour, stories and secrets can have positive effects. Anecdotes and stories, particularly those relating to children and sex, are told as moral tales. People often told me horror stories of the treatment of children (never those in The Park although there was evidence that many were inadequately cared for), and in so doing, delineated proper relationships. For instance, Dina told me one day that she had heard a strange sound from the dumpsite behind her house. She ignored it initially, thinking it was just children playing, but when the sound persisted, she went to investigate and found a baby wrapped in a blanket and carefully placed in a plastic bag. No one else was around. She reported the case and eventually a young man from a neighbouring shack settlement was arrested. His girlfriend had left him with the baby while she sought a job. Frustrated by his inability to comfort the crying child, he abandoned the baby. Rather than indicting the man for his inability to care for the child or to ask for assistance from others, Dina interpreted the story as an indictment of the woman for being an inappropriate mother and leaving her child in the care of a man. A gendered moral of women's responsibilities and men's incapacities is embedded in the tale and its telling.

In communities in which well-being rests on intimate knowledge, gossip serves as an alert to matters that might need redress. So too secrets. For example, people often conveyed to me the news of someone's illness by hinting that they were HIV positive. 'It's supposed to be a secret but ...', I was told time and again. The circulation of information couched as 'secret' in this way has the effect sometimes of allowing people to talk about things otherwise frowned on, unsanctioned. One such was Lorraine, whose partner had died of what were said to be AIDS-related complications. A sickly woman, she gave birth to a premature child. Everybody 'knew' she was HIV positive, but few people broached the topic. She had told friends whom she trusted to keep the secret of her HIV-positive status secret. They in turn, told others, so that soon it was common but unspoken knowledge that she was ill. When people came to visit, they concentrated their concerns on the child rather than on the woman, in this way offering support without stressing the nature of the illness. They brought her food 'so that the baby will be strong', and visited regularly ostensibly to chat, but in doing so, helping unobtrusively to care for the child. Here rumour had the effect of creating surreptitious support – a community of 'knowers' who rallied around. Forms of support can be silently offered because everyone knows the secret and knows that it is 'secret'. Secrecy does not mean 'unknowable' but 'undiscussable', codes of speech and propriety work to replace speech with gesture and silence, and, in this case, support tactfully offered.

In the cases I have cited above, secrecy and gossip work together to enable relationships to be sustained without need to name suffering explicitly. But sometimes they can undermine relationships. People who are considered to be gossips are thought to be vengeful and dangerous. Stories are understood as being most detrimental to social life, undoing relationships, replacing trust with doubt. There is here a fine line between sociability and danger. Sometimes stories spill over into violence, particularly where sex and drink are involved. Stories (rather than tangible evidence) of sexual misconduct are often sufficient to precipitate domestic abuse. The model of person that shapes conduct in the settlement holds that in matters of seduction, women are passionate temptresses, men are insanely jealous and that stories bear sufficient likeness to truth to incriminate. Where infidelities occur or are suspected, they are generally considered to be a woman's fault. Even a suggestion that a woman has been unfaithful is sufficient 'evidence' for a severe beating. Language is imprinted on the body when stories precipitate physical abuse.

Language is not just about communication but about social relations: about one's being in relation to others. We inhabit the world through language. It pre-exists us; we are always already implicated in and by it. It is saturated in power. A large body of literature shows that language is not simply descriptive, a word corresponding with a thing or state. Language acts with force in the world. As the philosopher Michel Foucault has shown, it shapes our notions of truth and gives form to social institutions. J.L. Austin distinguishes between language's illocutionary and perlocutionary force. The former is descriptive, the latter effective. In perlocution, the force of language exceeds words. One can see this most clearly in witchcraft accusation, where words hint at more than themselves, where they suggest and give form to powers that harm. In so doing, fear, danger, violence and isolation are released as social vectors, interpretation runs amok. One can see language's perlocutionary effect too in rumour, which, as Veena Das (2001) notes, may render the world uninhabitable and, importantly, irrecuperable: the world cannot return to what it was in the afterward of rumour and the actions taken in its name.

It is not always palatable to live with clear-sighted realism about the world one inhabits. In fraught, raw circumstances, truth may give way to an imagination that is two-fold. In its ugly forms – skelling, rumour, verbal abuse and insult – it mirrors the corrosive world and the grossness of material conditions. It undermines, humiliates and wounds, cruelly undercutting one's own and others' achievements. A sense of instability and unpredictability in the world is echoed in linguistic forms that have the power to destabilise one's sense of self and placement in the world. Such forms of language mark the limits of recognition and acknowledgement of another as human. People will often say of those who skel that 'she treats me like a dog' – by which they mean a cur not a pet. Used in these ways, language is dangerous and destroys.

Sometimes stories offer a flight of the imagination from the real into a kinder world that offers more possibility for living generously, if only in the moment. The imagination draws people to a place without limitations, away from the narrowness of truth and reality. The stories that Raymond and others tell, beautiful fantasies, may make people feel better, more able to cope with a world awry. And yet in some ways they are possible only when one is not quite there – when alcohol has a mild hold on the tongue, or events present themselves to imagination in such a way as to be transformative. Imagining another life does not lack its own dangers: it is easy to move too far and too quickly from reality – making one 'bonkers', mad, demented. Language can invert: the mad, delirious and dying may speak in words that cannot be understood. The trickster is a charmer, but also a danger. An oiled tongue may lead to soft words or hard fists. Laughter may cut or heal. Words can make or break a sense of solidarity and community. They can solidify existing stereotypes or create something new – a place of dwelling.

From the Park to the Village

ABOVE **Aubrey signing a subsidy application under Sandra's watchful eye.**

ABOVE RIGHT **Dina posing on the bulldozer preparing the new site for The Village.**

RIGHT **Sandra and Dina pose with workers and officials at the new site.**

BELOW **The first houses being erected.**

ABOVE LEFT **Demolishing The Park.**

TOP **Wissie mending while the settlement is bulldozed around her.**

ABOVE **Razing the remainder of the old site.**

BELOW **Those who did not qualify for subsidies were left homeless.**

ABOVE **The last houses in The Park**

LEFT and ABOVE Packed and waiting to move.

BELOW RIGHT and LEFT Oom Price, one of the *eerstemense*, was the first person to move to The Village; Dina and Sandra pose with Oom Price and Meitjie and friends.

Illness and accompaniment

'You only get sick in this place. People die around here. The woman who died the
other day hasn't even been buried yet ...'

Auntie Maggie, 2004

'Once people know you have AIDS, they stop worrying about you. Then you'll lay in
your house all alone .... When they find out that you have that kind of disease,
they stop taking notice of you and they all just kind of drift away from you ...'

Lorraine, 2004

'Illnesses don't ask you for your permission'

Clive, 2004

Michael Taussig notes that, 'Health is part of the human condition, as is disease,
and the incidence and manifestations of both are heavily determined by the
specificities of social organisation' (1992: 102). In other words, how we get sick
and with what illnesses is not merely a question of chance but has to do with the
way society is organised – and particularly with structures of inequality (see also
Singer et al. 1992). Veena Das takes this argument a step further. She proposes
that 'culture works to distribute pain unequally in populations' (cited in Wikan
1999: 62). Her unusual characterisation of culture is suggestive in relation to
thinking about illness. Our ways of making the social are revealed not only in
our social institutions but in our culturally framed responses to illness, dying
and death; in the distribution of ill-health across populations; in the cycles of
wellness, illness and suffering that punctuate life and living; and in the ways we
deal with these. How do we understand the body and its vulnerabilities? How do
people live with uncertainties of the kind that illness introduces into social life,
and with what effects? What kinds of attention do sick people receive? How does

illness reshape relationships to community and language, to social forms and to experience? The answers to these questions rest heavily on local conditions as these are experienced over time.

Much social science research relating to illness is diagnostic or prognostic in its scope. So much and yet so little is known of how people make sense of daily life in the face of illness, or about its impact on accustomed modes of sociality and ordinary ways of relating. Local understandings of the body, the ways that social relations and language are moderated to encompass illness and the adjustment of ordinary routines to accommodate or refuse it, remain in many respects opaque. It is here that anthropology, with its commitment to local worlds and fine-grained social analyses, has much to offer. The discipline's focus on relationship and sociality, its attention to history and context, and its methodological tools offer a means to understand the effects of illness on individuals and their relationships, the worlds they inhabit and the forms of sociality illness makes possible or denies.

One of my first and lasting impressions of The Park was how terribly ill many of its residents were. Most had or had been ill with tuberculosis, not an uncommon complaint in the region that has the dubious acclaim of having one of the highest TB infection and multi-drug resistance rates in the world.[1] People's illness episodes were both acute and chronic. Over the duration of my research, a growing proportion of people drew disability grants for conditions ranging from severe diabetes, to lung damage caused by tuberculosis, to arthritis and amputation. Malnutrition seemed rife. Alcohol use was common and for some this gave rise to addiction and abuse. Several children and some adults exhibited signs of foetal alcohol syndrome. Many women described themselves as *vol stres* (full of stress), *senuweeagtig* (tense, nervous – or, as it was translated in the local vernacular, 'on my nerves'; see also Swartz 1998: 142–66), or as having 'high blood' (pressure), or as being *pap* (soft, weak), without *krag* (power). Daily routines were shaped by medical regimes and needs. Anne described the demanding regime of medications she took to manage her *suiker* (diabetes) and 'high blood' among other serious medical conditions; Vicky told me that alcohol was her anti-stress medication and had to be consumed at regular intervals in the day. Bernie described her *snaakse* (strange) turn when she became *pap* and hypertensive, and the dreams that accompanied it which she read as signs of impending death. Conversations and interviews were interrupted by patients visiting the DOT[2] worker in the settlement to receive their medication. Gerald, a volunteer on HIV medication trials, explained that from time to time he would 'go off' the medications so that he could be properly sociable. Anna *met die een been* (one-legged Anna) regaled me with scarcely coherent accounts of her attempts to secure a disability grant. Ou Rose became too ill to get up from her pile of blankets on the floor but entertained us with her stories from that position. Charmaine described how she would share her prescription asthma drugs and painkillers with people who asked her for them and told me how, 'If I start feeling funny then I just take [someone else's] tablets'. Frieda's man died and when I went to pay my condolences I learnt that her financial position was precarious. She was now responsible for the sizeable debt they had run up at a spaza shop, a debt that had previously been secured with his disability grant. Katryn's house was filled with sick siblings for whom she had to care. Wissie and Brian both had TB and were bed-ridden for months on end. Wissie was desperate for plums and grapes, the picking of which was one of the main sources of income for casual workers in The Village, but access to which was prohibitively expensive in the local shops. Brian died in 2004, one of many residents who died in what ought to have been the prime of life. Wissie died two years later.

I was always bombarded with questions – Did I know whether the *druppels* (drops) and Afrikaans 'remedies' (over-the-counter herbal preparations) were good for epilepsy, for headaches, for sterility? (I had no clue: such remedies were not then part of my health-seeking repertoire.) Could one wash someone with AIDS without incurring the virus? What about sharing their food? How does one manage household resources eroded by the costs of medication and absence from work? These questions gave rise to intense conversations about diagnosis and cures and different ways of understanding how ill-health settles in communities. And, of course, I was given advice, primarily about pregnancy. It was medically unsafe for a woman my age to be childless, I was warned; a complete 'scrape' or 'womb clean' (D&C) was the best way of ensuring conception; the sex of a foetus could be told before birth by the hue of the *lineas negra* or whether the pregnant mother became pretty (a girl child) or ugly (a boy). In addition, the names of doctors most likely to assist one with obtaining a disability grant; the best *druppels* for a nagging cough; and home remedies for tiredness, irritation, anxiety were offered.

Whenever I visited after an absence, people would begin our conversations by asking, 'Have you heard?', and relating to me the names of those who had died, and the reasons for their death. Over time, HIV/AIDS began to figure in their accounts, initially in undertones and later prominently. Between 2001 and 2003, more than thirty of the eight hundred people living in The Village died,[3] mainly of diseases related to poverty, including TB, and diseases compounded by HIV seropositivity, and of violence. Very few have lived long enough to die a death not associated with illness or violence – to die 'of old age' (*ouderdom*) as it was locally known. In dry, sociological terms, the number of dead accounted for almost four per cent of the population over two years.[4]

In this community, as we have seen, life's contingent quality has long been apparent and the forms of social stability that exist have been wrought with great effort from insecure and unstable grounds. Social conditions are such that it is difficult to make daily life coherent and people's humiliations are frequent. Illness and unseemly death – from violence, from the diseases that disproportionately affect the poor, deaths that are the product of forms of social neglect (be they deliberate policies or the product of inadequate attention) – are part of the humiliations they endure, and people have had to become accustomed to their management and to the instabilities of social life that illness aggravates. Cecil Helman, a medical anthropologist, describes such people as 'time poor' (2006: 4), by which he means that their lifespan will remain short by comparison to the 'time rich', who are able to afford the new medical technologies – 'life extension' and 'life enhancement' technologies – that will extend their term of life. The distinction between time-rich and time-poor is useful, not least because it points to the different ways that class inflects health and illness. In South Africa, average life expectancy at birth is estimated at 51 years (Macfarlane 2004: 11). The Western Cape's estimated life expectancy is higher, at 62 years (ibid.: 18), but those living in similar contexts to people in The Park can expect a much lower lifespan with more years ill.[5] Clive commented casually, 'I'll probably die (vrek) when I'm forty'.[6] In South Africa, the distinction between time-rich and time-poor people rests less on access to life extension and enhancement technologies than on healthy lifestyles, freedom from violence and basic access to healthcare and medication. Socio-economic class becomes a general proxy for health, poor people tend to be sicker and to die younger than the rich, who are more likely to suffer 'diseases of lifestyle' and to have access to the resources to manage these illnesses.

Local models of the body and illness

Poor people are accustomed to the knowledge of their (collective) vulnerability. As Janine commented, 'We're born sick. Newborns come into this world sick and they stay that way'. The customary gift at baby showers is a remedy (for colic, sleeplessness, irritability, teething, sore stomachs, coughs, running noses, wind) selected from a pre-circulated list. In middle-class communities the gift is usually of clothing; medicines are seldom given. One might say that the babies of poor women come into the world surrounded by remedies as protective devices. Janine was surprised when I commented that this was a class-related phenomenon: middle-class people expect health not sickness for themselves and their children, and ill-health marks a crisis in everyday life rather than a constant accompaniment to it.

People I knew in The Park/Village had experienced, among others, work-related ill-health (accidents, pesticide poisoning, sunstroke); environmentally induced illnesses, such as those that accompany living in inadequate housing with insufficient water and no sanitation; diseases associated with poverty; diverse respiratory-tract infections; stomach disorders; cancers; arthritis; psychological disorders and stress-related illnesses. A range of models of bodily function and susceptibility circulate in everyday life in The Village and biomedical and other explanations are sought for their illnesses. 'Close living' and the drugs and alcohol to which people turned to manage stres exacerbated inter-personal tensions (a psychological model of distress) and 'jaloersheid' (being jealous), and the eruptions of violence left many scarred and some dead.[7]

People understand their bodies as vulnerable not only to disease and discomfort caused by external agents ('germs', working conditions, etc.) but also to reckless passions. Anger and violence are thought to be caused by excess heat, itself caused by passion. Passion's heat quickly frictions into physical violence, particularly when fuelled by alcohol and/or jealousy. It falls to Rastafari to cool down heated emotions through words, a process called 'reasoning'.[8] Here, language is imagined to have the capacity to soothe the passions and avert social tensions and violence. So powerful is the folk model of heat and cold in shaping ideas about conflict and its mediation that it was implemented as part of the allocation of houses in the new site. Seeking to ensure 'racial integration' but anxious that integration might trigger interpersonal conflict, leaders allocated a Rastafari-headed household to each section of the new settlement. Rastafari were expected to act as calming influences and to mediate potential (racial) conflicts. As a result, the built environment is shaped by the folk model of the body and passions writ large. A local model of the body was given material form in the allocation of houses and the distribution of different sectors of the population within the settlement. The models of the body are metaphors and analogies for other relationships, giving rise both to what Scheper-Hughes and Lock (1987), drawing from Victor Turner, call 'the body social' and to a material distribution of bodies in geographic space.

Conversations about illness are frequent and people speculate about symptoms and diagnoses drawing on a wide range of experience and diverse models. Biomedical models overlap with and exist alongside other models of the body. Sometimes this gives rise to contradictory interpretations which people must then navigate, as when an HIV-positive Rastaman participating in an antiretroviral (ARV) trial[9] smokes zol as part of his daily rituals. Dagga smoking (apart from being illegal in South Africa) is prohibited by the medical regime which administers ARVs for the drug trials in the expectation that the body that receives the drugs is 'uncontaminated' by other drugs. Ideas about purity and contamination in two different systems of understanding the body work against one another. For the Rastaman, marijuana is part of a religious ritual that creates a pure self, united with a higher being and one's fellows. For the medical profession, marijuana is a pollutant that may decrease the efficacy of the drug trials. It creates an impure body that is an inaccurate measure of the efficacies of trial medications.[10] Patients, who draw on a range of models, seek diverse ways to deal with their discomforts and illnesses while biomedical practitioners argue impatiently that 'these people' do not know how to follow prescriptions, are prone to addiction and unable to care properly for themselves by sticking to the rules of biomedical regimes. Here, biomedicine arrogates to itself the authority to make diagnoses and to offer judgements that are framed as neutral but are in fact freighted with moralistic judgements about how the relationships between people should work. As Taussig notes, 'Maladaption is … not a thing, but a purely normative concept traveling under the guise of scientific jargon' (1992: 103). He adds that such concepts 'smuggle in a particular intention of value by making it appear to be like a fact of nature' (1992: 103). So naturalised are the moral judgements that they become part of people's everyday consciousness of themselves. I have heard those afflicted with TB, for example, describe themselves ashamedly as 'non-compliant'.

There is a tendency in the medical anthropology literature to measure 'local' models against a 'universal' biomedicine, so that the local is understood as that which is different from biomedicine (see, for example, Helman 2000). But biomedicine is localised in everyday life for residents; it does not stand outside of the ordinary. Its technologies and diagnostic categories are part of people's ordinary worlds and are invoked and subject to interpretation and contestation in people's everyday activities of making sense of experience. Let me give an example. Hearing a terrible commotion one day, I followed the sound to where a growing crowd was trying to soothe a young woman who was thrashing about, running blindly, stumbling, falling to the floor. A visitor to The Park, her illness histories were not known to residents. Someone was sent to town to call an ambulance (cell phones did not exist then and there was no call-box in The Park at that stage) and as people tried to calm the woman they speculated about her affliction and its treatment. Some said she was mad; others that she had epilepsy; still others that she was spirit-possessed. Those who said she was possessed offered two different explanations: either she was possessed by demons or had *amafufunyana*. Three different models of affliction operate here – a psychological model of madness, a biomedical model of epilepsy and a model of possession that identifies a spiritual affliction. Each called for different modes of treatment and different practitioners – a psychologist or psychiatrist, a medical doctor, a *sangoma* (traditional healer) or a religious healer. The ambulance arrived, the orderly diagnosed epilepsy and tried to sedate the woman prior to hospitalisation. Some of the bystanders who felt she was spirit-possessed stopped him, arguing that if she were possessed then sedation would do more harm than good by curtailing the spirit's activities. Here, too, different models of risk operate: one model that calls for sedation in order to reduce the body's thrashing; another that calls for non-sedation so as not to antagonise a causative agent, an alien spiritual presence. In the event, the medical orderly was prevented from sedating the woman. As I recall, she was not hospitalised then but, having calmed, was taken to a healer in a nearby village. She did not return but gossip had it that she was later admitted to hospital.[11]

In this example, part of the process of 'diagnosis' was social – differing models of the body and its afflictions were brought into conversation, different diagnoses given and a range of options offered. Contestation and conflict over these diagnoses was part of the process through which community members reached a decision about how best to treat the afflicted woman. All the models I have described are equally 'local' in the sense of being part of a repertoire of knowledge and explanatory models from which people draw in assessing the immediate situation. Those who espoused a biomedical intervention would not exclude different healing models in other instances. Unlike the standard analytic model that, as I described earlier, sets 'local' knowledge in opposition to a universalistic biomedical knowledge, biomedicine is but one of a range of possible 'local' ways of understanding and interpreting affliction. What distinguishes biomedicine from other regimes is that the state is implicated in the provision of care.

Taxonomies of illness

I have argued that biomedical knowledge is part of local knowledge. It is often localised further through close assessment of the body, interpretation and reinterpretation. For example, while biomedicine describes TB in terms of stages of severity assessed on the basis of symptoms, diagnoses are brought into residents' local discourse through careful attention to the effects of the illness on the appearance of the body. Local taxonomies are descriptive: people differentiate between 'vet TB' (fat TB), 'maer TB' (thin TB), 'mooi TB' (pretty TB), 'lelik TB' (ugly TB), 'vinnig or gallop TB' (fast TB) and 'touched by TB'. When the afflicted person does not lose weight or appear ugly, s/he is considered to have either vet or mooi TB. 'The TB hasn't made her thin or anything like that: she still has her full figure' as one person described it. Lelik or maer TB characterises those on whom the disease has wrought much physical damage: 'When your health deteriorates quickly and you look shrivelled and things like that' said one woman. Vinnig or gallop TB is a hindsighted diagnosis. Taking its toll quickly, those who suffer from it usually die, often unexpectedly. A 'touch' of TB is to have experienced a mild form, to have had the disease diagnosed and treated before deep damage to the lung tissue – 'scarring' – has occurred. Those who have had 'a touch' will always be short of breath, prone to respiratory illnesses and weak, but, cured, are not drastically incapacitated afterwards.

Naming in this way renders idiosyncratic the experience of illness and of the suffering that may attend it. The proliferation of descriptors associates disease with a particular body and its experience of illness in a particular time and place. The effect is to take the familiar but homogenous, abstract and depersonalised biomedical categories and personalise them, making them responsive to the particularities of person and context.

Skin is the first organ scanned for illness's marks: serious illness – TB, cancer and now HIV – is thought to darken and discolour. People with TB talk of how they note that their skin has gone 'black', and of how, a few weeks into effective TB treatment, the skin returns to its 'yellow' colour. Sometimes people describe the very ill as being dark as 'makwerekwere', the local term for foreigners from elsewhere in Africa. South Africa's historically horrifying relation to physical classification haunts in the assessment of health and illness in the post-apartheid era.

Interpretation is based on intimate knowledge of gendered modes of comportment and people's daily habits. Older women surreptitiously assess young women for 'tell-tale' signs of pregnancy: changed gait, widened hips, potbellies and 'bigger bums'. Donna, for example, speaking about the early stages of her pregnancy, recalled that it was her mother who alerted her to her nascent pregnancy:

> I didn't know that I was pregnant because I wasn't showing. The only difference was that I became fairer and my mother used to ask me: Donna, why are you so yellow? You're black. You can't be yellow. And look how you're standing ... Like someone who's pregnant!

Signs are not self-evident and must be interpreted. Inferences are drawn from particular observations and people's knowledge of context, personalities and behaviours. As Lorraine commented of her neighbour,

> Look, TB makes you thin (teer jou uit) ... I've heard them say that if you have TB it sometimes turns to AIDS. And so that's how you can tell if someone has AIDS because his skin becomes darker (swart). When you have AIDS your skin becomes darker. But I mean [her] colour has changed again. She's light of complexion again, but now they're drinking again. They think their bodies are doing better now so they can have a few more glasses without getting sick again. But that's the time when they are actually making things worse for themselves because alcohol dries

one up inside. I mean it takes away your veins and all your blood vessels. That's why you don't feel like eating. You don't feel like eating but you'll grab the wine bottle because it enters your body faster than food .... And you know there was a time when [she] picked up some weight again and she looked good but when I saw her recently she was as thin as she is now .... When people around here find out that they have some kind of disease they start to drink because they think that the alcohol will cure them ... [But] the alcohol just makes things worse. It only incites the disease and you're likely to die quicker.

Here, careful attention to individual appearances and behaviour over time is contextualised in local knowledge about how people respond to illness and health. A description of behaviours is linked to an assessment of the process through which illness and alcohol eat at the body, rendering it meagre and reducing one's relationships.

Deaths too are distinguished on the basis of appearance and the illnesses that people know one another to have: the deaths of elderly people known to have had TB were considered to have been caused by TB alone, as were those of the very young and children; younger people with TB were increasingly often assumed to have died of 'AIDS and TB', irrespective of the causes recorded on death certificates. As Paul Farmer (1993) found in his study of HIV/AIDS in Do Kay, Haiti, explanations for illness rest on local moralities in which models of innocence and sexuality – and thus appropriate gender behaviours – are important in explaining illness. The AIDS-related death of the first school-going teenager in The Park was frequently explained as having occurred through a contaminated blood supply or injection in hospital, and not by sexual transmission of the virus.[12]

HIV/AIDS and the hardening of descriptive repertoires

I visited Dina one day after I had been absent for a long time. As had become her custom, she began her narration with a litany, counting off the deaths of her neighbours on her fingers. As she did so, she asked whether 'people overseas' were affected with 'die virus' (HIV). She did not believe me when I told her that in many places abroad, HIV seropositivity is considered a chronic condition that can be managed with drugs and a healthy lifestyle. Identifying seven people who had died in the preceding few months, she worriedly commented that only a few days previously she had heard that President Mbeki said he knew no one who had died of AIDS[13] so how come she knew so many? Her tone was not accusatory but questioning: how is it possible that two such different lifeworlds and forms of experience should exist side by side? Her questions were particularly poignant in that, as I discuss below, the adoption of a biomedical explanation for the relation between HIV, illness and death was not automatic and its acceptance still rests on precarious grounds.

Just as we are accustomed to thinking of our model of the body as stable and individual, so too we anticipate that taxonomies of illness – the ways we classify and categorise states of deviation from good health – are fixed. But, like understandings of the body, taxonomies are fluid, subject to revision as times and contexts change, and as different explanations are put to the test and critically evaluated. Responses in the face of illness and premature death are various and differ over time. At the turn of the millennium in The Park, HIV-related illness or AIDS deaths were social diagnoses that were made on the basis of a range of factors including the age, relationships and everyday behaviours of the sufferer. In this community, most residents have acknowledged the virus's presence among them for less than a decade. Prior to this, many people denied that the virus existed at all. Their denial suggests the weight of stigma that attaches to an illness like HIV. Denial may be a coping mechanism (Deacon, Stephney and Prosalendis 2005; see also Fassin 2006). If something does not exist then one does not have to deal with it. It also points to the limits of direct speech, indicating what people feel they can and cannot address directly (a theme to which I return). Faced with state and medical arguments about their susceptibility, some resorted to conspiracy theories to explain the presence of the virus: HIV as an experiment in mass extermination sanctioned by the apartheid state; divine retribution for morally unsanctioned behaviour; witchcraft or neighbourly envy.[14] A conversation in December 2000 illuminates this further: Charmaine said that the HIV/AIDS rate was high, but that people did not die of AIDS. Rather, they died of TB or towery (witchcraft). She added that toormoord (witchcraft murder) is a product of jealousy. Again, passion comes to the fore as an explanatory model for ill-health. Although such notions are often depicted as 'local' responses, they are not in fact, as Paul Farmer (1993) and Adam Ashforth (2002) have shown: AIDS is often described in terms of what Farmer calls a 'sent sickness'. Witchcraft 'belief' is often thought to be the product of ignorance, but as E. Evans-Prichard's (1937) study of Azande oracles long ago showed, and anthropological work ever since has confirmed, it offers a way of making sense of events and experiences that seem otherwise inexplicable.[15]

There was a time in The Park, not that long ago, when TB was considered a cause of death in and of itself, irrespective of the age or gender of the afflicted person. Then, people were also thought to have died of ouderdom (old age – although few people lived long enough to qualify for this appellation), 'high blood' and 'sugar sickness' (diabetes), of cancer and diarrhoea, of longontsteking (lung infection – used to describe a range of respiratory infections, but most commonly pneumonia), of 'maagpyn'/'maagseer' (stomach cramps, diarrhoeal diseases) or of hunger. These causes have seldom been mentioned as causes of death in recent years. More recently, local taxonomies of illness and death differentiate between 'TB', 'TB and AIDS', 'AIDS', 'diarrhoea' or 'maagpyn' and 'cancer' as causes of death.

TB, which has gradually come to subsume other terms for respiratory infections, is now increasingly associated with HIV seropositivity.[16] Ponkies described the link between TB and HIV/AIDS as an overflow: improperly identified and treated, TB spills over into AIDS, she said, an assessment that is widely held by residents. 'Wasting' (away), formerly associated with cancer or diarrhoeal diseases, is now attributed to AIDS, except if the afflicted person is old (cancer) or very young (diarrhoea).[17] Those whose illnesses were extremely painful and prolonged were considered to have died AIDS deaths, again, often irrespective of medical diagnoses. Those who died alone, unattended or destitute were thought to have AIDS. (It is in part for this reason that state pauper's burials are widely disparaged.) This model of the body is striking in the way it expresses both bodily and social shrinking: the body turns inwards and social relations are narrowed. At worst, the individual dies alone and is buried by the state, in the absence of kin, friends and the rituals that mark life's proper ending. Fear marks a retreat from the social. Notwithstanding the positive campaigns to destigmatise HIV – such as the 'fight the disease not the person' model – people are fearful of being stigmatised and often pronounce their proper medical diagnoses in deliberate attempts to deflect the negative associations of HIV/AIDS.

In recent years, residents' earlier models of reading symptoms and relating them to diagnoses have narrowed further: HIV is now assumed to be a base condition of almost all illnesses. Local symptomatology increasingly rests on an assumption of a 'weak system' and on that basis an evaluation of the body's changing external signs is undertaken. Young people and women in their early middle ages in particular are subject to the scrutiny and evaluating gaze of parents, neighbours and friends who assess health in relation to sexual behaviours, skin colour and changes in body shape. The immune system has come to the fore as an explanatory model for people's vulnerability, and HIV and AIDS figure increasingly prominently in explanations for adult illness and death. So prominently in fact, that HIV seems to have become the primary explanation for ill-health, even when in biomedical terms, the virus is not present in the body.

An earlier, nuanced taxonomy of illness seems to be being substituted by a more homogenous classification: AIDS. Even death by cancer, long resistant to incorporation into the AIDS-death model is increasingly being classified locally as AIDS-death, and indeed 'cancer' is increasingly used by residents as a euphemism for HIV/AIDS. People are described as having died of 'that cancer'; HIV/AIDS is implied by tone, intonation and gesture – a drop in the voice accompanied by a sidelong, significant look. The shift need not be unidirectional. The ways that illness categories are used in social life are, as I have shown, flexible and responsive, and what currently appears to be a singularisation of illness may yet be undone as time passes and as ARVs become increasingly available. However, by the end of my research in 2005, AIDS seemed to have become a basic premise of everyday life, the *a priori*, unstated condition on which social life and relationships were built. At the same time, however, people did not necessarily speak openly of AIDS as it manifested in the community, and people with HIV seropositivity seldom revealed their HIV status publicly.[18] Instead, the causes of illness were speculated about, and sick people were often the subject of gossip. HIV seropositivity is 'read' through its effects on moods and social behaviours. One young woman described to me a woman she and others believed to have had HIV seropositivity: 'When she was drunk she would dance in the street and sometimes she would lie *kaalgat* (bare-assed/stark naked) in the road, and that's how people knew', she said. A woman who began seeing '*mannetijes*' (little men – the implication is that she was delusional) was thought to be afflicted with AIDS. Behaviours that lie beyond local convention, mood swings or inappropriate emotional responses become symptoms through which (potential) illness can be read and identified.

The shifts I have described above do not mean that other classifications fall away and are entirely replaced by HIV/AIDS as diagnostic categories in local thought. Biomedical explanations exist alongside a range of others, sometimes displacing them and sometimes being eclipsed by them, depending on the precise circumstances in which the topic of illness arises and the specific questions to which diagnostic categories are addressed. Rather, the conjunction of high death rates and fear of HIV seropositivity produces a reification of illness categories and a transformation of the conditions assumed to underpin ill-health. In this context, mortality narrows and hardens descriptive repertoires. The scope of HIV/AIDS is increasingly seen as the base condition of illness and is assumed to encompass diverse illness experiences. Yet, at the same time, the diagnosis limits the means through which understanding is possible, foreclosing the range of explanations for ill-health and death. For many, this has been confusing. During conversations with residents in recent years, I have been asked to explain the relation of HIV and poverty, to advise residents (usually, but not only, women) as to whether or not *towery* (witchcraft) exists and if so, to explain what its relation to illness is and, if not, to explain why people act as though they believe in it.

Alongside the reification of categories has been a growing uncertainty about susceptibility. I have been asked by several people whether TB causes HIV/AIDS, whether this explains why TB seems so resistant in the present, and whether someone with TB is necessarily HIV positive. One young woman asked me whether rich people ever caught the virus, another told me that HIV was a disease 'in the air', a phrase she interpreted to mean that its means of communication was airborne, and which draws in part on immediate knowledge about TB infection. Locally, before the English acronyms of HIV and AIDS caught on, HIV was described as 'vuilsiek' (lit. dirt disease, a venereal disease), an appellation that is also used to refer to sexually transmitted diseases more generally. Vuilsiek has moralistic overtones, implying symbolic pollution generated by deviation from social ideals. A young woman described HIV as a 'vrouesiekte' – women's sickness – spread by women's failure to adhere to local ideals of chastity and discretion encapsulated in the gendered model of ordentlikheid that we have already encountered. The descriptor assumes women to be culpable.

Increased social 'certainty' about HIV seropositivity as illness's cause has led to a consolidation of ideas about causation and recourse. As fears of HIV/AIDS increased, a model of the body as vulnerable to others (and not just 'germs') gained ascendency. This is not unimaginable (STDs are not uncommon in South Africa, after all, and models of ill-health caused by witchcraft are widespread) but in the absence of a biomedical cure, the body was seen as increasingly susceptible to the ill-wishes and evil-doings of others. At the same time, some felt that it could be protected through recourse to towery. More recently, the suggestion that illness might be caused by witchcraft has been (partially and perhaps temporarily) replaced by medical models. In part this is owing to the ongoing efforts of local health workers and community leaders to offer biomedical explanations for ill-health and to try to stop people seeking cures by visiting toordokters, who, these officials felt, were quacks, stealing money from the poor by offering false cures and still greater false hopes. But the acceptance of the biomedical model has brought with it an uncertainty about government's role in health provision. I was frequently asked why it is that white people in South Africa seem not to experience the same kinds of illnesses or the same rates of mortality, why they seldom attend state hospitals and why black people continue to undergo hardships in the aftermath of apartheid. My answer – that the political economy of hardship set in place by colonialism and sedimented under apartheid perpetuates inequities and will take generations to redress – resonated with people's understandings but seemed feeble in the face of suffering. Sophisticated local knowledge of the political economy of health, etched in first-hand experience of its inequities, is undermined by scientific models of HIV infection and AIDS-related death that hold that HIV is an 'equal opportunity' virus, and scientific models themselves are questioned with local understandings of inequitable access to health care. Confusing state responses to HIV/AIDS have further complicated local understandings. The slow and contested 'roll-out' of ARVs; the highly controversial 'natural remedy' approach of the previous Health

Minister, Manto Tshabalala-Msimang; the state's contradictory stance on disability grant access for those with low CD4 counts, and so on combine with the difficulties people already face in relation to access to health care facilities and create confusion among residents as to what remedies are available, effective and whether they are entitled to access them or whether, as one person put it to me, 'antiretrovirals are only for the rich' (see also Leclerc-Madlala 2005). Poor residents are mocked by a state-of-the-art private hospital and clinic that stands at the entrance to the road that leads to the section of town in which they live. They can scarcely find the minimum sum that allows them access to the state hospital, let alone cover the costs of a taxi if they do not qualify for an ambulance or if it is too slow in coming, and when a visit to the hospital is required, often go into debt with neighbours, or, if they are in good standing, with *subeen* owners, to make the sum that will grant access. The local state hospital in the area has fewer than two hundred beds, the nearby day hospital lies across a busy highway and is badly understaffed so that patients wait for hours in the draughty waiting room. The chronically ill and close-to-death are often sent home to die. Their suffering brings ongoing uncertainties that fold into lives already rendered precarious by poverty.

While patients speak well of the staff and the treatment they receive at the state day clinics and hospitals, they complain that it takes great effort and time to get access to state medical attention. The messages they receive and the ways they interpret information are confusing or even contradictory. During an ante-natal check-up, Lorraine took an HIV test which came up positive. An earlier partner had died of HIV-related illness, but, she said, they had not been sexually active at the time. The doctor asked whether she had cared for him, shared food with him. His questions were presumably directed at assessing the extent to which she might have come into contact with the virus in the ordinary modes of care, but Lorraine understood him to be saying that

> I didn't get it from a man ... that I picked it up somewhere. So when he said that I had picked it up somewhere, I tried to think where it could've happened. But then he said that I might have gotten it from someone's food I was eating or something like that you see .... During that time he spent at the hospice, he always asked me to eat with him ... so I'm wondering if that's how I got it. But it can't be. ... I always fed him but he'd always tell me to eat with him. I didn't want to be funny (offensive) so I ate with him ....

Here, gestures of care are scrutinised for their possible role in causing illness. Ordinary sociability becomes suspect, patterns of generosity in care are thought to render one vulnerable.

There is no necessary connection between these understandings of HIV infection and knowledge about prevention of sexual transmission. Knowledge, attitudes and practices do not necessarily coincide. Knowledge that condom-use offered a means of protection against transmission seemed widespread among residents. Young people had learned about HIV and condom-usage at school and it had been confirmed by community health workers.[19] In everyday conversation, people joked about condoms; they spoke of using them; they knew that condom-use could reduce the chances of HIV transmission; they knew where to obtain condoms.[20] One woman added that she had been told by nurses at the local clinic that she should always make sure that she and her boyfriend washed before and after sex so that people would not smell the sex and sweat on her and accuse her of illicit sex, exposing her to accusations of being HIV positive.[21]

Speaking uncertainty

Those afflicted select whom to speak to about their illnesses. One young woman who was diagnosed as HIV positive when pregnant described her response to the doctor and staff at the clinic where she was diagnosed, who apparently told her not to tell everyone about her disease:

> The doctor probably meant that ... once people know about your illness they'll stop keeping company with you, you see. If you hear that I have AIDS then you're going to stay away from me completely. Or maybe you wouldn't want to eat anything I ate or if I eat something and offer you some, you might say that you don't want any because you know that I have AIDS ... because you're afraid that you are also going to get it, you see? So that's how you become lonely and depressed and you start thinking that you're going to die soon or ... you commit suicide, you see? You could have lived longer but you cut your own life short.

But she also commented on the real dangers of social isolation that might accompany revelation:

> Once people know you have AIDS they stop worrying about you. Then you'll lay in your house all alone ... No one comes to visit you or encourage you ... or just talk to you or anything like that. You lay all alone in a dark room, waiting for your death. Now, you see, when no one knows about your illness, you die quicker, that's why I say if you have any kind of malady, it's better to surround yourself with people ... so that you can talk about your problems with them.

Her decision was to tell a select few:

I said to him: 'Doctor, I think I have to tell my friends about this so that they know what's going on because I don't want them to find out about it after I am gone.' Because, you see, that's the time when people will gossip about it. I keep saying it's better to tell your friends while you're alive, but you also have to know who to tell. You shouldn't tell people who, when they get drunk, will shout in public 'Hey, you have AIDS'. The thing is, you can't tell everyone because when people sometimes quarrel, they throw your disease in your face, you see .... I told all my friends about it. I just wanted to see their reaction towards me, you see. But all of them said, 'we're going to support you', and things like that. And I said to them: 'yes, that's why I told. I wanted to see if you were going to support me'. But so far they've all been very supportive.

She claimed to have told only seven people, all close friends and neighbours, selected on the basis that she felt that they were reliable, that they could be trusted not to reveal her secret. But their discretion was not as reliable as she had hoped – after all, three outsiders, I and two research assistants, had been told by one of her friends that although it was secret we should interview her about her HIV seropositivity.

Despite this selectivity, illness seems to attract gossip. It is as though this casual speech takes up residence in the bodies of people known to be ill. A visit to the clinic, doctor or hospital renders people – particularly women – vulnerable to neighbours' speculation. As the figure of language's informality, imbued with fear and negativity, rumour and gossip find a home in a suffering body and rest there. They are oddly tenacious and difficult to dislodge. The force of such words is powerful: many women I know, particularly the young and attractive, now try not to go outdoors too often lest they be accused of 'rondlopery', of seduction and of potentially spreading the virus. The potential to be the subject of gossip has the effect of shaping where, when and how one moves. Thus informal modes of speech have powerful effects in moulding how one occupies space. Increasingly, house doors are closed, sociality is constrained indoors. These models draw from and reinforce local notions of gender propriety: as we have seen in earlier chapters, men are not constrained in the same ways.

Silence may be one social response. It does not mean ignorance. People have generated creative ways to speak about or infer the presence of HIV and other aspects of social life that might pose dangers to social relations and that therefore call for guarded talk. Although people now seem to have good general biomedical and social knowledge about the virus and are willing and able to speak abstractly about it, they tend to speak elliptically when its presence is close or immediate. Such coded speech is understood by those who are part of the speech community that has developed it and after a while is used in ordinary speech. Codes become naturalised in everyday habits of communication. For example, if a resident describes some as having *vuilsiekte* (dirt sickness) or '*that* cancer', it would now be understood as a reference to HIV seropositivity without the use of the words HIV, virus, AIDS or their vernacular equivalents.

Language, danger, care

I want to think for a moment of how language is implicated in ordinary care-filled interactions. It requires skill and judgement to know how and when to speak of illness or its threat in ordinary social circumstances. A particular discretion becomes necessary in asking after the health and activities of friends and neighbours and one must become adept in its use and suspension. Language must be melded and accustomed modes of sociality moulded to guard against giving offence or causing harm. Care must be tentatively offered and one must be sensitive to the framing of requests, alert to hints and subtle undercurrents in conversations. Metaphor abounds. This is, of course, not new. Susan Sontag has written powerfully of the ways that metaphor shapes our experiences of illness (1978, 1989). At the same time, new words and forms of language are inserted into public discourses previously moulded by elaborate forms and relations of respect and avoidance that come close to prudery, or the crude terms through which public reference to sexual matters is otherwise often made. Precise, immediate and direct terms for bodies and sex – vagina, intercourse, penis, extra-vaginal sex – supplement and sometimes supplant these forms. A new vocabulary has come into being: phrases like 'AIDS orphans', words like 'seropostitivity' and acronyms like HIV, AIDS, VIGS and TAC[22] need little explanation for the South African lay public nowadays. In public discourse there is a solidifying of linguistic forms at the same time as social forms dissolve, crumble and are reworked under the weight of illness.

In contexts where words take on formerly unanticipated valences, speech acquires new dangers. Public talk may become hazardous – South African newspapers have reported cases where someone has declared their HIV-positive status only to be attacked and in some instances killed. Sometimes, people have spoken out boldly about the disease that they see taking its toll on the lives of family and friends. Some have taken the brave step of revealing their HIV status. For others, the possibility of the virus's presence is secluded, hidden, held quietly to the self, intimated but never revealed. For some, rumour, scandal and gossip are ways to speak its contours. The effect of these forms of speech may be to alienate those about whom it is used. Rumour – a form of speech that cannot be traced to its origins – floats free of social responsibility even as it may have devastating effects on social relations. In its most extreme form, as Veena Das (2001) notes, rumour may lead to death. This has been the case where individuals have been murdered when their seropositive status was made public. Some of the linguistic forms are subtle, or rest for their full acknowledgement on the unsaid. Here, the extra-linguistic has an important role in meaning-making.

Let me give some examples to clarify. Once, as I was leaving a friend's house after a long and wide-ranging conversation, catching up on news and events that had occurred in her community while I had been away in the USA for a year, she drew me outside her house, away from her children. Discreetly turning her back on the neighbouring houses, she said, 'I must ask about my life', and asked in a worried tone whether I thought she had gotten thinner. I did not know how to reply and said only that she looked no thinner than the last time we had met. I asked if she was feeling concerned. She replied, in what may seem a non sequitur, that her daughter, aged three, still breastfeeds intermittently through the day.

It was a small incident – less than a minute's conversation, on which a stranger might not even remark, and which, twenty years ago, would probably not have been uttered or, if uttered, not have carried the same terrible weight or sense that it did in the pre- 'roll-out' context of South Africa, 2003. Part of our conversation earlier that afternoon had been about the fact that she suspected her husband of taking lovers and she was not certain he used condoms when he was with them. We had spoken before of what she experienced as the slow erosion of her relationship. She had gone for HIV tests more than once in the last two years. She had once told me of her anxious reading of natural signs as she waited for the result of her first HIV test: she had bought the local newspaper on the way to the clinic to collect the results and the wind had caught it, scattering the pages. In that moment, she said, she had seen her life spread to the winds and feared the worst from the results of the test.

HIV was implicit in the question she posed to me. Simply describing her weight and her daughter's occasional nourishment was a delicate alert that she was concerned about her own HIV status and also about what we have come to know as 'vertical transmission' or 'mother-to-child transmission'. I knew that she asked me about her appearance in connection with 'the slim disease' and its possible effects on her child, and she knew that I knew, but neither of us said anything more.

It was a moment that continues to haunt. She had taken such care with framing the question so that it seemed innocuous – a woman asking another woman about her looks. She had put the question almost casually, in such a way that neither of us could go further without breaching its frame and the discretion it impelled. Yet, it was prefaced with a murmured comment – 'I must ask about my life' – and a gesture that pulled us to the protective shadow of a house, out of sight of the neighbours. The missing premises of her question did not need stating: in some contexts one need not speak of HIV/AIDS to invoke its presence. Sometimes, naming does not illuminate and may endanger. Silence or elliptical speech such as this may be the response: a way of holding one's harmful knowledge away from others, protecting them. The cost to the self of these modes of knowledge may be high: anxiety, doubt and the erosion of trust echo the uncertainty about the presence of the virus. In such contexts, qualities of attentiveness become crucial. Where one cannot admit painful experience in words, lest it cause pain to the listener, the listener must bear the responsibility to do more than simply listen; to take note of gesture, pause, location, to read between the lines, to interpret and reinterpret and then to act in response, obliquely. There are dangers: over- or under-interpretation, misrecognition, improper attribution of tone, gesture, euphemism.

In speaking or not speaking of illness, new forms of delicacy are called forth. Sometimes these forms are too fragile to carry the full weight of experience, particularly in relation to the expression of emotion. Here, attentiveness calls for a means to engage with another person in ways that do not usurp experience but allow for forms of sharing that, even though only ever tentatively, may reassure or console, offer solace or support, or simply a place of respite. In this way, words may find a home in the body of another, and experience may rest even when not explicitly stated.

Naming is ambiguous. Illness named – a diagnosis – may offer a means to understand experience and possibly to intervene in healing. But it may also reduce the person, shrinking a life to a single category of health or its absence, reducing diverse roles, relationships, personal characteristics to a singular status – 'the ill' – thereby diminishing the person and the contexts of everyday life. Or it may offer a reprieve from judgement. An example: frustrated at the slow distribution of building materials after a terrible fire that razed large sections of the settlement, Gerald, an 'out' HIV-positive community committee member, started to shout at the people queuing for goods. His voice was loud, the language ugly and people were angered, but they explained his behaviour away – 'it's the illness speaking', they said. Here his mood was attributed to his seropositivity status, rather than to external or subjective causes (the heat of the day; the loss of his home; the damage done to the community; the fact that the fire had meant that people had to seek shelter and assistance from one another, stretching meagre resources still further; the unruliness of the crowd seeking materials, his frustration at being unable to manage the allocation process efficiently).

Where an illness comes to occupy the self, caring is at stake. Writing of the reification of illness, Michael Taussig (1992: 83–109) notes that it disguises a power relation in which the joint attempt to make mutual sense of an experience of ill-being is reduced to an asymmetrical relationship in which medical practitioners are rendered experts and patients must become responsive to their knowledge. In this way, a diagnosis comes to subsume the person (see also Sontag 1978), so that all (social) experience is explained by a diagnosis. When people identify others as being HIV positive, rather than as having HIV seropositivity, it is as though illness comes to be all-encompassing – as though one is one's viral load status.[23]

A proliferation of language indiscretions surrounds the ill person – one might say that gossip and rumour take up residence in the body. Along with these, the contradiction: forms of silence at the outer edges of a social circle surround a sick person. When illness incapacitates, forms of avoidance may take hold, such as the failure to address individuals, to touch them, to speak directly with them. Often conversation happens around the sick person, rather than with him or her. Sometimes there is partial inclusion. Sometimes, however, the person is abandoned. Language ebbs and flows around the ill, sometimes withdrawing as the sick person approaches death. Holding open a space in which someone deathly ill is still included in ordinary language interactions marks a struggle to extend the courtesy of speech to those not easily recognised as part of the living.

This struggle is echoed in the deadening effect of a named diagnosis; the medical insistence on terminology and the specification of the medical term to a body that encompasses the person so that one becomes/is the illness (Taussig 1992). As we have seen, people familiarise such diagnoses by using adjectives (such as classifying an illness as *vet* or *maer* TB). The noun resurges in death's aftermath when illness is named explicitly – '*Sy het gesterf. Sy't* AIDS *gehad*' (She died. She had AIDS). In death's afterward, the noun has singularity, power and finality. Naming in this way is not necessarily a judgement or judgemental. It is a statement of fact – fact that rests on social experience rather than biomedical diagnosis.

What I hope to have shown so far is that language is a site of struggle in relation to illness and care. Patterns of speech may be particular to specific communities and may implicate caring in different ways. For biomedical practitioners, a singular diagnosis becomes the basis on which one relates to another. This establishes a power hierarchy in which the patient's intimate knowledge of his or her body and experience is homogenised into an illness category. The benefit: tailored treatment. The risk: that one loses sight of the complex ways in which people fashion themselves and everyday life in specific historical contexts. Ethnographic materials demonstrate the complexity of speaking of experience and of attending to one another. Gossip can act as a veil, protecting too direct a gaze. It can also be a shroud. Naming may illuminate and offer sustenance by indicating that one's own experience is not utterly unique – that there are others who have similar experiences and suffer as one suffers. One might say that it affords a kind of welcome into a community of suffering; diagnosis as greeting. But it may also cause suffering, as when one's illness status comes to be of more significance than one's relationships in everyday life. It is to the making and holding of relationships in the presence of illness and the face of death that we now turn.

Care of the ill; tending to death

Of illness and dying, Alphonso Lingis writes,

> This dying concerns me; one is not free to justify the death of the other, not free to justify, with the imperatives of my own tasks or those of the common work of civilization, leaving the dying of the other to him or her. (1994: 175)

His words are echoed in the actions of those I know who attempt to care for the dying. In the community, people mobilise around their ill families, friends and neighbours. Indeed, the presence of family and friends is one of the markers of a 'good death'. Other indicators include dying quickly, without pain or suffering, without violence, without causing hardship to others, 'at the right time' (that is, quietly, of old age). Good deaths are not common, and the presence of those who care is sometimes all that can be offered to offset hard avenues to death.

I visited Maggie, an old woman who was caring for her brother from whom she had long been estranged. He had shared her house for a short while some months previously, but they argued constantly and the fighting got on her nerves so that she had taken ill, and eventually she had asked him to leave. A few days prior to my visit, he had arrived unexpectedly, and sickened fast. She slept on the concrete floor while he lay on her only bed, so thin he scarcely wrinkled the blankets. All that was visible was the top of his head. He did not move for the duration of my visit, and died shortly thereafter. Afraid that he might die in her absence, she had not gone to work at her twice-a-week char job for the duration, and in the absence of an income, had become reliant on gifts of food from neighbours. He was the fourth person that she had taken into her home and cared for. The first was her sister, who suffered epilepsy, who had had to leave because 'The doctors are too far. It's difficult to try to wake people and to call an ambulance and stuff like that, because she usually gets attacks at night. That's what it's like around here. What else can you do? You just have to accept it'. The second was a friend, Rina, registered as her dependant in the housing subsidy application forms. Rina's illness had become too great for Maggie to manage and at the time was 'lying in hospital'. Along with her concern for her friend's well-being, Maggie was anxious about the implications of her possible death for issues of inheritance. The third was a visitor to whom, some months previously, she had offered her bed. The visitor had spent the previous few months shifting from place to place in the region, seeking friends and family who might care for her. Maggie had known the woman from many years before, and, with the assistance of neighbours, one of whom had once worked as a nurse-aide, tended her till she died. It took the woman three days to die once she began to die in earnest, I was told, and it was a terrible death, 'an AIDS-death', hard and painful. 'There were sweat drops on her face and she had staring eyes and terrible bedsores and a swollen mouth' they said. Many people, hearing of the horror of her dying, were too afraid to help care for her or even to visit. Those who had helped care slowly fell away until only two remained to assist. The task of care horrified them: they recalled with sorrow the woman's suffering and their helplessness in its face, yet they did not abandon her. When she died, they arranged a funeral, desiring that she not be buried as a pauper.

The state offers only cremation to those too poor to afford private burial. Cremation is considered ignominious, and people make great efforts to bury their dead themselves. One woman lamented that her partner had been cremated by the state because she could not afford a funeral. There was no funeral ceremony, she said; no sharing of food with the community. And now there is no place to go sometimes and sit and talk or think, nowhere to lay flowers on anniversaries. The dead man's sometime employer had arranged for a state cremation thinking that it would save the widower the expense of a funeral, but her neighbours were scandalised at the lack of ceremony and skindered that her husband had been buried like a bergie, destitute and lacking in friends and relationships. A friend's thoughtful suggestion that she treat what would have been her twenty-first wedding anniversary as an occasion to grieve was warmly received: the suggestion, quietly offered, gave her a dignified means to reclaim her status as a decent widowed woman and to find a home for loss.[24]

The local cemetery is only one of a number of sites for burials. The movement patterns associated with urbanisation are frequently reversed in death when the body is sent to be buried elsewhere. This is particularly the case among recently arrived Xhosa-speakers, for whom there is a strong moral injunction to return to be buried where one's umbilical cord is buried, the place where one's ancestors rest, 'home'.[25] Afrikaans-speakers who originate outside the city are also often returned in death to their birthplace to be buried.[26] Burial may bring migration patterns full-circle.

Funeral arrangements are complex and the timeframe considered fitting for burial depends less on chronological time than on what one might call social time; the time it takes to make sure that the body is in the correct place for burial and the appropriate people present to witness and perform rituals. Funerals generally occur from several days to two weeks after death in order to give sufficient time for these arrangements to be made.[27] During that time, customs of caring for the living differ. For example, Xhosa widows usually stay in seclusion in a room emptied of furniture. Tended by women, they rely on the goodness of others for their sustenance and seldom go outdoors until the funeral. They ought not to engage in domestic chores, including cooking for themselves: visitors bring uncooked foodstuffs – flour and oil chief among them – which are prepared by kin and neighbours. Vigils associated with the deaths of Xhosa-speakers usually last for about a week before the body is buried or taken elsewhere for burial. Sometimes funeral arrangements involve intense family negotiations as the appropriate kinsfolk to perform rituals are sought. All funerals in The Village include a Christian service, a ritual procession to the graveyard (if the person is buried locally) and the sharing of a meal after the ceremony. The absence of a community hall in The Village made it difficult to complete these ritual processes and people expressed great dissatisfaction about the fact.

Despite the range of time within which a funeral might occur, in all cases, timing is delicate. A body left unburied too long reflects badly on kin: it is assumed that the reason lies in kinsfolk's unwillingness to shoulder the responsibilities of caring for the dead. That in turn implies discord and alienation and casts the dead person in a poor light as someone who had been unable to maintain social ties during life. People are anxious not to appear to disparage the dead and yet there are real constraints involved in funerals, which are costly, especially if the body has been stored in a private morgue as often is the case when the state hospital morgues are too full. Those responsible for the funeral must pay for the morgue, for the costs of transporting the body to the site of the ceremony and then the burial site, for the ceremony, the gravediggers, the food that is ceremonially shared by all those who attended the funeral and others besides. The lack of a funeral appals local residents and where possible, community members pay for the funerals. Residents are expected to contribute R10 (a little more than a US dollar) or as much as they can afford towards the costs of a funeral, with the expectation that others will do the same for them should it be necessary when the time comes. Part of living then lies in cultivating the relationships that secure dignity in and after death. Some people have already made provision for their deaths. Funeral insurance and burial associations account for a large portion of the expenditure of those with regular and reliable incomes, and are considered requisite among Xhosa-speaking residents of the community, many of whom plan to be buried at home.

In the aftermath of death, new questions arise relating to inheritance and the intersection of law and custom. Questions arise about forms and protocols of burial ritual to be followed and about burial sites. The demands of the dead on the living are onerous; the social etiquette and cultural rules associated with adequate, let alone proper burial, arduous. These are not particular to The Village. Across the country, undertaking companies boom, cash loan centres open alongside the funeral parlours, entrepreneurial cameramen make lucrative livings filming funerals. Ministers and male agnatic kin are in demand to perform their ritual specialities, and ritual processes are revitalised and reworked. In the process, culture is reified, old conventions receive new valorisation and new social forms emerge and crystallise. Some conventions may liberate but others may reinforce pre-existing forms of inequality, such as that between women and men, or between young and old.[28]

The fact that people are familiar with death's presence, the existence of sometimes beautiful, sometimes inadequate rituals to comfort the living, does not render them blunted by death's presence or its injustice. Frequent association with dying does not, as some have argued (Scheper-Hughes 1992), necessarily render people stoic in death's presence. People's first topic of conversation when I visit The Village is carefully recalling who died, when and how. Their chronology of death consists of accounts given in particular, even graphic detail. Even where causes are known or surmised, death tears the social fabric, angers, hurts and puzzles. We should not mistake brusqueness in care for an erosion of the capacity to care. Nor should we anticipate that grief's temporality is immediate. As theorising from Freud to the present shows, grieving may arise unexpectedly in a present far removed from its source in the past.[29]

Stories of the availability of care in The Village have reached others living nearby: the homeless and destitute, those unable to access care from kin or the state. Some find their way to this community and beg assistance from residents. Although many residents cite this as a new phenomenon, in fact it is not. The community has always had a reputation for taking in the ill and The Park once had a section informally known as 'the hospital', where the destitute and ill came to live and to be cared for. But now, some of the residents are angry, believing that ill people are usually HIV positive and will spread 'their diseases' among the healthy. They would prefer that no one unknown come to the area. It is a cause of great tension, with people taking sides over the issue. Uncertainty, already deeply engrained in social life for so many, is engraved still deeper as the social effects of the virus are countered with blame, denial, misinformation and accusation, and with qualities of care that are demanding in their unrelenting nature. In this context, talk about rejection imposes limits on the conditions of welcome.

The horror of Maggie's friend's death that I have described above left a deep impression on some of the residents. After her death, there was talk of setting up one of the houses in the area as a hospice of sorts but the idea has at present floundered on the practicalities of finding funding, training carers and on the sheer scale of illness. The work of caring is arduous – feeding, cleaning, wiping, lifting, moving, washing, demonstrating concern, sitting, talking, touching, improvising, recalling the dying to life, mustering their energy, reminding them that they are yet part of the living, even when they cease to interact and lie staring unblinking at an unceilinged roof. And allowing them to die, ensuring that they are in company, not alone. Even touching is made difficult for some in the face of the terrible devastation that illness wreaks on the body. It takes enormous resources – emotional and material – and extraordinary resourcefulness to care for the ill and to bury the dead with dignity. Material resources, always slim, are stretched ever thinner, and people's emotional capacities too may be stretched to their limits.

Sometimes people are unable to care; they have reached the limits of their abilities to respond to suffering. If this happens, kin and neighbours are castigated. Sometimes, the weight of caring is heavy and guilt may burden those who find themselves stretched beyond their capacities and their means. Sometimes, anger abounds. As social scientists, we do not yet have a way to think adequately about 'uncaring', its causes and its effects. Nancy Scheper-Hughes (1997) has described as 'life boat ethics' the limits to care she observed in Brazil's favelas. She argues that recurrent deaths blunt grieving and limit the capacity to care about the living. Her argument suggests a moral failing. It is sometimes true that people suffering from terrible illness and close to death are abandoned in their distress. For example, one day in The Village my research assistants Robyn and Janine encountered a man who, terminally ill with cancer, had been sent home from hospital. The members of his household were revolted by his illness and his inability to care for himself. Slowly they withdrew their care, eventually leaving him alone and unattended. When Robyn found him, he had not been cared for or cleaned for many hours. She called for assistance from neighbours and began to wash him, restoring care and acknowledging the fact of his humanness. A few others responded and joined her in tending the man. He died some days later. Many were incensed at the man's treatment and members of his family were avoided when news of their failure emerged. His wife, who died a few years later, and stepdaughter, who left the settlement, were widely disparaged and many considered them to be rou (raw, in the sense of socially unfinished or incomplete). In such cases, we need to understand more closely the contexts and understandings that precipitated a lack of care. I argue that it is symptomatic of a social failure – something larger than the failure of a relationship between individuals and indicative of the failure of social institutions.

But it should be noted that such instances were few. Although the quality of care may have been wanting, most ill people were adequately cared for by a range of people, usually kin, friends and neighbours, and almost always women. The state was noticeably absent from ongoing forms of care for the very ill.

Revised social forms

Much social theorising assumes that societies and cultural systems are robust. The effect of illness and death and discourses about these on their current scale is to remind us that what we call social relations are the product of efforts expended over time. We need to know of the forms of such effort and of the moments when it fails or cannot be sustained. We might consider a relationship with someone (potentially) deathly ill to be a kind of welcome – an avenue into what remains of life and living. Welcome works by not insisting on recognition as a prior condition or event. It assumes the lowest common denominator of recognition: that the person approaching death is human.[30] Its trust is predicated on willingness to risk. Nowhere is this more apparent than in the complexities of 'disclosure', in which one may literally risk life.

There is an assumption in much of the discourse around HIV/AIDS that public disclosure of one's seropositivity immediately attracts negative social response – stigma. While this may indeed be the case, close attention to a single instance suggests that stigma is not a generalised response, an automatic consequence of disclosure, but arises at particular moments in an individual's social interactions.[31]

Gerald tested HIV positive in the late 1990s. So too did his wife Lien and one of his two children. He disclosed his status to his community in 1998. He had been offered an opportunity to live in a closed community but he rejected it, saying that he felt it important to return and disclose his status, to be an example to others in the area. For a while, people insulted him and he was shunned, but he persevered and remained in the community, taking on community leadership tasks when he was well enough. Sometimes when he got angry or upset and raised his voice or yelled threats and abuse, people would mutter about him, but they were usually cautioned by others who attributed his changed moods to the virus.[32] A Rastafari, he had cut off all his prized dreadlocks in August 2001 because when his son pulled his hair in play, it fell out in his hands, scaring the child to hysterical tears. Once, he showed me his medication regime. A volunteer for ARV drug tests ('a guinea-pig', he called himself), he had to take five different medications at different times. The first tablets were to be taken after breakfast, the second set, two-and-a-half hours later, the remainder after meals through the day and evening. Neither he nor Lien had work. They relied for an income initially on a small salary he received for his work in organising the community, and later, after that dried up, on payment for odd-jobs for one of the spaza shop owners; on receiving food in exchange for dagga from other residents and on the proceeds from the sale of dagga to residents of nearby towns. Frequently there was no food in the house.

In 1999, Gerald had fallen very ill and come close to death, but had recovered. Residents say that his recovery is to be attributed to their prayers. After that, he was certified too ill to work and received a state disability grant. He prided himself on the fact that he seldom had to accept handouts from neighbours and visiting NGOs, but was unaware of the fact that neighbours frequently kept the household supplied with small quantities of food. They would send children with covered plates of food and a message that they had cooked too much, in order to spare Lien the humiliation of accepting charity from those only a little less poor than she. Nevertheless, it was an unusual day when the family had more than one meal. His wife was too ill for most of their marriage even to continue with doing the occasional odd jobs for other residents in the community for which she had previously been paid a small amount. A reserved, delicate woman, her health had long been bad. In 2001, she told me that she had asthma, TB, vallende siekte (lit. 'falling sickness' – epilepsy), swart long ('black lung' – a reference to the scarring left by TB) and 'die virus' (i.e. HIV). A shy person, she was a little afraid of the world outside her home environs, especially given the scandal that had attached to her when her husband first announced his HIV status. She frequently spent days indoors or on her stoep, sitting quietly with her baby. Her first visit to the CBD of the city in whose environs she had grown up was made in 2001, when she was 27. Then, for the first time in her life she caught a train. She was senuweeagtig about the prospect for days before, and excited too – it was the furthest she had ever been from home and she was anticipatory about the visit. The purpose of the forty kilometre trip, which required considerable organisation, was to consult her husband's doctor about her growing ill-health.

Her husband, too, was less than sanguine about his regular hospital visits to the city. They made him nervous, he said, and he claimed that he was un-able to sleep in the days preceding the two-hour journey by train and minibus taxi to the centre of town. In the morning, before setting off, he would wake extra-early and smoke a big zol to calm his nerves and take away the hunger pangs. His doctor always commented that he was looking well, and he would agree, 'Yes, I'm irie'. Little did the doctor know that was indeed the case. One of the medicines made him very sleepy, and, he said, bad tempered. It hindered his business because he could not stay awake throughout the day and he was rude to potential customers. Every now and then, when the 'side'-effects became too much to bear, he would 'self-test', stopping taking the medicines so that he could spend the daylight hours awake, working, socialising, tending to his beautiful garden, full of vegetables and marigolds.

Between 2001 and 2002, Lien and their baby, Jerry, spent much time in and out of hospital. Scarcely a month went by when they had not been hospitalised for periods ranging from a few days to several weeks. They also lived outside the community staying with family members who could care for her and the child. The household was in a constant state of fusion and fission as she and Jerry came and went and the regularity of care and meals for the two remaining members was in flux. In 2002, Jerry died. On 1 January 2003, six months after her son's death, Lien, who had been terribly ill and weak for a long time, also died.

Gerald faced the terrible decision of what to do with her body. Friends tried to persuade him to have her cremated because he did not have enough money for a funeral. The night before the cremation he decided he could not go through with it: 'I couldn't burn her: she was my wife', he said repeatedly. He borrowed money from friends and approached a benefactor who paid for Lien's body to be released from the morgue. The funeral was small; only immediate family attended and he did not invite people from The Village. I do not know whether his son was cremated or buried.

Gerald's explanation for their deaths varied. Sometimes he simply said that both had been too ill and could no longer live. Once he blamed the hospital for failing to provide adequate care. Once he suggested that a business deal in which he had been involved had gone wrong and his erstwhile partner had attempted to bewitch him but that the punishment had missed him and been deflected onto Lien and the baby instead. (Some people referred to him behind his back as 'Badluck', implying that he both experienced and caused it.) In each case there is a different locus of responsibility marking different degrees of intimacy: a virus; the state; his business; his partner and, by extension, himself. The different loci suggest that the individual is the site of complex relations – individual sexual relations, business relations, citizens' relations with the state all intersect in Lien and Jerry's illnesses and deaths.

Some in the community, angered and saddened by their deaths, began to insult Gerald openly, calling him 'AIDSgat' (AIDS arsehole) and worse. Some threatened him physically. His business and political relations soured. Those who had supported him found themselves unable to intervene in his defence. He became afraid for his life and left the community in which he had lived for at least twelve years. He sought shelter and comfort with relatives, moving from place to place in the area as his welcome grew thin. His living son, HIV seronegative, went to live with other relatives, far from his friends in the community in which he had grown up. For a while the father and son had little contact, until Gerald went to live with his mother in a shack settlement, calling for the boy to accompany him. Gerald did not visit friends in his erstwhile home, fearing to go there. He later told me that the accusations and jeers hurled at him masked some people's wish for his death: he said that he knew 'secrets' of community leaders and that as he was sole witness to their corruption, with his death they would be free. Once again he intimated that his illness was caused by personal malevolence.

Here, illness intersects with local politics to produce what may be a form of paranoia. Deaths signalled the dissolution of family and community, of relationships that might otherwise sustain. That the family had remained so long in the community is a testament to the work of friends and neighbours who cared, not solely in material terms (although that mattered), but who performed the work of social care – rebuking those who would reject, smoothing over uncomfortable incidents, checking discretely on their well-being. It is testament too, to each individual's own ongoing effort to remind others of long-lasting relationships, relationships that predated illness and scandal and which were in this way made to endure. But, it seems that the deaths of the woman and child were the solvent of social efforts, the site at which blame and anger and fear overcame the work of making social relationships that could endure suspicion and distrust, and the point at which old relationships were inadequate to sustain the weight of loss and sorrow. In this case, grief has the form of anger and rejection – the individual is cast out of the body social.[33]

What happens to someone rejected by the community? The work of making and tending social relations is ongoing. Gerald's rejection by and ejection from his community was simultaneously an exclusion from a psycho-social and physical space and also an ejection from the temporality of intimate relations. For a time, until he went to live with his mother, Gerald was considered by residents of The Village to be a *bergie*, his life unfolding unconnected to meaningful others. 'He's living on Busy Corner' was the disdainful response to my enquiries about his whereabouts. The tone was dismissive: those who live on Busy Corner are considered unable to care for themselves or create and maintain enduring relationships. The temporal scale of Busy Corner is fractured and transitory; continuity of anything but discomfort is hard to sustain. Gerald's return to his mother was a return to a recognisable sociality, one that centres on kinship and the continuities through time – genealogy – that it offers. Bringing his son to live with him there consolidated his sense of return to kinship's time and the belonging it affords. Gerald died in 2006. His son continues to live with his grandmother.

In the face of illness and death, social forms are consolidated or revised. As we have seen, kinship relations come under new scrutiny and may be reworked. Let me give another example. Once, a middle-aged woman I know asked me to take photographs of her and two babies. She positioned the group with care – herself and the twins in the pushchair in front of the gate to their new house, tall sunflowers smiling behind their heads. The children wore new clothes that she had sewn for them. I did not recognise the children – her own children having long since grown to adulthood – and asked about them. She explained that they were her daughter's babies who had been sent to her to be cared for after their mother had died the previous month. She stated the cause of death simply and straightforwardly – 'It was AIDS', she said. The other two children, older, had remained with their father's kin in the Eastern Cape. The photos I took were to be sent to the children's father to show him and their siblings that the babies were still well, loved and well cared for. Some time later, she told me she was afraid that now that the father had seen how beautiful, healthy and well-cared for the twins were he might assert his claims over them and send someone to steal them away from her, undoing the relationship she and they had so carefully wrought.

In another instance, I sought Benjy to give him photographs I had taken of his family at his request. He was not to be found: ill, he had moved back to his birth-town in the Karoo – a place he had not lived in for at least fifteen years. There, he hoped, family would care for him as he weakened. He had rented out his small house in The Village in the hopes that the income would sustain him in the absence of a pension or disability grant. His son and the boy's mother had not accompanied him: as the boy put it, 'my father's people are not my people'. The woman had disappeared and the boy, aged 15, no longer attended school and was living 'here and there', staying with friends until his welcome wore out and then moving on. The stabilities in his life – a home and regular attendance at school – were destroyed, and although the youth cast his life as one of adventure and excitement, its cost, in terms of building ongoing relationships, was high. Benjy's illness undid a set of social relations, expelling the child from portions of what had been his kin network, and the new relationships forged to deal with immediate circumstance have a quality of happenstance and contingency and are unlikely to afford the kind of security and predictability (limited as these may be in that context) that will stand in sufficient stead in the long term.

Patterns of dispersal such as these are widespread as people leave urban areas to go to kinsfolk elsewhere, often in rural areas, to be cared for and to die. The movements bring about separation and reformulations of family, and with them, a reworking of relations that draws on and echoes and sometimes inverts the social geography of migration, separation and movement that were instituted by colonialism and apartheid.

Illness and deaths bring with them struggles within families and between families and different community, legal and cultural conventions. Notwithstanding the implication of much social theorising that its time is constant, unfolding predictably, in fact, the social is made in its punctuation by crises. Illness and death are two such, and they come now at times that an earlier generation would not have anticipated, affecting the young in death and younger and older generations by the death of middle generations that ordinarily bear the responsibility of caring. Time's expected flow is punctuated with the growing absence of a generation. The punctuation is accompanied by the presence of what Lingis calls 'a strange time' (1994: 173): the temporality imposed by dying. He reminds us: 'Dying takes time; it extends a strange time that undermines the time one anticipates, a time without a future, without possibilities, where there is nothing to do but endure the presence of time' (ibid.).

Dying entails both this quality of time that 'is drifting', at the same time as there is a renewed urgency and imperative to care. One might interpret the abandoning of deathly sick people by their relatives and by the state as an inability to manage the kinds of demands that this temporality imposes. Illness, death and talk of illness and dying insert new forms of time into daily routines and everyday life. Caring is pierced by waiting; plans are hollowed by uncertainties; time becomes rigid and drifts simultaneously. It is within and across these qualities of time and not solely those of chronology, seasonality and genealogy that social worlds are crafted and refashioned. The return to life involves, as we have seen in Gerald's case above, the crafting of relationships so that they again take a recognisable and socially sanctioned form.

Death, singularity, accompaniment

Lingis writes movingly of our relation with others in death. 'We know ourselves in our mortality', he says (1994: 159). Death calls the singular into being:

> Born in a place that another vacates, summoned already by a death that is my own, apprehending the possibilities open singularly to me, I discover the others in their otherness, in the places and the possibilities that are for them. The others who pursue their own singular powers also trace out possibilities they cannot actualize and leave for me. In the handshake that recognizes our kinship, we exchange messages and resources. (1994: 172)

For Lingis, it is in the recognition of singularity that death impels, and in the relation to the other that this is rendered possible, that human sociality is made.

His frame offers a way to think through the implications of how illness distributes relations in everyday life and to consider the ways in which the social is crafted from the conditions of possibility at hand.

As I have shown in this chapter, the ways we understand illness are not simple or uniform but shifting and under scrutiny. Biomedical models are part of local repertoires, domesticated through interpretation and careful attention to the particularities of individual lives and social relationships. Age, gender, past histories, individual peculiarities all enter the process of diagnosis. Diagnoses shift over time and are contested; people draw on a wide repertoire to explain ill-health. The repertoire is not 'culturally exclusive': A Xhosa-speaking person is as likely to discuss *druppels* as an Afrikaans-speaker; the latter makes use of a model of witchcraft that a more culturally bounded model would associate with 'the Xhosa'. Biomedical remedies are sought by all and state-provided biomedical care is increasingly people's first port of call once self-assessment and community networks have failed.

Increasingly, however, HIV/AIDS introduces to the present a homogenising tendency. Diverse experience is read through its lens, interpreted in its frame. One effect is a hardening of categories through which social life is experienced and explained, structuring them in ways that produce a homogenisation of social explanation and emotional responses alongside a proliferation and fragmenta-tion of experience. At the same time, social life continues to be refashioned. For many now, the virus, its suspect(ed) presence or forms of illness associated with it are the backdrop of uncertainty against which the ordinary activities of the day take place, the invisible grounds on which everyday life is made. Here, AIDS is not like other illnesses – life's shadow-side – but its foundation.[34] This is not to say that it will remain such, but to note that for a period of time in which remedy (ARV medication) was not available to sufferers, HIV/AIDS was understood as the basis on which social life had to be built.

Taussig argues that 'Charged with the emotional load of suffering and of abnormality, sickness sets forth a challenge to the complacent and everyday acceptance of conventional structures of meaning' (1992: 109). While I agree that this is true, his model suggests that illness is somehow outside of everyday relations. My own argument, presented here ethnographically, has been that illness is woven into the uncertainties of everyday life – it is part of how the structures become the conventional and taken-for-granted aspects of life. In thinking about this process, I find the rhetorical concept of 'enthymemes' apposite. Enthymemes refer to the unstated principles that ground arguments and anticipate the turns they will take. It seems to me that, for the time I write about, HIV/AIDS was an enthymeme of everyday living and dying. The illness foregrounds an ethical responsibility, what Lingis describes as an imperative to accompany the ill or dying person. It may be part of our task as scholars to understand this, and if Lingis is correct, to find ways to make it work in creating and sustaining forms of sociality that are generative in the face of illness, in time's uncertain presence and death's rub. This may offer a form of hope – not in terms of a narrative of redemption or recuperation or recovery – but in terms of accompanying another through life's unfolding and ending. In an interview on hope with Mary Zournazi, Lingis says, 'Hope is to hope that things can be born in your life' (2002: 41). Compassion, he notes, is like hope (2002: 39), and it calls one to accompany another.

It is the act of accompaniment, rather than co-residence or kinship or even shared histories per se, that accomplishes 'the community'. It may be for this reason that when a man died alone, in agony, abandoned by his family and friends, people in The Village were so distressed. 'Where were the people who were supposed to look after him? It was their duty to look after him. ... if you are going to leave that person to perish, then he'll die for sure'. And yet, as scholars we are called to ask about the kinds of community that come into being when one is called to accompany others to premature deaths.

Ordentlike huise, ordentlike mense

ABOVE LEFT **Unloading in The Village.**

ABOVE RIGHT **Aunty Maggie and Fiela moving house.**

BELOW **The Village**

LEFT **Gladys in her** *makhoti* **finery, and Xolelwa, pose in The Village.**

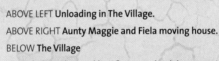

ABOVE **Settling in**

BELOW RIGHT **Janine's gentleness won her a special place in residents' hearts.**

BOTTOM **Baby (left) and Bernie laugh over photos of the move.**

BELOW LEFT **Aunty Jane and her grandchildren**

LEFT **Gerald and Cudo take a quiet moment after the frenzy of the move.**

ABOVE LEFT **Holland, Des and their son, Son, in The Village.**

ABOVE RIGHT **Eric waiting for church at Raymond's house.**

RIGHT **Petronella poses in front of Aunty Baby's display cabinet.**

BELOW **Dina (left) and Aunty Evalyn share a joke in Dina's new house.**

Conclusion
Raw life, new hope?

Clive: My life is almost over. I'm already 23. I'm 22, going on 23.

Janine: You're 22 years old, Clive! Your life is hardly over!

Clive: No, I'll be too ashamed …. It seems to me like I'll never get anywhere.

Carmen: Especially in this place, where nothing ever happens.

Clive: It's true. We don't get anywhere. Our dreams … I've been praying to God for such a long time but nothing's happened. There's no progress. Each year we become worse off instead. You have to look out for yourself. You have to sniff around (*skarrel*) for a life.

Janine: *Skarrel?*

Clive: Yes. If you can't do that then you'll really become a *bergie*. It's true.

These words, drawn from a wide-ranging conversation between Janine, Clive and Carmen one day in 2004, are deeply distressing. The words dismay not only because they discount the considerable gains that have been made in the post-apartheid period, but because a young man is so willing, so able, to see his life as over when it has only just begun. Or, by his reckoning, is half over, given that he expects (not unrealistically, given the paucity of medical care, the extremes of poverty, his occasional forays into dangerous forms of male prostitution, and the devastating closeness of HIV/AIDS, TB and environment-related illnesses) to die by the age of forty. Humiliation, dreams thwarted, questions of progress and its opposite, the rendering of human life in animal terms, the nearness of social isolation and the real possibilities of absolute destitution are all mentioned in the short extract. And yet as we have seen earlier, Clive and others live fully, sometimes with abandon, often with humour, 'on the edge'.

Clive's assessment makes me wonder, 'What is a life in this context?', and 'How does one live it?' When I visited The Village in 2009 to share the draft of this book with some of the residents, Clive was the first person I saw. He was carrying a bright umbrella and wearing a baby-papoose, with a tiny infant fast asleep on his chest. He was caring for her while her mother worked. In so doing, he made his body available to the child, loaning his time to her life. In local understandings of personhood, this is what differentiates life in community from a life on the streets, what makes a person a person not a thing. For residents of The Village, the ultimate degradation, the thing to be cautious of, is to end up as a *bergie* – unable to care for oneself, someone whose primary dependence is on alcohol or drugs rather than on people. Such a person is represented by residents – some of whom have come perilously close to this form of life – as having life but not fully living. In other words, a life worthy of the name is created by being dependent on others, and that dependence is precarious. It must be nurtured through extremes of passions and circumstances. Maintaining relationships is central to survival, to a sense of oneself as a person, and to one's sense of belonging. The forms of sociality that emerge in the ugly terrain of such contexts are often improvisational in character. Little can be taken for granted: not one's relationships, nor one's well-being; not even one's dreams. The possibilities of living sweep between two poles: at one end, trying to adhere to a model of decency that often seems to mock one's every effort but that offers the reward of respect or at least a partial acceptance; at the other, forms of wild abandon that risk abandonment.

I have characterised life in The Park as raw. These forms of rawness have their origins in earlier times. They exist elsewhere, in shantytowns and in the poor suburbs of the city (see Salo 2004), where gangsterism has long provided an alternative form of social security to impoverished residents and where the cruel boundaries of the formal economy cause informal, grey and shadow economies to predominate.

In 2006, South Africa Housing Minister Lindiwe Sisulu announced that all shack settlements would be eradicated by 2010. While a laudable goal, it was unrealistic and unlikely to solve the pressing problems of urban-rural poverty and urban migration. The provision of housing to poor people in urban areas, while important, has not necessarily directly ameliorated people's living conditions beyond the basics of shelter. There is a fine line between 'upgrading' and the creation of new 'poverty enclaves' and their formalisation in the built environment. The post-apartheid state's policies to ameliorate living conditions have run up against poor service delivery and mismanagement of funds and the sheer scale of lack. The fact that the Western Cape is attractive to job-seekers from elsewhere, combined with the City of Cape Town's poor management of resources and slow response to urban planning needs, has meant that far from decreasing in number, shanty towns have proliferated in the post-apartheid period. Apartheid's historical legacies endure in the present. It is well known in policy circles and in South African society in general that there is a real danger that unless economic benefits accrue to poor people, educational outcomes are improved, welfare programmes sustained and opportunities (jobs among them) offered, interventions such as housing initiatives will be little more than aesthetic acts that cast responsibility for material and social maintenance and communal well-being back onto the 'poorest of the poor' whose individual, social and material resources have been eroded by long histories of dispossession, alienation and social aggravation.

In her critique of liberalism, Elizabeth Povinelli (2007) describes such worlds as 'rotten'. She argues rottenness and privilege are hinged together by a particular liberal imagination writ into both intimate and ranked social relations. Her description of privilege is telling. She considers it a form of amnesia 'that many people consider life as something that can be counted on, at least for a certain length of time, for long enough to be able to forget about its limited nature' (2007: 80). And she comments that 'This amnesia does not infect many others' who live in 'a vastly reduced, almost uninhabitable landscape' (ibid.). While she is referring to the lifeworlds of indigenous Australians here, the description is apposite to life in The Park and, to a lesser extent, The Village, where, as we have seen, regularity and rhythm are hard won and precarious and life's sharp edges cut all. Povinelli would not object. Her critique is levelled at the liberal diaspora, which, in the afterward of apartheid, South Africa has entered, if only partially. Colonial and apartheid's illiberal discourses of race and rank have been replaced by a liberal discourse of the self-made person, who, given the right conditions (in this case, houses, franchise and the rights enshrined in the Constitution), is anticipated to become otherwise, new. Where that does not happen, as when people are unable to live up to the ideals prescribed by their understandings of ordentlikheid, the failure is disguised as an individual or genetic failure rather than as one of structure or history. And so, where individuals or families or indeed whole communities (however defined) are unable to accomplish the 'potential' that access to housing (itself indicative of democracy) ostensibly offers, they are written off – the 'those people' of disparaging elite discourse.

The link between the two possible forms of life I have described here – ordentlikheid and rawness – lies in the continuities of capitalism, at first in racial form and now in the ideology and practice of the neo-liberal market economy, somewhat mitigated by state welfare. In South Africa, what Povinelli describes as a genealogical society (based on rank and status) has not been replaced by one based on the autological subject (in which freedom is understood as the sovereignty of the self), whatever the rhetoric. Genealogy (which in South Africa took and takes the forms of particularly savage race, class and gender relations) continues to structure the possibilities of action, self-making and life in the post-apartheid context. Genealogy is disguised in the liberal rhetoric of self-making and possibility. What residents and others decry as a lack of 'moral community', or the continuities of 'the bush', or the presence of 'rawness' and violence in everyday life, are then explained away in terms of individual failings: drug and alcohol addiction, inadequate money-management, living only in the present, an inability to plan for the future, a lack of respect for life. '*Hulle's net bosmense*' (they're just bush people) is how one resident of The Village put it. Her words enfold several meanings. Taken literally they mean 'they live in the bushes'. At a metaphoric level, the phrase means 'they are raw', and read in relation to the pernicious evolutionary ranking that endures in South Africa, means 'they are uncivilised'. I regularly hear people say dismissively, 'You can take the people out of the bush but you can't take the bush out of the people'. Other phrases are equally unkind: one city councillor described residents as 'that motley crew', and argued that people's ongoing poverty was the result of a failure to make an effort or to recover from life's hard knocks. These remainders, reminders and presences are also explained in terms of lack of role models, lack of opportunities, lack of ability to recognise these and poverty's effects in enabling only *ad hoc* interventions that militate against sustained visions for the future. Such accounts do not acknowledge the erosion of the grounds on which social worlds are built, or how they are shaped by historical processes. They do not recognise the struggles to hold together a daily life worth living. They do not admit that people's efforts to establish stable emotional and material zones and continuity and coherence in everyday social relations are complicated by the emotionally and materially draining problems of entrenched and enduring poverty, violence and illness. They do not acknowledge the effects of individual, genealogical or structural histories in limiting opportunities, curtailing prospects. And they may not admit the ways in which new interventions made with the best intentions may replicate older structures.

Auyero describes 'poverty enclaves' in Argentina as the product of 'the withering away of the wage-labor economy, the official indifference of the state, and the breakdown of the organizational fabric of these territories' (2000: 93). He suggests that such areas are likely to become functionally split from the rest of society. He describes three forms of violence: interpersonal violence, structural violence (in the form of mass unemployment) and state repression. His argument revisits in a haunting way earlier debates about the marginal relation of shanty residents to 'mainstream' society. Janice Perlman's *The Myth of Marginality* (1978) offered one of the strongest critiques of marginality during that period. She argued that far from being unrelated or marginal to formal economies, residents of shanty settlements enabled those economies, providing a source of cheap, surplus, endlessly exploitable and renewable labour. In other words, rather than being marginal to society, shack settlements were asymmetrically and tightly bound into it. By the turn of the millennium, however, she, like Auyero, has found that marginality has become a reality (Perlman 2005) through forms of social exclusion that act perniciously against the poor.

Both authors focus on economic relations. Neither addresses the ways in which social ideals held by the mainstream are incorporated into everyday lives and ideals of poor people and structure aspirations at the same time as limiting opportunities to accomplish them. This matters. The conditions that characterise the Argentinean and Brazilian cases that Auyero and Perlman describe are not exactly the same as those in South Africa, although there is no doubt that growing unemployment and ongoing social exclusion in South Africa are making themselves felt at the political level. No one could easily accuse the post-apartheid state's policies of bad faith. It is committed to redress for various forms of social ills. Yet remedies are often constrained by powerful normative discourses and prevailing global political and economic contexts. These articulate with local forms to produce forms of marginalisation that are limiting but may also be productive for those who inhabit them. People struggle against forms of vulnerability and social invisibility and they sometimes succeed in making gains. Thus margins are sites of both subjugation and creativity, zones in which possibility and constraint play off one another, often in unpredictable ways.

The South African state's attempted remedies for colonialism, apartheid and their historical remainders have been couched in a framework that guarantees individual, cultural and social rights, including socio-economic rights, in a constitution widely regarded as one of the most progressive in the world. But they have been implemented in a neo-liberal capitalist context that has been shaped by global pressures (Koelble and Lipuma 2005; Robins 2005), which has in turn shaped how remedies are understood and enacted. State policies attempt with varying degrees of success to engage the historical residues and social consequences of colonialism and apartheid. They do so in shifting global and local economic contexts, which have influenced a move from the Reconstruction and Development Programme (RDP) with which the newly democratic South African state commenced ruling, and under the auspices of which state housing subsidies were established, through the more capital-friendly Growth, Employment and Redistribution Programme (GEAR), which instilled fiscal stability but was not able to alleviate poverty, to the most recent Accelerated and Shared Growth Initiative for South Africa (ASGISA) which aims to increase GDP and halve unemployment and poverty by 2014. The liberal democratic process and the procedures that have resulted foreground the individual and his or her rights rather than relationships, in a context that presupposes a radical break – post-apartheid – that does not in fact exist, particularly where the liberal ideal has sedimented as an aspirational norm.

My work with residents of The Park/Village over an extended period (1991–present) demonstrates the scale of social devastation caused by capitalism's colonial and apartheid forms. These have given shape and generational continuity to everyday lives edged in roughness. It also demonstrates the effort that goes into making everyday lives worth living and relationships worth having. Ongoing humiliations include being poor in an environment that stresses the accumulation of goods and the accomplishment of prescribed social forms – marriage, the nuclear family, privacy, home-ownership, steady employment, health among them – as markers of distinction, markers to which people desperately aspire and against which they are measured and found wanting.

Despite the move to formal housing and the amelioration of basic living conditions that this enabled, forms of rawness endure in The Village. Changing people's environments does not necessarily produce radical social change unless accompanied by changes in their material circumstances. This is important to acknowledge in the context of present state policy which aims to eradicate shacks but which has not yet been successful in equitably redistributing wealth, resources and opportunities. Real wages for workers have declined since 2000, despite positive growth in the economy, and the gap between rich and poor is widening. While state social grants have been made more widely available, no one can imagine that they are adequate or sufficient to the maintenance and well-being of families.[1]

In the context of dire impoverishment, histories of violence and social injustice manifest as interpersonal violence, crime, illness and untimely death. Residents frequently tell me stories of abuse and abandonment. They describe themselves and others using words more apposite to the life of animals. Older residents lament what they see as a growing insubordination of young people. I am told that there is an increase in drug trafficking. The Village has not escaped the scourge of tik (crystal methamphetamine), an extremely cheap and easily manufactured drug that has flooded the Western Cape, bringing violence and the destruction of lives and property in its wake.[2] Several of the young people who appear in this book are now said to be tik-heads. While ARVs are now available, poor people are still likely to bear the brunt of the burden of ill-health, both in their bodies and in social relations stretched to breaking point to deal with the vagaries of inadequate material resources and state care. People are still reliant on personal networks to access work opportunities, and these are becoming less effective in the face of a large and growing pool of potential labour. In the post-apartheid era, reports of violence against children and women have increased.

Roughness endures in the present as people struggle in almost impossible conditions to attain ideals that themselves are underpinned by a kind of violence: the implicit violence of being called to be other than one can be and the violence that underwrites a specific model of *ordentlikheid* which is heavily classed and gendered in nature. I have argued that people internalise normative models about the good life and how to live it. Many seek to accomplish and adhere to a liberal model of decency that is extremely difficult to achieve. Residents are aware of this and comment both cynically and despairingly on it but, nevertheless, for many *ordentlikheid* seems the only way out of the everyday rawness of life unless one is prepared to run the risks that are so clearly described in the extract with which I opened the chapter.

On Tuesday 11 December 2007, the daily newspaper, the *Cape Times*, ran two articles about The Village. '"Model" settlement loses soul to vice, apathy and friction' ran the headline of one (Life supplement, p. 3). The other, alongside a story about legal challenges to the state's urban relocations policy, began 'The impoverished people living in a Reconstruction and Development Programme (RDP) housing project ... say they have been "dumped" by local authorities' (p. 5). Both articles describe the lack of amenities; the presence of *subeens*; and the failures of local authorities, state policy, private enterprise, civil society and the residents themselves for 'crippling social problems', including unemployment, alcohol and drug abuse, child neglect and domestic violence. Estimates of unemployment vary between seventy and ninety per cent. Residents are unmotivated and many have stopped seeking work. Care workers report that children are neglected and that parents trade food packages for alcohol. A trustee of The Consortium that donated the land on which The Village is built is quoted as saying 'the community has done little to help itself'. Residents and care workers concur. Asked 'What is good here?', Heibrey, Ponkies's youngest daughter, now a care worker, is reported as saying, 'Lots of the children are very talented. Give them a stage and they dance like Michael Jackson, sing like Whitney Houston. These are things that need to be stimulated, to give them hope'.

Hope has loomed large in much of the discourse of making a better life in South Africa, and in this community particularly. Over time, like others in South Africa, those who came to be resident in The Park/Village hoped to be permitted to live as citizens, free of racial and other discriminations. They hoped to live in town without legal restriction and police harassment. They hoped to be granted access to basic amenities and later hoped that new housing would give rise to new possibilities for self-formation and social respect. Many of those hopes are social in character, oriented towards redressing historic wrongs. Historically, they have given rise to mass action, protest, insurrection, delicate negotiation, an inclusive vision of the future. Much has been accomplished but, as is clear in this study, the legacies of structural violence endure. In The Village, it seems that the scope and scale of what people can imagine as redress have narrowed to the individual and to the very young. Stimulating children's desires to sing and dance – that is, to be children – is too little to ask.

Residents agree. When I visited in 2009 to share the news that I had completed the book, there were signs of renewed social effort in the community. Dina and Sandra and Clive and Bernie commented on the palpable sense of possibility in the settlement. Community leaders had formed a 'citizens group' focusing on education in rights. There were moves to identify and remove tik dealers. I was told that there had been fewer deaths than in the years immediately after the move to The Village. A women's group, aptly named 'Hope', had started. These facts alert us to the ongoing nature of making social worlds worth inhabiting in the face of hardship.

In making everyday lives, people juggle with terribly limited possibilities at hand. These are not 'choices' in the sense implied by liberal notions of the sovereign subject. Their improvisational quality is suggestive of the kind of temporality that violence and poverty instantiate. The result for many extremely poor people is a kind of ontological insecurity and the production and contestation of forms of rawness that may appear to be self-willed but are in fact historical. The post-apartheid tragedy is two-fold: that rawness exists and that individuals believe that they are solely responsible for it.

Endnotes

CHAPTER 1

'Teen die pad, Die Bos' (Alongside the Road, The Bush)

1   These are pseudonyms. 'The Bush' was renamed 'The Park' in about 1995, after the first democratic elections and when it became clear that not only would the site be accorded recognition but that residents might soon obtain formal houses. The new houses, built a few kilometres from the site of The Bush/Park, are known as The Village. The names also map a slow formalisation of the sites—from bushes under which people sheltered to more formal residential arrangements. Throughout the book, I use the terms appropriate to the time period about which I am writing at any given time.

2   Unless otherwise stated, all translations are from Afrikaans words.

3   In 2006, South Africa ranked 121 of 177 countries on the United Nations Human Development Index (http://hdr.undp.org/hdr2006/statistics/indicators/17.html, accessed August 2007). In other words, twelve years after transition to majority rule, it remains an extremely unequal society, and the gap between rich and poor is growing.

4   The distinction is the basis for Michel Foucault's elaboration of biopower, a form of power over populations. For an excellent exploration of this in a South African context, see Alex Butchart (1998).

CHAPTER 2
'I long to live in a house'

1   The common English term, vagrants, which gives its name to the laws under which many people were prosecuted, does not have either the poetic ring of bosslaper, or its accuracy.

2   'n Dop is a measure of alcohol. Banned in the 1960s, the dop system, under which farm labourers were paid in part in alcohol, was central to management of farm labour. In 1998, Dopstop research (www.dopstop.org.za) found that almost ten per cent of farms surveyed gave daily alcohol to workers. The individualised provision of alcohol seems largely to have ended, but there is a bustling smokkel (smuggle) trade in alcohol; individuals buy alcohol at wholesale prices and resell to workers.

3   The terms 'squatter' and 'informal' settlements reflect differences in legal status at the time. Squatting was illegal in terms of the Prevention of Squatting Act. Informal settlements, although sharing many of the physical characteristics of squatter camps, had a degree of legitimated, if not quite legal, standing.

4   There has been massive urban growth in the city and many farms on the periphery of urban areas have become low density, middle- to high-cost housing estates.

5   She uses the Afrikaans word 'huise' which translates as both houses and homes. I have used whichever term seems most apposite to the conversation.

6   Die Bos is the name of the farm onto which The Park had backed. When I first began working there, the settlement had no formal name and residents referred to it variously as 'Die Bos', 'ons plek' (our place), 'die kamp' (the camp), 'die plakkerskamp' (the squatter camp). Later, they began to refer to it as 'the ghetto'. The area was renamed The Park in 1995, and was replaced by The Village in 2001.

7   In the event, within six months after the residents of The Park had moved to The Village, almost every yard was fenced. Residents purchased wire and wooden posts and a couple of men resident in the community charged R20 for their labour in erecting the fences.

8   Later, when residents had moved into formal houses, one man explained to me that the forms of privacy that private property created were inimical to sociability. He said that in The Park if a neighbour had played his music too loudly, one could complain, but now that there was private property, the neighbour had the right to do as he wished and no one could intervene. While certainly not an accurate representation of the relations that private property engenders – the majority of legal cases have to do with conflicts between neighbours – his comment is nevertheless revealing.

9   South Africans in general are high consumers of alcohol. As a result alcohol consumption is not as stigmatised as the use of drugs. The consequences of alcohol-use for individual and public health are horrific. One in five patients treated for alcohol problems is under 20 years of age; foetal alcohol spectrum (FAS) disorder rates are high, affecting one in twenty-five children in the Western and Northern Cape; alcohol-related illnesses and accidents make up the third highest cause of death in the country (http://www.mrc.ac.za//public/facts13.htm, accessed 31 August 2007). Several of the children and some of the adults in The Park were visibly affected by FAS. Mandrax and marijuana were easily and cheaply available in The Park. 'White pipe', a mixture of Mandrax and marijuana smoked in a broken bottle was the most common form of heavy drug use.

10   A recent study of violence on commercial farms in the Western Cape (REACH 2007) found that half the respondents had experienced sexual violence, and one-third of respondents under 12 years had experienced sexual abuse, usually committed by relatives or neighbours. Alcohol and stressful living conditions were implicated in violence. Many of the residents of The Park had previously lived on farms. Domestic violence was common (Ross 1996).

11   People frequently described their lives and world in terms more apposite to animals. Janine and I translated spuls as 'horny'; it implies 'being in heat' like an animal. The other common word was jas, a slang version of jag, to hunt. There is a predatory sense in how men spoke of women.

12   Some residents say that drug use, particularly the use of buttons (Mandrax, active ingredient Methaqualone), is preferable to alcohol-use because buttons do not stimulate lust or

jealousy, whereas alcohol is thought to produce both. Developed as a sedative, Mandrax is highly addictive. Although banned in 1977, it is widely and cheaply available on the Cape Flats, where it is usually smoked as 'white pipe', crushed and smoked with marijuana (*dagga*) in a bottleneck. Users report aggressive feelings when it starts to wear off.

13   Pierre Mayol notes of wine consumption in a working-class district of Lyon, France, that even though it undoes social distinctions and prevailing moral codes, drunkenness is opposed to revolution (social change) because it inaugurates an orientation to time – nostalgia – that is opposed to that of revolution. Rather than being directed to the future, drunkenness 'brings the subversive dreams about the social to a halt, because in its extreme manifestation, it is a dismissal of History' (1998: 94). 'Drunkenness remains, fundamentally, a pathos for the ego. Revolution, on the contrary, assumes a belief, an uprising, a rigor, an assortment of competing forces, and even more, an insertion into the social thickness that it is a question of transforming' (1998: 94). Perhaps the root of the despair some people expressed about alcohol-use after the move to The Village lies in their anxiety that it effaced the possibilities of change they so desperately sought.

14   There was no piped water supply to the shack settlement. Water was available at a tank, which was open at specified hours. Residents purchased water at a cost of R2 per 20 l.

15   Ironically, the development discourse of 'model communities' was used by the apartheid state to justify forced removals in terms of the Group Areas Act.

16   Proper sanitation has long been a core concern in housing and development discourse in South Africa. Early proposals for site-and-service schemes, which provided stands with piped water and toilets, were rejected by residents of informal settlements. Further exploration is beyond the scope of the chapter.

17   Residents' concerns about payment were not ill-founded – at present, rates and arrears are high and mounting. In January 2004, only 41 residents had made any payment at all. All community leaders were in arrears. In 2000, the state introduced free basic services at a minimum level for impoverished households.

18   Indeed, fires were frequent in The Park and two massive fires between 1999 and 2000 razed more than half the shacks in the settlement in each instance.

19   Ironically, the phrase has religious undertones; in a Christian context, God is described as being unchanging, always the same. My thanks to Marlon Burgess for this observation.

20   Domestic workers are particularly required to submit in this way, even as they see the underside of the lives of their ostensibly 'decent' employers.

21   Further detail is provided in Chapter Six.

22   There has, as yet, been insufficient attention to the modes of children's moral decision-making in relation to violence and the family in South Africa. Important exceptions are Reynolds (1995, 1997, 2000) and Henderson (1999).

23 The stress of life rematerialises in Chapter Six, and the transformation of *deurmekaar* lives into *ordentlike* ones is a theme I pursue later in the chapter.

24 In fact, teenaged pregnancy is not new despite the current moral panic about it (Mkhwanazi 2004). Most women in the settlement bore their first child while still teenagers. These children were often 'grown up' by their grandmothers (see Chapter Four). That there were a number of teenagers who had babies in the period 2000–2005 has more to do with the particular demographic of the settlement coming of age (there were few children between 8 and 16 in the settlement in 1991 when I began research) than with a historical change in reproductive patterns. Amoateng et al. (2007: 99) show that some forty-four per cent of South African women bear a first child before marriage. They do not state the average age of first pregnancy but according to the Census data for 2001, approximately thirty per cent of women bore their first child before the age of twenty (Statistics South Africa 2005: 76).

25 Many residents had been very ill, and several had told me that they were 'holding on' until they moved into the new houses. In the first few months after the move, two men were murdered and four adults and a child died of illnesses. See Chapter Seven.

26 For South Africans, the term is not neutral but is racially indexed. 'The community' usually refers to poor, black urbanites. It imposes a spurious similarity and congruity of goals. See Thornton and Ramphele (1988).

CHAPTER 3

Sense-scapes: senses and emotion in the making of place

1 Rastafari would not use the word zol among themselves, instead using *chullus* (chalice) to describe marijuana cigarettes and the rituals that accompany their use. However, zol was the word commonly used – by Rastafari and non-Rastafari alike – to describe such cigarettes to me. Its use indexes me as a double outsider: white, not a Rasta.

2 This is his nickname, acquired because his previous job had been in one of the security companies that proliferated in the post-apartheid era. Very few people in The Park were known by their given names; most were known only by nicknames. As most people had more than one nickname, acquired through different social networks (family, friends in The Park, friends outside The Park, work relationships, etc.), calling someone by a nickname immediately situated the relationship and social network. Very few people, even close friends, used or even knew one another's surnames. Had it not been for my survey work in which I specifically asked for surnames, I would have known the surnames of only two people, both leaders.

3 In 'Walking the City', Michel de Certeau writes that 'the panorama-city is a "theoretical" (that is, visual) simulacrum, in short a picture, whose condition of possibility is an oblivion and a misunderstanding of practices' (1988: 93), a fiction rendered by a 'voyeur-

god' who has made himself alien to 'murky intertwining daily behaviours' (ibid.). De Certeau argues that the people who are imagined as constituting the city have no temporal depth, no history. It is this 'universal subject' who is presumed to 'read' space as though it were a cartographic representation; a map. Tim Ingold has characterised this mode of knowing as that of the surveyor whose task is to combine data 'to produce a single picture which is independent of any point of observation' (2002: 191), and, one might add, which rests on a notion of time as standardised (Harvey 1996). Yet, as Nadia Seremetakis (1996) has shown, sensory experiences are modulated by history and historical processes change the possibilities of the experiential. In other words, while developers and planners imagine a universal person as the inhabitant of cities, the actual inhabitants are beings whose experiences are shaped by historical processes and who experience space differently from one another as a result of those processes.

4   Writing of cartographic representation, Stephania Pandolfo notes that bird's-eye views became popular in Europe during the Renaissance. She comments that the view from afar and above, from a fixed standpoint, granted the painter 'the privilege of presentness' (1997: 34). Citing Corbin, she compares this (footnote 40, p. 320) to Persian miniatures which encourage active participation (and thus a sense of temporal unfolding) on the part of the person examining a painting, not privilege and presentness. The latter creates a viewer, the former, an itinerant. Cartographic presentness is achieved at the expense of historical depth, and the visual replaces movement as a means to engage space.

5   De Certeau argues that in the last three hundred years the map has become dissociated from stories (itineraries, tours, pilgrimages), pushing away 'the operations of which it is the result or the necessary condition' (1988: 121), leaving in their stead only the abstract representation that, he argues, colonises space (ibid.; see also Mbembe 2000). Maps are common currency in modern life, and in that sense, if De Certeau is correct, then we are all made complicit with our own abstraction and colonisation. Edward Casey hints at this too, arguing that 'disembodiment is a geographic ideal' (1996: 49, footnote 24).

6   Even this is not as straightforward as it sounds. Discussions with South African urbanites who have visited cities in the US, for example, reveal common difficulties in navigating. Urban South Africans tend to give directions in which a sense of the individual's orientation and movement are implicit, and often directions assume features in the landscape (for example, 'when you reach the station, turn left; carry on straight till you reach Main Rd and turn right'). There is, in these directions, a sense that the instructor is following the route in the imagination: the instructions carry a sense of embodied experience and imply an interpersonal relationality; the instructor accompanies the walker in the mind. American urbanites tend to give more abstracted directions, using the cardinal points of the compass ('go west on 110th') and linguistic

clues (for example, 'avenue' or 'street' signals direction and not, as in South Africa or England, a type or quality of road and its urban/rural/suburban location). Americans generally offer directions that are individualised (not relational) in relation to a more abstracted realm.

7 Ian Hacking (1998) describes the emergence in French psychiatry of a classification of 'dissociative fugue' to describe people who 'wandered' compulsively. They were considered mentally unstable, to lack firm grounding and a home was an indication that something was amiss.

8 De Certeau's lieu(x) has been translated as 'place'. An alternative might be 'sites' but this would not do justice to the openness of De Certeau's concept. De Certeau's terminology seems awkward in English, where space is usually used to refer to the abstract and place to the domesticated or known. I have used his rendition of space/place in relation to discussions of his work and the more usual English understandings in relation to Ardener's work. De Certeau's argument about 'the proper' is particularly germane in relation to an understanding of colonial, modernist and apartheid spatial planning, a topic that is beyond the scope of this paper (but see for example, Pinnock 1989; Rabinow 1995; Caldeira 2000; Robins 2002).

9 Indeed, their lives have been marked by differences in their mobility. He claimed to have travelled widely in southern Africa, propelled, he said, by curiosity. She had been born near The Park and until she was already in her late twenties, had never been to the city centre, a mere forty kilometres away.

CHAPTER 4
Relationships that count and how to count them

1 Zolani Ngwane (2003) offers an excellent review and consideration of the large literature in this field.

2 It lies outside the scope of this chapter to discuss them in detail. Readers are referred to Wolpe (1972), Cock (1980), Burman and Reynolds (1986), Boonzaier and Sharp (1988), Reynolds (1989, 1997), Wilson and Ramphele (1989), Glantz and Spiegel (1995), Ross (1995), Ngwane (2003).

3 This clause is modified later in the form (p. 3) to refer to 'persons who are financially dependent on the applicant'. 'Spouses' are required to sign an affidavit that acknowledges that the details are correct and that s/he recognises that s/he is liable for prosecution if the details are incorrect or fraudulent (p. 10).

4 In total, 195 applications are officially recorded as having been made by residents of The Park. My wording here is deliberately elliptical. The housing list shows 195 successful applicants. Some people currently boarding in The Village were resident in the shack area and claim that they have made application, but that, although eligible, they did not receive housing. Their status remains unclear. Approximately one-third (n=62) of

the applications list women as the primary applicant. In seventy-one per cent of the latter cases, applications list only one adult applicant; twenty-four per cent of cases are accounted for by women as first applicant and men as second, and the remainder is accounted for by applications made by two adult women together. Thus, approximately twenty-four per cent of the total applications were made by households where no adult man is registered as having a material interest in the property. However, I caution readers not to rush to the conclusion that these twenty-four per cent of households therefore represent woman-only households in anything but general terms. Domestic arrangements in The Park are complex, and the absence of a male from the application does not imply that there is no man present in the domestic unit, or that men who are present do not have rights that can be actualised. Rather, as I show, it points to the difference in the ways in which relationship is reckoned in law and in practice.

5 A Griqua *dominee* visiting The Park once told me that it had been customary for the first-born child of a newly-wed couple to be 'donated' to one of the couple's parents, who were responsible for the child's upkeep and moral development. I have not been able to ascertain the accuracy of this statement, but it does suggest that current patterns of childcare have deeper historical roots – or that tradition is being carefully woven to legitimate contemporary practice. Linda Waldman (pers. comm. September 2007) notes that among Griqua 'grandmother' may refer to a woman's mother, or to a woman of her age, or to the sister of a woman's mother, or her cousin, or even the midwife who attended the birth. In other words, 'grandmother' does not necessarily signify a biological relation or even one that can be clearly (genealogically) described or delineated in a way that holds over time.

6 A Xhosa woman who had sent her infant son to the Eastern Cape to be brought up by her parents because it was safer to live there than in the squatter camp in Cape Town described how hurt and upset she was when she had visited over the Christmas holidays and heard her son address his grandmother as 'Mama'. She had carefully persuaded him that she was his mother not his sister and that he should recognise and address her as such. Ethnographic works by Reynolds (1989), Jones (1990), Henderson (1999) and Bray et al. (n.d.) address some of the emotional experiences of relations sundered in this way.

7 Children seldom call adults by their first or given names and use formal terms of address (*Meneer* or *Mevrou*; Mister or Mrs) only for teachers and complete strangers, usually white. People commonly use the honorifics *ouma* and *oupa* (grandma and grandpa), *tannie* and *oom* (aunt and uncle) followed by a person's first name or *bynaam* (nickname) to demarcate age differences and signal respect.

In 'western' reckoning Baby and Price, who are siblings, should stand in the same genealogical relation to Meitjie. Nevertheless, Meitjie holds that Price stands to her in the position of father and Baby as grandmother. The terminology may seem perverse given that western accounts of kinship, predicated on biology and genealogy, hold that the parental generation is closer and more responsible than a grandparental one, so one might expect that Meitjie would call Price 'Oupa' (grandfather), given that he is less than involved in her care, and Baby 'Ma', but for two factors: one, Meitjie knows her biological mother, and two, grandmothers stand in an extremely significant relationship of care. Meitjie's assessment is an accurate representation of local knowledge about kinship relations.

8 Rachel Bray's recent unpublished work demonstrates that HIV-positive mothers made careful decisions about their children's residence and cultivated kin relationships in order to secure their children's future care.

9 Of course, such ideas are likely to change when relationships are caught in the throes of controversies over property, requiring increasing legal intervention, and already legal contestation over property is increasing.

10 Such fluidity in relationships is not uncommon in postcolonial Africa. Ogden (1996) describes the range of possible subject positions that householding and sexual relations generated in Kampala and shows that a rich local taxonomy exists to describe these. See also Amoateng and Heaten 2007.

11 The phrase may have been 'Ons is vry nou': people speak rapidly and run their words together. If this was the phrasing then the translation is 'We're free now'. The way the phrase is spoken is wonderfully ambiguous.

12 Elaborate wedding ceremonies. The bride usually wears white, traditionally a symbol of purity, hence 'white wedding'.

13 It is common cause that men take little responsibility for the material upkeep of children born to vat en sit relationships. Over the period of my research, women have become considerably more assertive in using legal remedies to secure support for children, but their efforts are often frustrated by the slow pace of the courts and also by men's recalcitrance. Several women reported to me that the fathers of their children had 'thrown away' jobs when it was clear that they would be sued for maintenance.

14 Price did not contribute to her upkeep and in many respects he was dependent on Meitjie's care. However, because she was a minor, she was listed as his dependant. The privileging of age in the state's definitions obscures actual relations of care.

15 However, this law is circumscribed in some instances: RDP housing and some of the City of Cape Town's property interventions are two such. The case would have to be heard on its merits and in relation to the laws circumscribing convention.

CHAPTER 5

'Just working for food': making a living, making do and getting by

1 A reference to seasonal agricultural work. Many of the residents of The Park worked as seasonal casual labourers on wine and fruit farms in the area. A large number of

residents had either grown up or lived on commercial farms prior to settling in The Bush/Park, and many of them had worked on farms as children. Child labour is illegal in South Africa but the use of children as labourers continues. Those who live on farms are considered to be 'helping' their parents and learning the trade. They are not usually directly remunerated. Susan Levine (1999) has documented differential treatment of child workers in the nearby Breede River Valley.

2 Environmental health hazards include pesticide poisoning as a prime cause of illness among farm labourers in the Western Cape. See London (2003) and London and Bailie (2001).

3 Labourers are allocated a row to tend/harvest and, during the harvest, are usually paid per bucket of grapes harvested. Some young people were employed to harvest plums and oranges and some made *kleingeld* (small amounts of money, change) by *optelwerk* (casual work), collecting fallen oranges and *naartjies* (tangerines).

4 'Kitchen work' refers to work in restaurants; it is thus mostly evening work and transport home is usually included. Although a demanding job, because everyday daytime living noise made it difficult to sleep during the day in The Park, the fact that transport was provided was considered a major benefit. Poor people in Cape Town may spend up to twenty per cent of their income on transport costs (Kane 2006: 9).

5 All Rand amounts have been converted to the appropriate USD value at the time the data was collected.

6 The existence of such legislation does not mean that workers' conditions were necessarily improved: some farmers outsourced employment or sourced casual workers, and workers are covered by UIF only if they work for more than 24 hours a month. This disqualifies a large number of casual workers including domestic workers who work for three or fewer days a week. Despite the fact that it is a legal requirement to register domestic workers for UIF, a great many employers do not do so.

7 Some, members of 'numbers gangs' in prison, find it difficult to find work: the tattoos that identify them as members of prison gangs brand them to the outside world as 'skollies' or worse.

8 By the time I began work in The Park, however, most Rastafari were employed in the building sector. A few were skilled artisans (carpenters and bricklayers) and others worked as manual labourers. They all obtained their jobs by word of mouth.

9 While useful, averages such as this imply that incomes are regular and reliable, thus masking variation within the settlement and across the agricultural seasons, and disguise the terrible financial troughs faced by casual workers.

10 Unemployment Insurance is available to those who are registered with the Fund, and who work more than 24 hours a month. Employers and employees each contribute one per cent of the employee's salary to the Fund and employees can claim unemployment, maternity, illness, adoption and dependant benefits from it. Benefits

range to a maximum of sixty per cent of a worker's salary and are available for no more than 238 days in four years. See Unemployment Insurance Act no. 63 of 2001.

11 Seekings (2006: 49) notes that in 'no other country in the South does social assistance cover such a wide range of circumstances, reach so many of its citizens, or cost so much in relation to GDP'; by 2005, South African expenditure on welfare was the highest in the developing world, at three per cent of GDP (ibid.)

12 This is not new. Indeed, a 2002 study, 'the Getting By study' of 1 111 households in the Eastern and Western Cape revealed that 'pensions compete with wage-earnings as the most important source of income in poor households' and that in rural black households the state pension accounts for seventy-five per cent of income while among urban households comprising black and coloured residents, pensions account for approximately twenty-nine per cent of income (Moller and Ferreira 2002 reported in This Day, 23 February 2004). Similar findings have been made for KwaZulu-Natal (Adato et al., n.d.) and the Northern Cape (Waldman 2007).While it is true that state grants and pensions generated extensive networks of reliance in The Park/Village, it should not be assumed that grants automatically revert to discrete household units or that recipients disburse to the same people.

13 The Coloured Labour Preference Area (1955) applied to an area demarcated by what came to be known as the Eiselin Line.

14 Tensions, doubtless fuelled by others, grew to a point where community leaders decided that instead of transferring intact sections of the settlement to the new suburbs so as to retain the bonds of neighbourhood, as had earlier been decided, each section of The Village would consist of 'Coloured' residents and at least one Xhosa-speaking family and one Rastafarian household. Later, community leaders described this social engineering as an experiment in developing racial tolerance in the community in order that it might become a model for others. There is an uncanny reversal here of apartheid's racial separations.

15 This phrasing is not grammatically correct but in common with my interlocutors, I shape the linguistic form to fit the grammatical demands here. The correct version would be hy/sy skarrel.

16 In 2001, only two people had completed Matric (the school-leaving examination) and most adults in the settlement had left school after completing Standard Five, well before the official school-leaving age of 16.

17 The architect of apartheid, Hendrik Verwoed, held that Black people were fit only for menial labour and should be educated no further than would befit them to perform such tasks.

18 Under apartheid, racial classifications determined when children were considered to attain majority. African children were legally able to work at 16 years of age, Coloureds and whites at 18 years (Burman 1986: 9). Although very young when she began working, Elise's family circumstances were such that she had to work.

19 So great is the violence that in 2007 the South African Human Rights Commission held hearings into human rights violations on farms.

20 Global trends towards 'streamlining' and focusing on 'core business', and post-apartheid legislation relating to agro-industries, particularly policies regulating wages and residence rights, produced some unintended consequences. Labour relations, including contracting and managing, was frequently outsourced to contractors, who employed people at minimum wages (and sometimes below) for short periods of time, thereby circumventing the progressive provisions of legislation that secured basic rights for agricultural workers. It is beyond the scope of this chapter to describe these in full: interested persons should refer to Du Toit and Ally (2003, especially pp. 16 and 24ff.) and Du Toit (2004).

21 The fourth young woman was offered a job but, lacking the necessary identification documents which had been destroyed in a fire that ravaged The Park some years earlier and had not yet been replaced by the Department of Home Affairs, was unable to take up the post.

22 Exceptions were the families that moved to The Village from a farm neighbouring The Park, as part of the estate development deal, and Oom Neels, who worked his whole life on a nearby wine farm until he was disabled and lost his job and with it residence 'rights' for himself and his family.

23 'Working for Water' is a state project that aims to eradicate alien trees from the Western Cape, particularly its waterways, in order to protect the fynbos, the Cape floral kingdom, the world's richest plant biodiversity.

24 She reported that it was common practice for women to secure jobs on the project and then 'fall' pregnant, thereby ensuring that they received paid maternity leave. This is an excellent example of skarreling, making as broad a use as possible of existing opportunities. I am not sure of the extent to which her claims about pregnancy are true, but according to the Department of Water Affairs which is responsible for the project, 'Following the high incidence of unwanted and unplanned pregnancies in Working for Water projects, WfW joined forces with the Planned Parenthood Association and UNFPA to provide reproductive health care training and support to workers' (http://www.dwaf.gov.za/wfw/SocialDev/, accessed 18 September 2007). Even as anecdotal evidence, Charmaine's comment does point to the importance of proper state support for maternity leave, something as yet not available to non-working women in South Africa. Charmaine uses the Afrikaans phrase 'Sy met die lyf geraak het' (She became with life) to describe being pregnant. Her use of this phrase rather than the more common 'Sy's swanger' or 'Sy verwag' – 'She's pregnant' or 'She's expecting' indicates that she is speaking to someone with whom she is not familiar, hence using an ordentlike turn of phrase to mark her respect for an outsider (see Chapter Six).

25 I do not have data pertaining to the frequency of premature birth among residents

of The Park but many of the children born in the early period of my research were reported to have been premature.

26 The phrase she uses for disability grant, *ongeskikte geld*, also implies 'not good enough' (Linda Waldman, personal communication September 2007)

27 There is a contradiction in that men are ideally held to be responsible for household well-being but in practice it is women's work and incomes that go into supporting the household.

28 In his Budget speech of 2006, the Minister of Finance, Trevor Manuel, commented that South Africans needed to learn to save. Since 2006, Reserve Bank Governor Tito Mboweni has repeatedly upped the repo rate in an attempt to curb consumer spending and encourage saving.

29 Savings groups known as *stokvels* or *gooi-goois* (Afrikaans) or *imigalelo* (Xhosa), common throughout the country (see Lukhele 1990; Ardener L & Burman 1995), were not very common in The Park/Village, as most people felt themselves unable to make the kinds of commitment to regular payment that they required. But among the few households that engaged in cooperative sharing of this nature, moral imperatives ensured that obligations were met. A number have purchased goods on hire-purchase agreements, a point to which I return below.

30 In this, he offers an important counter to Michel Foucault's less optimistic use of the terms. For Foucault, both are power systems: strategies are the means through which war is enabled and tactics are the procedures through which bodies are placed in relation to one another in classificatory and normative systems that govern by creating subservience to law, order and peace (1995: 168).

31 This is true even where some people engage in illegal activities.

32 A reference to a local cartoon strip created by Stephen Francis and Rico Schachel that depicts relations between a middle-class white employer and a black domestic worker who invariably gets the upper hand (see www.madamandeve.co.za).

33 Anecdotal evidence offered by researchers at the Medical Research Council (Bourne, personal communication, June 2001) suggests that people moving from shacks to formal housing suffer malnutrition as a result of the changes in or collapse of previously existing commensal relations, brought about by strong social pressures to conform to ideals of self-sustainability associated with urban dwelling. In such instances, the social pressures to be seen 'not to be poor' have profound material consequences.

CHAPTER 6

Truth, lies, *stories* and straight-talk: on addressing another

1 Several residents reported that they had fared poorly at job interviews because their Afrikaans did not match the 'higher' form sought. As Clive put it, 'it's ('higher' Afrikaans)

not really the kind of Afrikaans we speak'. This is a major understatement: the Afrikaans in common use in The Park/Village is regionally specific. It makes use of many invented and slang words, and is tonally characterised by what is known (disparagingly by outsiders) as the Malmesbury brei (in which the letter 'r' is pronounced at the back of the throat). Tone is indicative of class status: the brei is marked low class.

2   It is for this reason that biography is offered at many African funerals; the social recording of death is the apposite moment to sum up a life. See Comaroff and Comaroff (2001).

3   For example, while employed as a farm labourer Raymond and friends used to hunt jackals and porcupines for food. His description of laying a trap for a jackal, waiting and being disappointed time and again is detailed with knowledge about the animal's habits and crosscut with folklore about its wiliness. He says that the animal bit off its paw while caught in the trap, then waited alongside its severed paw to attack the trappers. 'Anyway, he lay there waiting for us, pretending to be dead .... When we were a few metres away from him, he flew up and jumped on my back. Just look here! .... He bites and scratches. He attacks you with his paws as well as his mouth! You should've seen his fangs! ... [L]uckily that paw was lying with his other nails that could've ripped me apart. But those three paws and his mouth were bad enough! I peed and I almost pooped my pants! ...'

4   Judith Butler (2005: 36) writes, 'So the account of myself that I give in discourse never fully expresses or carries this living self. My words are taken away as I give them, interrupted by the time of a discourse that is not the same as the time of my life'. Adam Philips too is puzzled by the 'I' present in speaking. In reflecting on the I of psychoanalytic free association, he wonders whether the process is one of revealing what is authentically (one might say, essentially) present but hidden, or of creating the self. Is the process one of midwifery or of creativity afresh? He wonders whether a revolutionary autobiography might not make the word 'self' redundant: 'Where once we had described a person ... we would now be describing drifts of attention' (2006: 99).

5   This poses challenges to researchers, who are usually of a different class and social status. Ethnographic research obviates such suspicion to some extent. My initial lack of fluency in Afrikaans gave residents the edge over me, but the status differential instilled by apartheid remains. Janine's presence, her familiarity with similar social environments and her marvellously quick and witty Afrikaans were important in offsetting people's anxieties during interviews.

6   People often spoke about violence – usually violence that other people, particularly children – had encountered, and did so in graphic detail. Women very seldom told of their own experiences of violence, even though domestic abuse was common and women frequently bore the marks of men's rage.

7   Radcliffe-Brown (1940) offered a structural-functionalist theory to joking relationships and their counterpart, avoidance practices, by arguing that they served to maintain equilibrium between individuals and groups potentially in conflict. He later noted a structural principle: that avoidances are practised in relation to those of 'ascending generation' while joking relationships characterise relations between those of the same generation (1949: 135). Brant (1948) challenged the approach by cross-tabulating ethnographic data from a sample of societies and showing that the correlation between sexual partner preference and joking relationships is weak. In 1949, Radcliffe-Brown reiterated his theory, in response to Marcel Griaule's critique of the comparative method. Of interest to my study is Radcliffe-Brown's comment that the joking relationship marks a special kind of friendship (1949: 134), one in which there is an imputation of a kin-like (but not kinship) relation based on reciprocity and also an obligation not to take offence. In other words, the reciprocal responsibility is to accept with good grace the exposure to which one is subjected in wordplay.

8   Sachs's comments arise in the context of the case of Laugh It Off vs. SAB Miller heard before the Constitutional Court of South Africa, Justice Moseneke presiding (CCT 42/04; full judgment available at http://www.constitutionalcourt.org.za/uhtbin/cgisirsi/20070825181133/SIRSI/0/520/J-CCT42-04). Concurring with the Presiding Justice's finding, Sachs prefaces his comments with the question, 'Does the law have a sense of humour?' He finds that, 'The Constitution cannot oblige the dour to laugh. It can, however, prevent the cheerless from snuffing out the laughter of the blithe spirits among us' (ibid.), and, in a footnote, cites Umberto Eco: 'Perhaps the mission of those who love mankind is to make people laugh at the truth, to make truth laugh ...' (note 34, p. 63). He continues: 'A society that takes itself too seriously risks bottling up its tensions and treating every example of irreverence as a threat to its existence. Humour is one of the great solvents of democracy. It permits the ambiguities and contradictions of public life to be articulated in non-violent forms. It promotes diversity. It enables a multitude of discontents to be expressed in a myriad of spontaneous ways. It is an elixir of constitutional health' (ibid., pp. 64–5).

9   It is worth noting in passing that many Africans consider it utterly rude to pass someone without greeting them. 'You pass a dog like that, not a person', is how one woman described it to me.

10 It is not an accident that, like its English counterparts 'voice' and 'vote', stem is the Afrikaans word for both.

11 The question of how one comes to be free is raised again in the context in which everyday language carries such symbolic violence. The sheer task of becoming truly free is revealed in its full scale when this is considered.

12 Perhaps my differential response to Mem and Hendrik's writings rests on a particular claim made by a child's distress. It may have to do with the fact that Hendrik wrote

about his own particular circumstances whereas Mem's reflections, although specific to her personal context, were reflective of a broader predicament facing other children too.

13 Raymond's words are particularly telling in that we had been discussing South Africa's Truth and Reconciliation Commission on which I had conducted research (Ross 2003). His words are an implicit castigation of those in authority and whites in general who failed to apologise for apartheid, to express remorse at its evils or to make adequate redress for the structural and interpersonal violence it generated and sanctioned. Life in The Park was a direct outcome of apartheid policies. Implicitly, Raymond is reflecting on the structural and historical limits imposed on the possibilities of his own life.

14 Didier Fassin (2006) warns against over-interpretation in relation to witchcraft. I agree with his anxiety that emphases on witchcraft may run the risk of reproducing stereotypes about superstition but note that it is in the nature of the language associated with witchcraft (metaphor and indirect speech) to invite over-interpretation. Witchcraft accusation 'works' by blurring the relation between a word and a referent. Pointing to language's excess, it invites people to interpret, re-interpret and over-interpret, in an almost compulsive way.

15 This is an interesting point in relation to Das's argument that rumour re-circulates prior, dormant histories and stereotypes that may engender violence. In the example I cite here, the possibility of rumour is met with the sanction of violence: violence precedes the language that is feared.

CHAPTER 7

Illness and accompaniment

1 According to the World Health Organisation (2005: 25), in 2003 South Africa ranked eighth in the world in terms of its estimated TB burden.

2 Direct Observation Technique: in order to reduce 'non-compliance' with TB medication regimes, community workers are responsible for administering scheduled drugs. In The Park, the DOT worker received a small salary. As the role was considered a job, community leaders allocated it to someone deemed in dire need of work. In 2003, that person was a woman who was mentally challenged.

3 I do not have data pertaining to deaths in The Park, but fieldnotes reflect that people were frequently ill, particularly with respiratory infections. When they became very ill, many left The Park to be cared for by relatives elsewhere. When people die they are usually buried elsewhere and not in the local cemetery and so records there are not of great use in trying to ascertain rates of death.

4 In the period 2005–2007 residents recall that at least twenty-seven people whom I knew had died. Respondents say that the main causes of death were TB and HIV.

Three of the twenty-seven were murdered. I do not have data pertaining to birth rates, but for the period under consideration, they were lower than the death rate.

5   The Healthy Life Expectancy for South Africa is estimated at between 41 and 43 years. That is, a newborn can expect to live a total of some forty healthy years, being ill for the remainder of the lifespan (Health Systems Trust, http://www.hst.org.za/healthstats/145/data). The Western Cape has the lowest adult mortality rate in the country: in other words, people resident in that province are likely to live longer (http://www.hst.org.za/healthstats/178/data). This is owing to the disproportionate prevalence of wealthy and middle-class people in the city, with access to good health care, both preventive and curative. However, these data obscure the shocking health conditions of the poor in the city.

6   *Vrek*, part of everyday slang, properly refers to the death of an animal.

7   Part of everyday life involves skirting the edges of violence; children quickly learn how to navigate adults' moods, to assess how violence is folded into time ('don't aggravate him in the evenings when he has a *dop* in him: rather speak to him in the mornings' I was frequently told), and to avoid the areas where dangers are likely to lurk.

8   To the best of my knowledge, Rastafari reasoned only with male miscreants; female neighbours and committee members supported or argued with women offenders, suggesting that the hot-cold model is gendered. I have not been able to explore this further.

9   By the time I completed my research early in 2004, the state's anti-retroviral 'roll-out' programme had not yet been fully implemented. The Rastaman was the only resident I knew to be receiving biomedical attention for HIV – and that because he was a participant in an ARV drug-trial.

10 It is not inevitable that biomedicine will regard marijuana as contaminating – in California, for example, it is used in conjunction with chemotherapy as it is believed to relax the body and make it receptive to the drug regimes (S. Levine, personal communication, February 2006). There is a strong lobby among some biomedical practitioners in South Africa to make marijuana available as part of cancer treatments but to date it has been unsuccessful, as have been attempts by Gareth Prins, a Rastafari, to have *ganja* legalised. He argues that for Rastafari *ganja* is an important part of religious practice and curtailing its use is a contravention of the Constitutional guarantee of freedom to practise one's religion (Gareth Anver Prince vs. The President of the Law Society of the Cape of Good Hope and Others, Constitutional Court, Case CCT36/00).

11 Anne Fadiman (1998) has described a similar case in America, in which a young Hmong girl, daughter of Vietnamese refugees, was afflicted with what biomedical practitioners diagnosed as epilepsy and her family and Hmong friends, as spirit possession. The tensions over diagnosis were such that the parents were accused of neglect when they sought to have her treated in the traditional manner.

12　While I cannot verify this, the point is that the local model of childhood rests on school attendance and sexuality; young girls who are sexually active are often disallowed to attend school (see Chapter Three). Since the young woman in question was still at school, the assumption in the community was that she was not sexually active and that transmission must therefore have been by means other than sexual.

13　In 2000, President Mbeki convened a Presidential Advisory Panel on HIV/AIDS that included scientists who denied that there was a link between HIV and AIDS. Mbeki's own statements on illness are derived from a political-economic approach – one which understands illness as the outcome of negative social and environmental factors and that seeks to locate illness in relation to the broader historical processes that give rise to inequalities in everyday life. He was quickly branded 'an AIDS-denialist'.

14　These patterns are not specific to my fieldsite; anthropological studies elsewhere in South Africa report similar patterns of explanation across different regions, classes and education levels (see Levine and Ross 2002; Robbins 2004; Leclerc-Madlala 2005).

15　By understanding ill-being as directed human malevolence arising from tensions in social relations, ideas about witchcraft are able to address the problematic questions, 'why me? why now?' without resorting to purely metaphysical or anarchic models – that is, without resorting to the idea that illness is caused by an omnipotent Supreme Being or ascribing to a view of the world that holds it to be chaotic, random or meaningless.

16　This is interesting in view of reports that find that although the national co-infection rate of TB and HIV is estimated at 66.4 per cent (Medical Research Council, cited in Thom and Cullinan 2005), the co-infection rate in the Western Cape is lower than elsewhere in the country, at approximately 50 per cent (ibid.). This finding does not mean that residents' perceptions are incorrect – it may be that impoverishment and social fluidity are implicated in the co-infection of TB and HIV. Bamford, Loveday and Verkuijl (2004: 222) report that 'HIV infection in a person who is already infected with TB increases the risk of developing tuberculosis from 10% in a lifetime to 7–8% per year', and state representatives fear that people will not seek TB treatment for fear of HIV stigmatisation (Medical Research Council, cited in Thom and Cullinan 2005). Statistics SA state that in 2001 TB accounted for twelve per cent of deaths nationwide (ibid.). This is in marked contrast to Bradshaw et al. (2003: 685) who estimate that TB ranks third as cause of death (after HIV/AIDS and homicide/violence) and accounts for five per cent of deaths in 2000. They argue (2003: 686) that Statistics SA under-reported AIDS-related death by reporting on explanations reflected on death certificates rather than underlying causes of morbidity.

17　Age is assessed differently for men and women. Women's ages are assessed in relation to reproductive cycles through the generations – a woman is defined as 'old' if she has grandchildren, irrespective of her chronological age. Men's ages are more usually calculated chronologically.

18 There is an interesting and as yet under-researched link between generation and willingness to disclose; anecdotal evidence suggests that younger generations seem more willing to disclose their HIV status than an older generation. There have been some innovative attempts to generate disclosure and modes of transparency in discourse about sex, sexuality and illness. The LoveLife Campaign is one, 'STEPS for the Future' – a video and training project that addresses far-flung communities through the medium of film – another (see Levine 2004a and b).

19 I do not know the extent of their or anyone else's condom-usage: in the context of participant-observation, it seems voyeuristic and too demanding of others to ask. However, one of the young women who participated in these discussions was pregnant, suggesting that preventive measures were less than successful.

20 State health-care workers had delivered a supply of condoms 'for the community'. They were kept by one of the leaders of the community and people were expected to ask her for them: as can be imagined, few people did.

21 Smell is an important and under-researched aspect of illness and care of ill people. Susan Levine (personal communication) reports on a conversation she had with young people living in shantytowns who complained that HIV/AIDS made people smell. A counsellor explained that the smell was not the disease per se but that of bodies left unwashed because it was too arduous to collect sufficient water to clean people. See also Henderson (2004).

22 VIGS is the Afrikaans acronym for AIDS; TAC stands for Treatment Action Campaign – a social movement that lobbies for effective treatment for HIV/AIDS sufferers.

23 Suzanne Leclerc-Madlala (2005) reports rumours that in KwaZulu-Natal people pay others with low CD4 counts to impersonate them in order to secure state disability grants. While I must stress that these are anecdotes, nevertheless, they offer complex insight into the relation of identity and illness, and people's desperation to access meagre state resources. HIV tests taken under false identities render the relationship between the reification of diagnostic categories and one's identity particularly complex. In 2005, Trevor Manuel, Minister of Finance, announced that disability grants would no longer be available to healthy people who have tested HIV positive.

24 The absence of a grave to tend is a cause of considerable distress. In January 2007 I went to visit Baby, whose daughter and son-in-law and *grootmaak kind* Meitjie had died in the previous year. Baby said that she had come to terms with the loss of her daughter because she had buried the woman herself and regularly tended her grave. Meitjie was a different story: Meitjie's father had taken her body from the morgue and buried her without ceremony. No one from the community, not even Baby, who had brought her up since she was a small child, was invited to attend the funeral and burial. Baby does not know where Meitjie's grave is and says that she is unable properly to mourn.

25 In Xhosa tradition, a child's umbilical cord is buried in the homestead, symbolically linking the newborn with the lineage. 'Home' is understood to be where the umbilical cord is buried, and people usually express a wish to be buried there.

26 Burial generally remains the most common and preferred means of disposing of bodies. There is an increase in cremation owing to the shortage of burial grounds in the city and a campaign to promote cremations. Nonetheless, almost everyone to whom I spoke desired a 'proper' burial and eschewed cremation.

27 Islamic funerals, by contrast, rely on chronological time: funerals ought to have occurred by sunset of the day of death if possible.

28 Elsewhere in the country, for example, a re-valorisation of tradition is linked with a resurgence of cultural nationalism. Women's initiation ceremonies, scarcely performed in the last century, receive new impetus (Ngxabi 2004; Mkhwanazi 2004), as does virginity testing (Leclerc-Madlala 2005; Scorgie 2002), defended by some as 'tradition' and attacked by others as an assertion of patriarchal power. Although the forms that responses take are locally particular, similar contradictory responses have been observed elsewhere (see in particular Farmer 1993).

29 Part of what rituals accompanying life-cycle events – birth, marriage and death accomplish – is proper chronology, a way of holding the past in the past. Where misfortunes arise in the present, they may be traced back to ritual processes improperly performed. The effect is that time's unfolding has not been properly secured (see White 2001).

30 Belonging, by contrast, engenders trust as a consequence of recognition, reversing the call. The form of trust associated with belonging, then, is epistemological before it is ontological. Belonging and the forms of trust associated with it call genealogy into being.

31 Isak Niehaus (2007) is also critical of simplistic assumptions between disclosure and stigma. He argues that AIDS is symbolically associated with 'being dead before dying'. It is this state rather than assumptions of sexual promiscuity that gives rise to stigma.

32 Many residents are alcohol and drug dependent and people are accustomed to dealing with the mood changes induced by such substances. Nevertheless, local conventions of respectability – *ordentlikheid* – valorise consistency and people who are 'always the same', even when drugged, are considered respectable.

33 In some ways, one might see his rejection as a form of scapegoating. As Georgio Agamben (1998) reminds us, rejection from a community is an age-old sanction and is central to the form of power he identifies as sovereign.

34 It is not accidental that Zulu poetry about the disease describes it with metaphors of eating (Henderson 2004) – metaphors that echo and reverse their usual association with joyful sex, food and generativity. Here the metaphor that describes the generative and ensures continuity and sociability is rendered dangerous.

CONCLUSION

1 There has been a huge increase in the numbers of people accessing state grants: up from some 2 600 000 in 1999 to 12 million in 2007 (http://www.info.gov.za/otherdocs/2007/developmentindicator/poverty.pdf accessed August 2007 p. 27). Social grants constitute some three per cent of GDP (ibid.). Grants most frequently accessed by residents of The Park were Old Age, Disability and various Child Care grants. While there is considerable debate about the usefulness of minimum living levels (MML), poverty datum lines and other measures of poverty, the South African state has acknowledged a need for a standardised measure of poverty and to this end has recently (2007) initiated a process to develop such. The MML is currently R431 per capita per month (2006 prices) or R322 per capita per month in 2000 prices (http://www.treasury.gov.za/povertyline p. 8 accessed August 2007). The bulk of the population of The Park lived on substantially less than this amount (see Chapter Five). The Gini coefficient, which is a measure of economic inequality, shows that inequalities remain extreme: in 1993, before the institution of democracy, it stood at 0.672 and in 2006, measured 0.685 (http://www.info.gov.za/otherdocs/2007/developmentindicator/poverty.pdf p. 24).

2 The drug is a stimulant, widely if clandestinely available, and very cheap. It is most commonly used by men in the 15–24 year age group. Studies have found that its use has increased radically since 2002 when studies began (http://www.mrc.ac.za//public/methamphetamine.pdf accessed 31 August 2007). Research by the Medical Research Council with teenagers has found a positive relation between tik use and increased sexual risk behaviours (Plüddeman et al. 2007).

Glossary of select Afrikaans terms

altyd – always

armoede – poverty

baasskap – domination, mastery

bandiet – convict

bedagsaam – considerate

bekeer – convert (i.e. a 'reborn'
Christian)

bekeerde – converted, reborn

bergie – tramp, lit. mountain person

besig – busy

bietjie – a small portion, a bit

bliktoilet – bucket toilet

boek – book

boekwurm – bookworm

boer – farmer; generic term for white
person, usually an Afrikaaner

boere – police

boontjies – beans

bos – bush

bosman – bush man

bosslapers – homeless people, lit. bush
sleepers

braggerig – bragging

brei – to pronounce the letter 'r' at the
back of the throat

dagga – marijuana

deurmekaar – confused, disoriented

die – the

dieselfde – the same

doodgenootskap – burial association

dop – drink (alcoholic)

druppels – drops

ek – I

eerste – first

eet – eat (of humans)

fynbos – Cape floral kingdom

gallyblik – charcoal drum

ganja – marijuana

gedrag – behaviour

geld – money

gesig – face

gevaarlik – dangerous

groet – greet or say goodbye

grootmaak (past tense grootgemaak) –
raise

half – half

hart – heart

hoe – how

hoekom – why

hoerdery – whoring, promiscuity

hoogmoedig – arrogant

huis – house

huisvrou – housewife

hy – he

ja – yes

jaloersheid – being jealous

kaalgat – stark naked

kind (pl. kinders) – child

klein – small

kleingeld – change, small amounts of
money

kraan – tap

krag – power

laatlammetjie – a child born long after
other children, often unexpectedly

land – country

langsaan – alongside

leefwyse – lifestyle

lelik – ugly

longontsteking – lung infection, usually
pneumonia

los – loose, wanton

ma – mother

maar – but

maer – thin
meisie – girl, girlfriend
man – man, husband
maniere – manners
mannetijes – little men
mense – people
moed – courage
moer-in – irate
mooi – pretty, nice
muurhuis – brick house
my – my
'n – a
naartjie – tangerine
nè? – not so?
nederigheid – humility
nie – not
ongeskikte geld – disability grant
opmaak – haughty
optelwerk – casual work
ordentlik – decent
ordentlikheid – decency, respectability
ouderdom – old age
pa – dad
pad – road, path
pap – 1. porridge (n.), 2. soft, weak (adj.)
papsak – packet (of wine)
plaasman – farm-dweller
plakkers – squatters
pypslaaper – pipe-sleeper
rof – rough
rondlopery – walking around, aimless
   wandering
rou – raw, rough, anti-social, unformed
saal – hall
sê – say
senuweeagtig – nervous
shebeen, subeen – an informal bar
sjambok – a rawhide whip
skandaal – scandal

skarrel – rummage, scrabble
skel – scold, shout
skelling – scolding
skinder – gossip
skollie – gangster, good-for-nothing
skool – school
skrop werk – scrubbing, housework
sloot – stream
smokkie – an illicit dealer in drink or
   drugs
snaaks – strange
spaza – small shop
speel – play
speurders – police detectives
spoggerig – natty
spuls – horny, in heat
stamp mielies – samp, crushed maize
sterf – die (of humans)
stoep – verandah
stories – harmful gossip
stres – stress
suiker – sugar, local term for diabetes
suiwer – pure
sukkel – struggle
swaarheid – difficulty, heaviness
swaarkry – hardship
swart – black
sy – she
taal – language, specifically Cape Flats
   Afrikaans
tik – crystal methamphetamine
tjommie – chum, mate
toormoord – witchcraft murder
towery – witchcraft
twak – tobacco
versproei – spread out, sprayed
vet – fat
vetplant – succulent
vinnig – fast

visie – vision

vol – full

vreet – eat (of animals)

vrek – die (of animals)

vrot – rotten

vrou – woman, wife

vrouesiekte – women's sickness

vry – 1. 'make out' (v.), 2. freedom (n.)

vuilsiek – venereal disease

waarheid – truth

waarom – why

ware – true, real

weggooi (past tense *weggegooi*) – throw away, discard

weggooi kind – abandoned child

weggooi mens – throw-away person

woes – fierce, furious

wreed – cruel, barbaric

wyn – wine

zol – hand-rolled marijuana cigarette

References

Adato, M, F Lund and P Mhlongo. n.d. 'Capturing "work" in South Africa: Evidence from a study of poverty and well-being in KwaZulu-Natal'. Unpublished paper, School of Development Studies, University of KwaZulu-Natal, Durban.

Agamben, G. 1998. *Homo Sacer: Sovereign Power and Bare Life*. Palo Alto: Stanford University Press.

Alvarez, A. 2005. *The Writer's Voice*. London: Bloomsbury.

Amoateng, A and B Heaton. 2007. *Families and Households in Post-apartheid South Africa: Socio-demographic Perspectives*. Pretoria: HSRC.

Ardener, S (ed). 1993. *Women and Space: Ground Rules and Social Maps*. Oxford: Berg.

Ardener S and S Burman (eds). 1995. *Money-go-rounds: The Importance of Rotating Savings and Credit Associations for Women*. Oxford: Berg.

Ashforth, A. 2002. 'An epidemic of witchcraft? The implications of AIDS for the post-apartheid state'. *African Studies*, 61 (1): 121–43.

Austin JL. 1962 *How to do things with words*. Oxford: Clarenden Press.

Auyero, J. 2000. 'The hyper-shantytown: Neo-liberal violence(s) in the Argentine slum'. *Ethnography*, 1 (1): 93–116.

Bamford, L, M Loveday and S Verkuijl. 2004. 'Tuberculosis'. *South Africa Health Review* 2003–4. Health Systems Trust. Accessed online: http://www.hst.org.za/publications/423 (July 2007).

Bank, L. 2001. 'Duncan's inferno: Fire disaster, social dislocation and settlement patterns in a South African township' in C de Wet and R Fox (eds). *Transforming Settlement in Southern Africa*. London: Edinburgh University Press, pp. 147–62.

Besteman, C. 2008. *Transforming Cape Town*. Berkeley: University of California Press.

Biehl, J. 2005. *Vita: Life in a Zone of Social Abandonment*. Berkeley: University of California Press.

Boonzaier, E and J Sharp (eds). 1988. *South African Keywords: The Uses and Abuses of Political Concepts*. Cape Town: David Philip.

Bourgois, P. 1996. *In Search of Respect*. Cambridge: Cambridge University Press.

Bradshaw, D, P Groenewald, R Laubscher, N Nannan, B Nojilana, R Norman, D Pieterse and M Schneider. 2003. *Initial Burden of Disease Estimates for South Africa, 2000*. Cape Town: South African Medical Research Council.

Brant, C. 1948. 'On joking relationships'. *American Anthropologist*, New Series, 50 (1): 160–2.

Bray, R, S Moses, I Gooskens and J Seekings (eds). n.d. 'Growing up in the new South Africa'. Unpublished manuscript. University of Cape Town.

Broadbridge, H. 2001. 'Negotiating post-apartheid boundaries and identities: An anthropological study of the creation of a Cape Town suburb'. Unpublished Doctoral dissertation, University of Stellenbosch.

Burman, S. 1986. 'Introduction' in S Burman and P Reynolds (eds). *Growing Up in a Divided Society*. Cape Town: David Philip, pp. 1–15.

Burman, S and P Reynolds (eds). 1986. *Growing Up in a Divided Society*. Cape Town: David Philip.

Butchart, A. 1998. *The Anatomy of Power: European Constructions of the African Body*. London: Zed Books.

Butler, J. 1997. *Excitable Speech*. London: Routledge.

Butler, J. 2005. *Giving an Account of Oneself*. New York: Fordham University Press.

Caldeira, T. 2000. *City of Walls*. Berkeley: University of California Press.

Casey, E. 1996. 'How to get from space to place in a fairly short stretch of time' in S Feld and K Basso (eds). *Senses of Place*. Santa Fe: School of American Research, pp. 13–52.

Clifford J and G E Marcus. 1986. *Writing Culture: The Poetics and Politics of Ethnography*. Berkeley. University of California Press.

Cock, J. 1980. *Maids and Madams*. Johannesburg: Ravan Press.

Comaroff J and J L Comaroff. 1991 and 1997. *Of Revelation and Revolution*. Vols 1 and 2. Chicago: University of Chicago Press.

Comaroff J and J L Comaroff. 2001. 'On personhood: A perspective from Africa'. *Social Identities*, 7 (2): 267–83.

Constitutional Court of South Africa (http://www.constitutionalcourt.org.za/uhtbin/cgisirsi/20070825181133/SIRISI/0/520/J-CCT 42-04)

Daniel, E Valentine. 1996. *Charred Lullabies: Chapters in an Anthropography of Violence*. Princeton: Princeton University Press.

Das, V. 2000. 'Violence and the work of time' in A Cohen (ed). *Signifying Identities*. London: Routledge, pp. 59–73.

Das, V. 2001. 'Crisis and representation: Rumor and the circulation of hate' in M Roth and C Salas (eds). *Disturbing Remains: Memory, History, and Crisis in the Twentieth Century*. Los Angeles: Getty Research Institute, pp. 37-62.

Das, V. 2007. *Life and Words: Violence and the Descent into the Ordinary*. Berkeley: University of California Press.

Deacon, H, I Stephney and S Prosalendis. 2005. *Understanding HIV/AIDS Stigma: A Theoretical and Methodological Analysis*. Cape Town: HSRC.

De Certeau, M. 1988. *The Practice of Everyday Life*. Berkeley: University of California Press.

De Certeau, M, L Giard and P Mayol. 1998. *Practice of Everyday Life, Vol. 2: Living and Cooking*. Minneapolis: University of Minnesota Press.

De Kock, A. 2002. 'Fruit of the vine, work of human hands: Farm workers and alcohol on a farm in Stellenbosch, South Africa'. Unpublished Master's dissertation, University of Cape Town.

Department of Water Affairs. (http://www.dwaf.gov.za/wfw/SocialDevII) accessed 18 September 2007.

Desjarlais, R. 1997. *Shelter Blues: Sanity and Selfhood among the Homeless*. Philadelphia: University of Pennsylvania Press.

Douglas, M. 1991. 'The idea of home: A kind of space', *Social Research*, 58 (1): 287–300.

Du Toit, A. 1993. 'The micro-politics of paternalism: The discourses of management and resistance on South African fruit and wine farms'. *Journal of Southern African Studies*, 19 (2): 314–36.

Du Toit, A. 2004. 'Forgotten by the highway: Globalisation, adverse incorporation and chronic poverty in a commercial farming district'. Cape Town: PLAAS (Programme for Land and Agrarian Studies) Chronic Poverty and Development Series No. 4.

Du Toit, A and F Ally. 2003. 'The externalisation and casualisation of farm labour in Western Cape horticulture'. Cape Town: PLAAS, University of the Western Cape and Centre for Rural Legal Studies, Stellenbosch.

Emmett, T. 1992. *Squatting in the Hottentot Holland's Basin*. Pretoria: HSRC.

Eriksen. T. 2004. *What Is Anthropology?* London: Pluto.

Evans-Pritchard, E. 1937. *Witchcraft, Oracles and Magic among the Azande*. Oxford: Clarendon.

Fabian, J. 1983. *Time and the Other: How Anthropology Makes Its Object*. New York: Columbia University Press.

Fadiman, A. 1998. *The Spirit Catches You and You Fall Down: A Hmong Child, Her American Doctors and the Collision of Two Cultures*. New York: Farrar, Straus and Giroux.

Farmer, P. 1993. *Aids and Accusation: Haiti and the Geography of Blame*. Berkeley: University of California Press.

Fassin, D. 2006. *When Bodies Remember: Experiences and Politics of AIDS in South Africa*. Berkeley: University of California Press.

Favret-Saada, J. 1980. *Deadly Words: Witchcraft in the Bocage*. Cambridge: Cambridge University Press.

Ferguson, J. 1985. 'The bovine mystique: Power, property and livestock in rural Lesotho' *Man*, New Series, 20 (4): 647–74.

Foucault, M. 1995. *Discipline and punish: The birth of the prison*. New York: Vintage Books.

Foucault, M. 2001. *Fearless Speech*. Los Angeles: Semiotext(e).

Geertz, C. 1973. *Interpretation of Cultures*. New York: Basic Books.

Glantz, L and A Spiegel (eds). 1995. *Violence and Family Life in South Africa: Research and Policy Issues*. Pretoria: HSRC.

Goody, J (ed). 1958. *The Developmental Cycle of Domestic Groups*. Cambridge: Cambridge University Press.

Gophe, M. 1999. 'Back to shacks as houses are sold to pay debts'. *Cape Argus*, 26 May, p. 5.

Griffin, S. 1992. *A Chorus of Stones*. London: Women's Press.

Guyer, J and P Peters (eds). 1987. 'Conceptualising the household: Issues of theory and policy in Africa'. Special Number of *Development and Change*, 18 (2): 215–34.

Hacking, I. 1998. *Mad Travellers: Reflections on the Reality of Transient Mental Illnesses*. Charlottesville: University of Virginia Press.

Harvey: D. 1996. *Justice, Nature and the Geography of Difference*. Oxford: Blackwell.

Health Sytems Trust. (http://www.hst.org.za/healthstats/145/data). (http://www.hst.org.za/healthstats/178/data).

Helman, C. 2000. *Culture, Health and Illness*. Butterworth-Heinemann: London.

Helman, C. 2006. 'Why medical anthropology matters', *Anthropology Today*, 22 (1): 3–4.

Henderson, P. 1999. 'Living with fragility'. Unpublished Doctoral dissertation, University of Cape Town.

Henderson, P. 2004. 'The vertiginous body and social metamorphosis in a context of HIV/AIDS'. *Anthropology Southern Africa*, 27 (1&2): 43–53.

Henderson, P. 2005. 'Mortality and the ethics of qualitative research in a context of HIV/AIDS'. *Anthropology Southern Africa*, Special Number on Ethics, 28 (3&4): 78–90.

Hymes, D (ed). 1974. *Reinventing Anthropology*. New York: Vintage Books.

Illich, I. 1973. *Tools for Conviviality*. New York: Harper and Row.

Ingold, T. 2002. 'The temporality of the landscape' in *The Perception of the Environment*. London: Routledge, pp. 189–208.

Jackson, M. 1995. *At Home in the World*. Durham: Duke University Press.

Jackson, M. 1998. *Minima Ethnographica: Intersubjectivity and the Anthropological Project*. Chicago: University of Chicago Press.

Jackson, M. 2002. *The Politics of Storytelling: Violence, Transgression and Intersubjectivity*. Copenhagen: University of Copenhagen, Museum Tuscalanum Press.

Johnson, B. 1990. *Stories, Community and Place: Narratives from Middle America*. Bloomington: Indiana University Press.

Jones, S. 1990. *Assaulting Childhood*. Johannesburg: Wits University Press.

Kane, L. 2006. 'Transport problems associated with poverty in South Africa'. *National Household Travel Survey Seminar: Understanding Travel Habits and Transport Conditions in Southern Africa*. Working paper, Urban Transport Research Group, Dept Civil Engineering, University of Cape Town.

Kerby, A. 1991. 'Introduction' in *Narrative and the Self*. Bloomington: Indiana University Press, pp. 1–31.

Koelble, T and E Lipuma. 2005. 'Traditional leaders and democracy' in S Robins (ed). *Limits to Liberation after Apartheid: Citizenship, Governance and Culture in South Africa*. London: James Currey, pp. 74–93.

Kristeva, J. 1982. *Powers of Horror: An Essay on Abjection*. New York: Columbia University Press.

Kundera, M. 1988. 'Sixty-three words', in *The Art of the Novel*. London: Faber and Faber, pp. 121–53.

Leclerc-Madlala, S. 2005. 'Popular Responses to HIV/AIDS and Policy'. *Journal of Southern African Studies*, 31 (4): 845–56.

Lefebvre, H. 2004. *Rhythmanalysis: Space, time and everyday life*. London: Continuum.

Levine, S. 1999. 'Bittersweet harvest: Children, work and the global march against child labour in the postapartheid state'. *Critique of Anthropology*, 19 (2): 139–55.

Levine, S. 2004a. 'Documentary film and HIV/AIDS: New directions for applied visual anthropology in southern Africa'. *Visual Anthropology Review*, 19 (1&2): 57–72.

Levine, S. 2004b. 'Steps for the Future (Actually, life is a beautiful thing): An introduction by the STEPS project staff'. *Visual Anthropology Review*, 19 (1&2): 8–12.

Levine, S. 2006. 'The "Picaninny" wage': An historical overview of the persistence of structural inequality and child labour in South Africa'. *Anthropology Southern Africa*, 29 (3&4): 122–31.

Levine, S and F C Ross. 2002. 'Attitudes to and perceptions of HIV/AIDS among young adults in Cape Town'. *Social Dynamics*, 28 (1): 89–108.

Lewis, O. 1959. *Children of Sanchez*. London: Secker and Warburg.

Lingis, A. 1994. *The Community of Those Who Have Nothing in Common*. Bloomington: Indiana University Press.

Lingis, A. 2002. 'Murmurs of life: A conversation with Alphonso Lingis' in M Zournazi (ed). *Hope: New Philosophies for Change*. New York: Routledge, pp. 22–41.

London, L. 2003. 'Human rights, environmental justice and the health of farm workers in South Africa'. *International Journal of Occupational and Environmental Health*, 9: 59–68.

London, L and R Bailie. 2001. 'Challenges for improving surveillance for pesticide poisoning: Policy implications for developing countries'. *International Journal of Epidemiology* 30: 564–70.

Lovell, A. 2007. 'Hoarders and scrappers: Madness and the social person in the interstices of the city' in J Biehl, B Good and A Kleinman (eds). *Subjectivity: Ethnographic Investigations*. Berkeley: University of California Press, pp. 315–40.

Lukhele, A. 1990. *Stokvels in South Africa*. Johannesburg: Amagi Books.

Macfarlane, M. 2004. 'Demographics' in *South African Institute of Race Relations 2003–4 Survey*. Johannesburg: SAIRR, pp. 1–40.

Madam and Eve (http://www.madamandeve.co.za) by Stephen Francis and Rico Schachel.

Malinowski, M. 1922. *Argonauts of the Western Pacific*. London, Routledge.

Manuel, T. 2006. 'Republic of South Africa Budget Speech 2006'. RP: 10/2006. Pretoria. Accessed online: www.treasury.gov.za.

Massumi, B. 2002. *Parables for the Virtual*. Durham and London: Duke University Press.

May, J (ed). 2000. *Poverty and Inequality in South Africa*. Cape Town: David Philip.

Mayol, P. 1998. 'The Neighbourhood' in M de Certeau, L Giard and P Mayol (eds). *The Practice of Everyday Life, Vol 2: Living and Cooking*. Minneapolis: University of Minnesota Press, pp. 7–15.

Mbembe, A. 2000. 'At the edges of the world: Territoriality and Sovereignty in Africa', *Public Culture* 12(1): 259–275.

Mbembe, A. 2001. *On the Postcolony*. Berkeley: University of California Press.

Medical Research Council (http://www.mrc.ac.za//public/facts13.html) accessed

31 August 2007,
(http://www.mrc.ac.za//public/methamphetamine.pdf) accessed 31 August 2007.

Meintjes, H. 2000. 'Poverty, possessions and "proper living": Constructing and contesting propriety in Soweto and Lusaka City'. Unpublished Master's dissertation, University of Cape Town.

Meintjes, H. 2001. 'Washing machines make women lazy: Domestic appliances and the negotiation of women's propriety in Soweto'. Journal of Material Culture, 6 (3): 345–63.

Merleau-Ponty, M. 1964. Phenomenology of Perception. London: Routledge.

Mkhwanazi, N. 2004. 'Teenage pregnancy and the making of gender identities in a post-apartheid township'. Unpublished Doctoral dissertation, University of Cambridge.

Moller and Ferreira. 2002. 'The Getting by Study' This Day February, 2004.

Murray, C. 1981. Families Divided. Cambridge: Cambridge University Press.

Nancy, J-L and A Smock. 1993. 'Speaking without being able to' in J-L Nancy (ed). The Birth to Presence, trans B Holmes et al. Palo Alto: Stanford University Press, pp. 310–318.

National Treasury (http://www.treasury.gov.za/povertyline) accessed August 2007 p.8.

Ngwane, Z. 2003. '"Christmastime" and the struggles for the household in the countryside: Rethinking the cultural geography of migrant labour in South Africa'. Journal of Southern African Studies, 29 (3): 681–99.

Ngxabi, E. 2003. 'Houses or homes?' Unpublished Master's dissertation, University of Cape Town.

Niehaus, I. 2007. 'Death before dying: Understanding AIDS stigma in the South African Lowveld'. Journal of Southern African Studies, 33 (4): 846–60.

Nyamnjoh, F. 2002. '"A child is one person's only in the womb": Domestication, agency and subjectivity in the Cameroonian grassfields' in R Werbner (ed). Postcolonial Subjectivities in Africa. London: Zed Books, pp. 111–38.

Ochs, E and L Capps. 1996. 'Narrating the self'. Annual Review of Anthropology 25: 19–43.

Ogden, J. 1996. '"Producing" respect: The "proper woman" in postcolonial Kampala' in R Werbner and T Ranger (eds). Postcolonial Identities in Africa. London: Zed Books, pp. 165–92.

Okri, B. 1993. Songs of Enchantment. London: Jonathan Cape.

Overing, J. 2000. An Anthropology of Love and Anger. London: Routledge.

Pandolfo, S. 1997. Impasse of the Angels. Chicago: University of Chicago Press.

Perlman, J. 1978. The Myth of Marginality. Berkeley: University of California Press.

Perlman, J. 2005. 'Marginality: From myth to reality in the favelas of Rio de Janeiro, 1969–2002'. Accessed online: http://www.megacitiesproject.org/Myth_to_Reality_Rio_1969–2002.pdf (February 2009).

Phillips, A. 2002. Equals. London: Faber and Faber.

Phillips, A. 2006. Side Effects. London: Harper.

Pinnock, D. 1989 'Ideology and urban planning: Blueprints of a garrison city' in W G James and M Simons (eds). *The Angry Divide: Social and Economic History of the Western Cape*. Cape Town: David Philip, pp. 150–68.

Plüddeman, A, A Fisher, C Parry, R McKetin and T Carney. 2007. *Methamphetamine Use, Sexual Health, Aggression and Mental Health Among School Going Adolescents in Cape Town, South Africa*. Alcohol and Drug Abuse Research Unit, Medical Research Council, South Africa.

Povinelli, E. 2007. *Empire of Love: Toward a Theory of Intimacy, Genealogy and Carnality*. Durham: Duke University Press.

Rabinow, P. 1995. *French Modern*. Chicago: University of Chicago Press.

Radcliffe-Brown, A. 1940. 'On joking relationships'. *Africa*, 13 (3): 195–210.

Radcliffe-Brown, A. 1949. 'A further note on joking relationships'. *Africa*, 19 (2): 133–40.

Ramphele, M. 1988. 'The position of African women: Race and gender in South Africa' in E Boonzaier and J Sharp (eds). *South African Keywords: The Uses and Abuses of Political Concepts*. Cape Town: David Philip, pp. 153–66.

REACH. 2007. 'Sexual harassment: Is it really a problem on farms?' Report of a fact-finding survey of farm workers conducted in 2006 by Rural Education, Awareness and Community Health. Accessed online: www.reach.org.za.

Reynolds, P. 1989. *Childhood in Crossroads: Cognition and Society in South Africa*. Johannesburg: New Africa Books.

Reynolds, P. 1995. *Paring Down the Family: The Child's Point of View*. Pretoria: HSRC.

Reynolds, P. 1997. 'Youth and the politics of culture' in S Stevens (ed). *Children and the Politics of Culture*. Cambridge, MA: Princeton University Press, pp. 218–42.

Reynolds, P. 2000. 'The ground of all making: State violence, the family, and political activists' in V Das and A Kleinman (eds). *Violence and Subjectivity*. Berkeley: University of California Press, pp. 141-70.

Rhoda, R. 2004. 'Letter to the editor'. *Cape Times*, 12 November, p. 4.

Rice, T. 2003. 'Soundselves', *Anthropology Today*, 19 (4): 4–9.

Robins, S. 2002. 'Planning for suburban bliss'. *Africa*, 72 (4): 511–48.

Robins, S. 2004. '"Long live Zackie, long live": AIDS activism, science and citizenship after apartheid'. *Journal of Southern African Studies*, 30 (3): 651–72.

Robins, S. 2005. *Limits to Liberation after Apartheid: Citizenship, Governance and Culture in South Africa*. London: James Currey.

Ross, F C. 1995. *Houses Without Doors*. Pretoria: HSRC.

Ross, F C. 1996. '"Vat Jou Goede en Trek": The effects of domestic violence in Die Bos' in L Glanz and A D Spiegel (eds). *Violence and Family Life in South Africa: Research and Policy Issues*. Pretoria: HSRC.

Ross, F C. 2003. *Bearing Witness: Women and the Truth and Reconciliation Commission in South Africa*. London: Pluto.

Ross, F C and A D Spiegel. 2000. 'Diversity and fluidity amongst poor households in Cape Town and the heterogeneity of domestic consolidation practices: Some cases'. *Tanzanian Journal of Population Studies and Development* 7 (2): 147–69.

Sachs, A. 2006. Judgement in Laugh It Off Promotions CC vs. SAB International (Finance) BV t/a Sabmark International, 2006 (1) SA 144 (CC).

Salo, E. 2004. 'Respectable mothers, tough men and good daughters: Producing persons in Mannenberg township'. Unpublished Doctoral dissertation, Emory University, USA.

Scheper-Hughes, N. 1992. *Death Without Weeping: The Violence of Everyday Life in Brazil*. Berkeley: University of California Press.

Scheper-Hughes, N. 1997. 'Lifeboat ethics: Mother love and child death in northeast Brazil' in R Lancaster and M di Leonardo (eds). *The Gender/Sexuality Reader: Culture, History, Political Economy*. New York: Routledge, pp. 82–8.

Scheper-Hughes, N and M Lock. 1987. 'The Mindful Body: A Prologemenon to Future Work in Medical Anthropology'. *Medical Anthropology Quarterly*, 1 (1): 6–41.

Schumaker, L. 2001. *Africanising Anthropology*. Durham: Duke University Press.

Scorgie, F. 2002. 'Virginity testing and the politics of sexual responsibility: Implications for AIDS intervention'. *African Studies* 61 (1): 55–75.

Seekings, J. 2006. 'Facts, myths, and controversies: The measurement and analysis of poverty and inequality after apartheid'. Paper presented at the 'After Apartheid Conference', Cape Town, 11–12 August. Accessed online: http://www.yale.edu/ macmillan/apartheid/apartheid_part1/seekings.pdf.

Seremetakis, C N (ed). 1996. *The Senses Still*. Chicago: University of Chicago Press.

Simmel, G. 1950. 'The Stranger' in *The Sociology of Georg Simmel*. New York: Free Press, pp. 402–408.

Singer, M, F Valentin, H Baer and Z Jia. 1992. 'Why does Juan Garcia have a drinking problem? The perspective of critical medical anthropology'. *Medical Anthropology*, 14 (1): 77–108.

Smetherham, J-A. 2007. '"Model" settlement loses soul to vice, apathy and friction', *Cape Times*, Life supplement, 11 December, p. 3.

Smetherham, J-A. 2007. 'People of RDP housing project say they have been dumped'. *Cape Times*, 11 December, p. 5.

Smith, J and I Wallerstein. 1992. *Creating and Transforming Households: The Constraints of the World-economy*. Cambridge: Cambridge University Press.

Soja, E. 1989. *Postmodern Geographies*. New York: Verso.

Solnit, R. 2006. *A Field Guide to Getting Lost*. Edinburgh: Cannongate.

Sontag, S. 1978. *Illness as Metaphor*. London: Allen Lane.

Sontag, S. 1989. *AIDS and its Metaphors*. London: Penguin.

South African Government Information (http://info.gov.za/otherdocs/2007/ developmentindicator/poverty.pdf) accessed August 2007 p.27. (http://www.info.gov.za/otherdocs/2007/developmentindicator/poverty.pdf) accessed August 2007 p.24.

Spiegel, A D. 1996. 'Domestic fluidity in South Africa'. *Social Dynamics*, 22 (1): 5-6.

Stack, C. 1973. All Our Kin: Strategies for Survival in a Black Community. New York: Basic Books.

Statistics South Africa. 2005. 'Stages in the Life Cycle of South Africans'. Report no. 03-02-46 (2001). Pretoria: Statistics South Africa.

Steinberg, J. 2004. The Number. Johannesburg: Jonathon Ball Publishers.

Swartz, L. 1998. Culture and Mental Health: A Southern African View. Cape Town: Oxford University Press.

Taussig, M. 1992. Nervous States. New York: Routledge.

Taussig, M. 1999. Defacement: Public Secrecy and the Labour of the Negative. Palo Alto: Stanford University Press.

Thom, A and K Cullinan. 2005. 'Provincial failures drive TB epidemic'. Accessed online: http://www.health-e.org.za/news/article.php?uid=20031190 (February 2006).

Thornton, R and M Ramphele. 1988. 'The quest for community', in E. Boonzaier and J. Sharp (eds). South African Keywords: The Uses and Abuses of Political Concepts. Cape Town: David Philip, pp. 29–39.

United Nations Human Development Index (http://hdr.undp.org/hdr 2006/statistics/indicators/17.html) accessed August 2007.

Waldman, L. 1994. Here You Will Remain: Gender, Violence and Movement on Farms in the Western Cape. Stellenbosch: Centre for Rural Legal Studies.

Waldman, L. 2003. 'Houses and the ritual construction of gendered homes in South Africa'. Journal of the Royal Anthropological Institute, New Series, 9: 657–79.

Waldman L. 2007. The Griqua Conundrum: Political and Socio-Cultural Identity in the Nothern Cape, South Africa. Londo: Peter Lang Publishers.

Western, J. 1981. Outcast Cape Town. Cape Town: Human & Rousseau.

White, H. 2001. 'Tempora et Mores: Family values and the possessions of a post-apartheid countryside'. Journal of Religion in Africa, 31 (4): 457–79.

Wikan, U. 1999. 'Towards an experience-near anthropology'. Cultural Anthropology, 6 (3): 285–305.

Wilson, F and M Ramphele. 1989. Uprooting Poverty: The South African Challenge. Cape Town: David Philip.

Wolpe, H. 1972. 'Capitalism and cheap labour-power in South Africa: From segregation to apartheid'. Economy and Society, 1 (4): 425–56.

World Health Organisation. 2005. World Health Report. Accessed online: www.who.org.

Yose, C. 1999. 'From shacks to houses: Space usage and social change in a Western Cape shantytown'. Unpublished Master's dissertation, University of Cape Town.

Zournazi, M. 2002. Hope: New Philosophies for Change. New York: Routledge.

Index

Page references in *italics* indicate where you can find a photograph or table relating to the index entry term.